# Successful
## Organizations
# ACTION in

# Successful
# Organizations
# ACTI⊙N in

A HANDBOOK FOR CORPORATE EXCELLENCE

Srinivaas M. Shiv Kumar Vembu, Vinod Kalkotwar
Jp Singh, Rupak Agarwal, Apoorve Dubey

PARTRIDGE
A Penguin Random House Company

**Editor**
Shanker.B

**Cover Design & Layout**
Shapes and Shades

Copyright © 2013 by Srinivaas M.

| | | |
|---|---|---|
| ISBN: | Hardcover | 978-1-4828-1538-2 |
| | Softcover | 978-1-4828-1537-5 |
| | Ebook | 978-1-4828-1536-8 |

First Edition: July 2012

**To order additional copies of this book, contact**
Partridge India
000 800 10062 62
www.partridgepublishing.com/india
orders.india@partridgepublishing.com

# CONTENTS

## ORGANIZATIONAL PRESPECTIVE

# HUMAN RESOURCES PRESPECTIVE

# OPERATIONAL PRESPECTIVE

# ABOUT THE AUTHOR (s)

**Srinivaas M. MS** is a B.Tech from IIT Chennai and a Post Graduate in Management (PGDM) from IIM Bangalore. MS is a co-founder & Managing Director of Master Mentors Advisory Pvt Ltd., a management consulting company, promoted by experienced alumni of the Indian Institutes of Technology (IIT) and Indian Institutes of Management (IIM) with a collective corporate experience of over300 years of which over 100 years is at CXO level He has over 20 years of rich corporate experience in leading Indian and Multinational Organizations like BPL Limited, Godrej & Boyce Mfg Co. Ltd., Bausch & Lomb India Ltd., HCL Infosystems Ltd etc., including over3 years as Managing Director of a BSE listed Indian IT company. Having worked in challenging roles across various functions like Sales, Marketing and General Management in senior levels of organizations, he has a tremendous understanding of the corporate environment. Being an avid reader and a keen observer, Srinivaas has accumulated a wealth of learning and experience, not only from his experiences, but also through his observations and interactions with professionals from a number of leading organizations.

**Co-authors: JP Singh—JP** is Post Graduate from IIM Kolkata (1984-86) and a founding member of Master Mentors Advisory Pvt Ltd. JP has over 25 years of experience in premier organizations like Lakme, Bausch & Lomb India Ltd. He served as the MD of Bausch & Lomb India for over 6 years. To help Organizations and individuals in realizing their potential by facilitating through, Strategic Consulting & Coaching to Enhance their Capabilities in the areas of Strategy & Marketing,

Leadership, Problem Solving/Decision Making, Innovation and Customer Value Creation

**Vembu Shiv Kumar—Shiv** is a Post Graduate in Management from Indian Institute of Management, Lucknow and a Founder-Director of Master Mentors Advisory Pvt Ltd. Shiv has 25 years experience as a Country Operations leader with proven track record across multiple industries and multiple consumer segments. Shiv has started up and scaled up operations of Organizations like Swarovski (Premium Fashion Retail) and the Nuance Group-Shoppers Stop JV (Large and Medium Format Travel Retail). He has also scaled up operations for Bausch & Lomb nationally (Ray-Ban) andregionally for Asian Paints.

**Apoorve Dubey—Apoorve** is the founding member of Master Mentors Advisory Pvt. Ltd. He is also the Founder and C.E.O of Kreyon Systems Pvt. Ltd, an IT and mobile application development company. He is the author of the international best-selling book, **"The Flight of Ambition"** published by Macmillan. Apoorve received his master's degree from the department of computer science and engineering, IIT Madras. He started his professional career as a software engineer. He has several years of experience in Industry & academics. He has worked as a technical architect and also streamlined several business processes in govt organizations' like MPEB, Indian Railways with innovative solutions. He is a key note speaker and has conducted several corporate sessions on leadership & management. He also works as a volunteer for NGOs to promote educational initiatives for taking quality education to the masses. The driving passion in his life remains to be able to contribute to the success of others. To know more about Apoorve and his work, you can visit www.theflightofambition.com.

**Vinod Kalkotwar—Vinod** has M.Tech. in Chemical Engineering from IIT Chennai and MBA in Marketing & Finance. He is a founding member of Master Mentors Advisory. Vinod has over 27 years of multi-faceted and hands on experience in industry, corporate banking, financial services and Investment banking. He founded boutique investment bank—Kalozal Consultants Pvt. Ltd. (Kalozal) in 2001. Kalozal specializes in raising capital (primarily equity—VC/PE), M&A, Strategic investment, Joint Ventures etc.

**Rupak Agarwal—Rupak** is a high-energy senior P&L leader with proven success in Strategy, Marketing, Operations, Customer Service and Financial Planning for organizational turnarounds and profitable growth. He has an impressive record of demonstrated results in multiple industries of IT products distribution, consumer durables, electronics & appliances, media, telecom services and real estate

Having held CXO and VP level positions with organizations like Godrej Properties, Reliance Communications, Bharti Airtel, HT Media, BPL Sanyo and Ingram Micro, Rupak has demonstrated his ability to infuse strategic leadership to unlock opportunities and drive growth trajectories. He has been recognized by Business India magazine and professional colleagues as one of the youngest General Manager at Hindustan Times and for his change management prowess, focused approach and speed. He has hired, trained and managed teams in excess of 1000 people and has demonstrated results in revenue growths, customer delight, capability building and coaching leaders.

Rupak holds numerous certifications and accreditations through The International Coaching Federation USA, SHL Training Academy UK and the NFNLP (National Federation of Neurolinguistic Psychology) USA. A visionary, motivational, lead by example, missionary change agent.

Rupak has an MBA from Indian Institute of Bangalore-India's premier-business school and a BE in electronics engineering.

**Special Thanks to: Keethi Jaya Tilak, Anilesh Seth, Sivaram Hariharan, Raghavendra Prasad, Srikant VN, Sundara Nagarajan, SS Alam, JaspalBajwa, Dr Naghi Prasad, Shankar Balakrishnan, KVV Satyanarayana & Kausthub Korde (TUV-Nord, India).**

The world is changing at the speed of thought. Businesses today face the stiff challenge of keeping up with the speed and continuously reinvent themselves to compete in the fierce global market. The market is evolving continuously and the consumers have more options than ever before. So, how does a company cope up with all the pressure of competition and staying relevant in a fast changing world? The most successful companies are those that are prepared to handle the changing landscape by staying ahead of the competition. They constantly change as per the demands of the market, while there are others who are left behind in this race. Polaroid is a great example of a company that revolutionized instant photography, however, it failed to capture market share in digital photography. The retail powerhouses like Kmart, Sears and Montgomery Ward could not keep pace with the rapidly changing needs.

However, the most successful companies constantly reinvent themselves—such as Wal-Mart, which ventured into low priced markets that the others could not exploit and also by using technology to outsmart its competitors. It is paramount that the companies stay relevant and look at every possible opportunity to reinvent as per the changing requirements of the market. They also need to act as change agents by shaping the future of markets they operate in.

Innovation is a process that constantly refuels an Organization. The differentiating factor between the companies that survive and those that do not is often the ability to adapt. Companies that do not innovate, they stagnate. Here is a look at the attributes of the most successful companies to reinvent themselves and staying relevant in the changing times.

## 1. Staying Customer Centric:

It is imperative for businesses to stay in touch with their customers and needs. Understanding the changing needs of the customer is a sure fire way for innovation.

## 2. Breeding Innovation:

Most companies around the world that are innovative conduct a series of experiments to help create new products and services or improve upon existing ones.

## 3. Creating value through novel ideas:

An idea that is translated into the product or service for the consumer is innovation. Successful companies create an environment where people are encouraged to come up with new ideas that improve the existing processes and solutions.

## 4. Keeping an eye on the competition and the market:

To constantly improve one must be aware of the market dynamics and the evolving needs. Market feedback is a great way to track and gauge the progress.

## 5. New products and innovations help the company to stay relevant:

Some companies like Apple follow a top-down approach in building their products and services. When Apple ventured into the cell phone market, it did not look at Nokia, RIMM and others. It followed its philosophy of 'Think Different' and created an iPhone that revolutionized the cell phone industry.

## 6. Understanding and addressing the needs of the customers better than the competition:

The companies that take care of the clients take the business. The idea is to address the problems that the customer faces and come up with the best possible solutions for them.

### 7. Encourage people to try, even though they may fail:

Great companies like Apple, Google, etc encourage their employees to experiment, without worrying about failures. The emphasis is on trying things and not necessarily on results.

### 8. Collaborations and build on ideas:

When people collaborate and intermingle they tend to come up with great solutions. Everyone is not an expert in everything, the idea is to make people learn from each other and build a synergy.

### 9. Attract, develop and work with the best people:

The best companies hire the smartest workers, train them and create an information pool to build the best products and services. The most passionate people end up creating the most innovative products.

### 10. Execution is the key:

The key to innovation lies in its execution. Ultimately, the ideas that bring value are those that get executed.

As organizations continuously reinvent themselves, the successful organizations are those that stand the test of time by sticking to timeless principles of eternal success at the same time balancing their urge for financial profitability, positive contribution to humanity and corporate sustainability.

**SUCCESSFUL ORGANIZATIONS IN ACTION** is an exciting effort from us to throw light on these fundamental principles of success as seen through the eyes of seasoned corporate professionals from their first hand experiences gleaned from over 100 years of corporate experience.

**Vembu Shivkumar**

Success through the pursuit of excellence is the goal of any organization. A lot of research has been done and a number of articles, blogs and books have been published on the secrets of successful organizations. Very often, we find that, what is successful today, does not stand to be a success another day. A number of so called successful companies who have been glorified in a number of earlier books have disappeared or gone down the path of deterioration. Enron & Lehman Brothers, which were rated as some of the finest companies are no more existing.

Success is never an enduring phenomenon, nor is it the end of the road for a company. For achieving success, a number of factors have to fall in place at the same time, while for failure a few slipups are sufficient. The causes for success today, may not be the same tomorrow as the market dynamics are changing rapidly. Organizations have to stay innovative, flexible and adapt themselves to the surroundings, while preserving their core values and ethical approach to survive and grow in the long term.

'**SUCCESSFUL ORGANIZATIONS IN ACTION**' aims to throw light on those success factors that have led the organizations to achieve tremendous results and achieve growth and glory. Through the eyes of seasoned and battle hardened professionals with more than 100 years cumulative experience in a number of successful companies, the book tries to expose to the reader a number of conventional and non conventional activities, strategies, tools and approaches that are employed by today's successful organizations to create new markets, outwit competition and create lasting value.

While a number of eminently successful companies are referred for various topics in the book, it is important to note that the factors for success and the number of such companies could never be exhaustively touched upon. Further, with the promoters and managements changing periodically, the approaches to the organization's development also changes and can lead a successful organization to a downfall or a period of reinventions for renewed growth.

However, the traits required for success of organizations are eternal and a study of these qualities in action helps us to learn from their experiences and lays down a faster route to our success or understands the behavior of our competition that could unsettle us.

We sincerely thank great leaders like Steve Jobs, Andrew Grove, Azim Premji, Bill Gates, Larry Page, Micheal Dell, Narayana Murthy, Sergei Brin, Shiv Nadar and a never ending list of great promoters who continue to amaze this world with their innovation and business leadership. They have provided inspiration to number of entrepreneurs across the globe to dream of success and execute their plans fearlessly and build successful organizations.

We would be forever indebted to inspirational leaders like Ajai Chowdhry & Jaspal Bajwa with whom we had first hand interaction to learn and fine-tune our skills through amazing experiences. These experiences have, inspired us to write this book to help entrepreneurs and smart businesses to go for enduring and ever lasting success.

We hope this book serves today's organizations, managers and entrepreneurs to shorten their learning curve and achieve more at their organizations. We sincerely regret in case any unforeseen errors have been written in any section of the book and appreciate the feedback that will help us to take corrective action. Please send in your observations, comments or issues if any to us at ms@mastermentors.in.

**Srinivaas M**

Building a billion dollar business is the dream of any entrepreneur. Most businesses are built around problems; the bigger the problem an organization solves, the bigger the business it builds. A great company is the best investment for future generations. It takes courage to build an enduring Organization that caters to the needs of people and society. It is intriguing that some Organizations have been in existence for centuries while others last for less than a decade. What differentiates the companies that stay vibrant and alive from those that die early? Why some Organizations scale and transcend the limit of time whereas others fail to expand? What does it take to build an Organization that constantly evolves with time?

An analysis of the performance of the top 200 global organizations reveals that, USA, UK, Japan, Germany, France and South Korea are home for most of the top global organizations with US based organizations contributing to over 40% of the total turnover with over 5 trillion dollar out of the 10 trillion US Dollar turnover contributed by these companies. For the purpose of this analysis, the companies of Chinese origin where over 90% of the turnover comes from State owned/supported enterprises have been excluded.

**Appendix 1** gives the list 150 of the finest and the largest organizations in the world that have stood the test of time and grown into over US$5 billion businesses giving employment to over 20 million persons. Indian Private sector has contributed to over 20 such companies in the list. There are over 60 organizations in the world that have lasted more than 100 years and are still thriving with profitable annual turnover of more than a billion US Dollars.

**Appendix 2** gives the list of over 60 such organizations that have stood the test of time contributing to a combined global turnover of close to 5 trillion US Dollars annually and employing over 9 million persons. The last 30 years have seen an accelerated growth in the launch of global organizations, which are gaining scale rapidly. The advent of internet and technological advancements happening at a rapid pace have spawned global organizations that are able to quickly take off and proliferate across the world with brilliant innovation and excellent execution.

While Automobile and Energy related organizations dominate the global scenario with over 18% of the total global turnover for the 200 biggest organizations globally, Technology with over 15% and Retail with around 10% are fast catching up with much higher growth rates, while Finance is stable at around 10% of the global turnover.

**Appendix 3** lists some of the finest global organizations operating on the cutting edge of technology. The convergence of internet, television and mobile technologies has led to a rapid rise of technology conglomerates like Samsung, Toshiba, LG and the like.

**Appendix 4** lists the organizations that have taken birth in the past 30 years, in the era of the internet and technological revolution and have grown rapidly into Billion US Dollar transnational organizations. Companies like Microsoft, Dell, Google, Facebook, Cisco, Amazon, eBay, Infosys, Cognizant adorn this list, while there are some companies, which are the offshoots of much older parent companies and are formed by a series of mergers and restructuring activities to take a new life and grow.

An analysis of the evolution of these global companies reveals the following: The companies came into existence on the pretext of solving some compelling problem through innovative solutions, methods or execution excellence offering a compelling value to the consumers.

For example, Thomas Edison founded General Electric when he originated the concept and implementation of electric-power generation and distribution to homes, businesses, and factories—a crucial development in the modern industrialized world.

Fortune favours the brave and in the business world, organizations who take calculated risks and invest their resources wisely have the highest chance to grow.

A solid value proposition and a scalable business mode with sound business logic is the cornerstone for the success of these greatest organizations. A product focus compared to just a service focus allows these organizations to capture the value in a standardized form while allowing adaptation to different markets as per the tastes of the respective target audience. This allows for a massive scale up across the globe with same quality standards maintained across.

These organizations through their evolution have continued to innovate, shaped the tastes, needs and wants of their target audience. They stood the test of testing times through their sheer persistence and adaptability.

Customer centricity and an R&D focus enables these organizations to come out with compelling propositions to their target audience at the same time maintain the novelty by launching newer versions and disruptive innovation led products & services continuously.

While in the initial stages of evolution, the influence of the core promoters has been overbearing, as the organizations grow, professional management is brought in to take care of the growth of the organization. Promoters step aside and their indispensability is replaced by a business catalyst & enabling disposition that leads to seamless integration of professional management to run day to day affairs. This will result in a seamless growth with no bottlenecks with an empowered decision making & ownership at all levels, It has been invariably found that acquisitions & mergers are an integral part of the story of the evolution of the global giants. Organic growth and control of organizations by closely held managements have led to constrained growth rates and those organizations, which have executed brilliant acquisition led strategies, have always experienced explosive growth rates. CISCO, a 43 Billion US Dollar Organization, is a classic example of an organizations growing into a global giant in a matter of 25 years, through a brilliant and calculated acquisition & integration strategy, as it acquired more and more cutting edge technologies & competencies in its domain of operation. While a number of times, the acquisitions do not take the expected shape and yield desired results, globally successful organizations, do not let these disappointments come in the way of their chosen paths and taken them in their stride.

Focus on global markets and not just the domestic markets are a common aspect of the world's most successful organizations. Global markets bring unlimited demand potential along with lot of challenges in the form of competition, adaptability to different cultures, managing people of different nationalities and the resulting cultural heterogeneity of the employee base etc. Organizations that are able to tackle these issues successfully, not only grow big, but also their economies of scale create humongous entry barriers to prospective competition.

India has its own share of Billion dollar organizations. There are over 50 Billion US Dollar organizations of which over 25 are ranked in the top 200 organizations in the world.

**Appendix 5** lists 50 of the finest Indian companies that have achieved an annual turnover of over one billion US Dollars contributing to over 500 Billion dollars of business annually employing over 2 million persons. Almost 50% of this turnover is contributed by 11 Public Sector undertakings controlled by Government of India.

The 21st century has seen some of the most successful organizations taking the global route to growth. It is but obvious that to achieve a rapid growth and compete on economies of scale, it is important for Indian organizations to focus on exports and also cater to the demand of the developed markets like US and Europe and also emerging markets likes Africa, South East Asia etc. This involves not only creating a presence across the markets, but also competing on quality at a competitive price with respect to the global competition. While companies like TCS, Wipro, Infosys and HCL have been highly successful in the Information technology domain, companies like Tata Steel Tata Motors, Larsen & Toubro and Mahindra & Mahindra have undertaken acquisition of global companies with access to developed markets and companies like Ranbaxy, Cipla, Dr Reddy's and Lupin Laboratories have grown to transnational pharmaceutical organizations.

**Appendix 6** lists some of the finest Multinational Indian Companies that have made world as their playground and have achieved phenomenal success in the global market place. Enterprising Indian promoters have understood the importance of going global to sharpen their competitiveness, attain economies of scale and also leverage their management capabilities in acquiring and turning around multinational organizations in distress at the same time gain by catering to the vast global demand for their products and services.

**Appendix 7** lists the top performing Indian conglomerates led by the Reliance group and the Tata Group which have become global behemoths as Indian transnational organizations. There is a definite realization among the dynamic, progressive and aggressive Indian organizations about the need to be externally focused in order to be successful.

It is indeed imperative to study the factors that are behind the success of these great organizations, that could inspire a number of entrepreneurs and smaller organizations to make a much deeper impact on a larger canvass leading to everlasting success.

Success of an Organization can be measured by its performance on 5 main parameters, Contribution to Environment & Society, Financial Performance, Operational Metrics, Customer Satisfaction & Employee Satisfaction.

Building successful organizations is a tough job, really tough one. Building one that stands the test of time is even tougher. It seems interesting, yet the most successful companies that stand amidst economic downturns, fast changing business scenario, competition and conflicts are governed by timeless fundamentals. These fundamental principles enabled these companies to evolve with time and endure during adverse situations. Here is a look at some of the governing principles that the greatest Organizations follow:

## 1. Vision:

A visionary company is built around principles. The underlying core ideology or the vision of the company is the foundation on which the Organization grows. While adapting and evolving as per the market needs, the brand values remains consistent. Coca-Cola has been in the market since 1886 and performed remarkably well maintaining its brand positioning, but sticking to its core vision of 'Bringing to the world a portfolio of beverage brands that anticipate and satisfy peoples; desires and needs.

## 2. A great workplace with best practices:

The best organizations are built around frameworks and systems. These companies are built around processes and frameworks that enable them to scale, replicate businesses and stay as market leaders. Some of these large incorporations have well structured and documented processes that made it possible for them to create a global footprint for a sustained period.

## 3. Method over Charisma:

Great Organizations are built on methods rather than individual brilliance. These systems are incorporated into the heart of their business and responsible for their strong positions for long time. They focus on knowledge sharing and building a continuity culture. These Organizations like 3M, Coca-Cola, GE etc have processes in place that make succession planning smooth.

## 4. Building Trust:

Trust is built when customers are able to derive value from companies' products and services over a sustained period of time. An amazing success story in recent times is that of Amazon. It started in 1994 and has redefined the way people purchase things. The trust has been built steadily by empowering the user with the power of informed decision-making and feedback. Ethical approach, value driven culture, concern to society, sincerity of purpose, unquestionable integrity make these organizations, a great companion to repose your trust on and make them the first choice to deal with, for any of your requirements.

## 5. Realistic Approach through marketing:

Great companies are ever vigilant to keep track of the changing market. They not only adapt to changes but also create a viable market through proper channels. Corning, a manufacturer of specialty glass products for last 160 years, analyzed the fast changing market opportunity. They are now one of the major suppliers for smart phone and tablet screens. Most of the old companies do not evolve with time but the leaders emerge even stronger by creating opportunities.

## 6. Innovation and understanding the dynamics of the market:

Creating an environment that promotes and encourages experimentation. Great innovations are results of endless experimentation and great companies prove it time and again. 3M started as a mine and failed miserably. The first president could not get a salary for 11 years. Yet with time it became one of the most innovative companies, with more than 60,000 products to its credit.

## 7. Satisfaction of the customer:

Any business revolves around the customer. The idea is to make the customer happy with the best products and services. Innovation that does not provide value to the end user is not worth it. GE has introduced goodwill and customer satisfaction program wherein GE Six Sigma black belts/management experts assist their customers in streamlining processes, cutting costs and resulting in optimized businesses for their clients, all free of cost. No wonder GE leads the pack among companies that score high on customer satisfaction. Technology giants like Google, Amazon are other great examples of companies wooing the customers by their excellent service.

## 8. Execution Excellence:

Successful organizations master the practice of translating thoughts and ideas into actions with speed, accuracy and cost effectiveness. This ensures that they are always ahead in the game with respect to their competitors in reading the market and in doing what is needed to always lead the same. Always, challenging the limits, continuously striving for excellence, never resting on past laurels are some of the hallmarks of thriving organizations.

## 9. Sustainable Development:

Successful Organizations are always conscious of the fact that they are meant to exist for generations and hence their strategies and tactics revolve around the long-term nature of their outlook. They are environmentally conscious and always adopt the TBL (Triple Bottom Line) approach of caring for People, Profits and Planet. It is not just profit alone that is the reason for existence at ethical, thriving and successful organizations. Environmentally friendly policies that will enable us to pass on a more habitable planet to our offspring, taking care of the society and working for the development of the people by focusing on corporate social responsibility will lead to a tremendous goodwill for the organization and higher valuations leading to sustained growth for the business.

Top organizations are built with timeless principles. What is needed is the top leadership to influx a need for improvement and growth. The most important thing is to stay ahead of your competition by constantly improving to suit the demands of the market. The most successful Organizations of the world are built around innovation. The business leaders not only innovate but also seize the market opportunities. They create a culture of continuous innovation and stay ahead of the competition by being different.

In the following chapters, we will examine some of the traits and practices; the organizations follow to court success and stay ahead in the business world.

# WHAT MAKES THE 21ST CENTURY DIFFERENT?

We are now living in an era, which is strikingly different from earlier centuries. What we used to achieve in centuries, we are in now in a position to achieve in decades and what we could achieve in decades, we are in a position to achieve in less than a year.

Innovations like 'Electricity' and 'Internet' have been at the root of most of the progress the mankind has made and responsible for tremendous boost in the productivity levels. The revolution in the telecommunication area has made, what was considered to be the staple diet for fiction writers, turn into reality. Robotics, Networking, Cloud computing, Telepresence, Extreme Mobility solutions, Individualized customer targeting, Unforeseen Customer Experience Focused capabilities, GIS, Big Data, Exploration of the universe and search for alternate locations for habitations etc are but few of the numerous innovations and discoveries that are being made and facilitated.

In the past decade, it was possible to get a hang on the innovations, inventions and discoveries as they used to be few and far between. The pace at which the world is progressing today, it is not possible for even geniuses to go to depth of even a small percentage of the inventions that are shaking the world every day, despite the unlimited power and productivity, search engines like 'Google' have placed in our hand.

At the route of all this is the unleashing of the power of the individual with the abilities conferred upon him by the power of automation, internet, networking and the collective learning of the past and this is enabling this continuous and relentless push to break down existing barriers. It is indeed worthy to repeat one of the greatest quotes of all times:

**"Give me a lever long enough and a fulcrum on which to place it, and I shall move the world".**
— *Archimedes*

We are having enough levers with us now and it is dependent on us how we use them and on what firm grounds, we place them.

Some of the trends we need to be conscious of:

- Movement from individualized approach to team based approach and now, groups of teams networked globally and collaborating together
- Movement from a one size fits all approach/batch processing, to more sizes for every individual
- Working in silos to collaborating with customers, competitors and the external environment
- Profligacy and generous spends to extremely focused and output linked spends
- Diversification and working on a broad area to working on an extremely focused area with razor sharp focus
- A few transactions with a customer to focus on lifelong engagement with his/her network and lifetime value
- Brute work to smart work, Idea creators to Idea catalysts for the entire enterprise

Burn rates to Value creation and Value capture rates, Family Managed to Professional and Organized approach, Focus on company value creation to overall value creation that will have a ripple affect on company's growth as well, 'I do everything' approach to 'Outsource to an expert', 'Solution Selling' to 'Solution Discovery and Insight Selling' and above all, a 'I Know all' approach to a continuous learning and evolution approach.

While we are empowered with new tools and are chasing new frontiers, it is important that we do not unlearn the good things from the past and be unmindful of the basics of sound and ethical businesses.

The speed of progress of creation of the tallest buildings should never undermine the importance of a strong foundation. Hence it is important to have a clear Vision, Mission, Strategic, Ethical and Value driven approach with focus of the triple bottom line of 'Planet', 'People' and 'Profits'. Any business that takes care of the society along with its focus on its bottom-line has a strong chance for continuing to grow strongly for generations.

Warren Buffet, Bill Gates, Larry Ellison, Sunil Bharti Mittal, George Soros, Li Ka-shing, Late Steve Jobs (a lot of work anonymously), Oprah Winfrey, Azim Premji have been a few of the greatest business persons of all time who stand firmly by the world, sharing the wealth they are creating for the progress of mankind and humanity. They are great role models that we have from whom, we can learn how to build sustainable, great organizations of the 21st century.

## THE SOLAR SYSTEM AND THE INFINITELY SCALABLE ORGANIZATION . . .

Ever wondered how some organizations' scale up infinitely, smoothly and systematically while some organizations implode being unable to manage the growth?

The analogy can be found in the operation of our Solar system. Our solar system consists of a number of celestial bodies like the stars, the sun, the planets, the satellites and many more.

Have you ever noticed how day after day, month after month and year after year, the same processes, the day, the night, the twilight occur in such a predictable fashion that you can predict the celestial occurrences thousands of years in advance?

Our solar system is a well-oiled machine with planets rotating around themselves to create day and night, deriving source of energy from the boss of the Solar system, the Sun, & revolving around the Sun with clinical precision to result in the days, the years and the seasons.

The planets in turn have their own satellites revolving around them by keeping safe distance among themselves.

Similarly we have infinite Solar systems in this huge universe and unimaginable number of celestial bodies living in harmony without colliding with each other for ages.

What we notice here is an intricate system of hierarchy (satellites, planets, stars, galaxy and so on) following a set of universal laws (attraction, repulsion, circular motion, reflection, force, energy and many more) with automated control and defensive mechanisms to defend themselves against any shocks (frictional force of the atmosphere to destroy asteroids crashing on to the earth etc) leading to amazing periodicity and predictability of the operations of the entire universe which is one of the main reasons behind the flourishing and ever-growing life on our planet.

Similarly any organization that wants to grow infinitely without any hiccups has to put in place such a foolproof system that is followed with precision and periodicity leading to predictable growth.

What we see here is the requirement of a set of Structures, Systems, Rules, Hierarchy, Processes planned in detail and executed to perfection. This will help when the organization experiences spurts of growth and also help it fix problems easily by isolating and addressing them when they occur. The leaders at various levels are like the planets, the Sun and the other stars in the galaxy around whom their subordinates are organized. The rules have to be laid out and followed with the single-minded objective, by defining and chasing the vision laid out. The head-office/top leadership including the CEO should impeccably coordinate the alignment between the objectives of various departments, divisions and branches, so that the resultant harmony and synergy will ensure that **the sum of parts is much more than the addition of the parts.**

Being Process driven will help the organization to manage the complexity arising out of growth. A process driven organization has systems in place to manage every activity across the organization both internally and in relation to the external environment. Systems can be replicated as required to manage the growth. But as the organizations grow large, the number of departments, types of activities and interactions internally and externally grow large giving rise to many challenges and contradictions. The organizations must have processes to review the systems periodically and also as and when situation arises, to manage such contingencies and redraw the systems to adapt to the evolving situation.

The same have to be followed religiously consistently for ever with control mechanisms to correct aberrations as and when they occur, almost instantaneously before any permanent damage occurs. Only then will the organization have the ability to manage growth of infinite dimension!

# STRATEGIC LEADERSHIP —LESSONS FROM THE UNIVERSE

Where else could we get learning's on Globalization, or should I say Universalisation, than the example of the Universe itself. Starting from The Big Bang & expanding to its current state . . . & still expanding! The origin was a very high concentration of mass & energy hugely compacted into a small space, probably smaller than an SME. Was it this energy of God, The Leader, that was The Driving Force, Passion & Desire that drove Him to create history? While it got Him to create The Big Bang & to lead the Universe to where it is, he used Good Orderly Discipline (Operating Principles) to guide the progress over time & space.

Lessons then, are many. The starting point of the journey has to be a Deep Passion, A Strong Desire to take on the challenge of expansion or, depending on the scale, Globalization; only the variables & complexity increase. No matter what the current size of the organization is, a huge accumulation of energy is a must to be able to start on the path. It is essential that a Leader has the Drive & the Vision which leads & guides the organization towards the future. We have examples like Ranbaxy, Dr. Reddy's to name a few, though not SME's now, but demonstrating the impact of such energy. In the absence of this, the initial energy can burn out. The initial energy has to last & last to ensure that the organization has enough fuel at all times, in the form of "The Entrepreneurial Drive".

A Leader then, is 'a person who leads' & Leadership is the 'ability to be a Leader'. What then, is 'Good' Leadership? Fundamentally, at the most basic level, the element of 'going in front' is an essential requirement to

7

be fulfilled. A Leader is also expected to have, depending on the field of operation, Business, Functional or Domain knowledge, specific to the area of operation. A good definition of Leadership that I came across is 'A Leader is someone you choose to follow, because you know that he/she can take you where you want to go, but cannot go alone'. This definition goes beyond just 'subject expertise'& 'going in front', to highlighting 'choice' & 'desired direction' on behalf of the followers as well! It allows for a conscious human being to make an active choice & to determine his/her future direction, so much a part of The Indian Ethos! The question then is about options available to be able to make a choice, rather than having to choose from whatever is available.

However, talking of Good Leadership, there is also the concept of 'Situational' Leadership. According to this, the approach should be changed depending on the context or situation. An approach valid in one situation may not be valid in another. So, a slightly broader view, encompassing more variables is proposed. Now what is the context that is generally kept in mind when choosing a Leadership approach? Very often, even when this is followed, the context remains very narrow . . . confined to one circumstantial dimension only i.e. a variation in approach/ action just based on situations & events or maybe depending on who the Leader is or what geography or domain he/she is involved in. Leadership should look at a much wider context . . . social, economic, psychological, physical . . . a holistic systems approach. A Bangalore city prospering in IT ignores the context of infrastructure or social inconvenience that maybe building up due to another variable that gets totally left out of the equation. While Delhi booms in real estate & infrastructure, social stress, intolerance, crime & road rage create a bulge and distortion of the picture at another place.

Good Leadership, at the cutting edge, is Life itself!! Like in life, a Dynamic Balance of various aspects has to be maintained . . . between yin & yang, masculinity & feminity. Good Leadership needs to attain a balance

8

between social, economic, physical & psychological variables. In most situations we see one-dimensional excellence at the cost of various other dimensions. The result is a time bomb ticking somewhere else. Depending on which area one is responsible for, one would maximize indices depicting performance in that dimension, sweeping the dust out from 'my house' onto 'the neighbors' front yard'. This does not really ensure a healthy, all round effort. Inflation & other pressures build up as a result of ignored variables, not built into the equation.

After all, 'A chain is as strong as the weakest link' . . . .

In the corporate world, to some extent 'The Balanced Scorecard' approach deals with such a situation, though not fully. Along with stakeholders' financial interests, it encourages measurement on the people, customers & process dimensions as well . . . definitely an approach in the right direction, but still needs broadening of the scope to include impact on society, environment & nature.

Neglecting any one dimension is like 'leakage' of energy from that 'weakest' point in the nuclear reactor . . . !! Balanced, well-rounded development, ensuring that social, economic, psychological, physical & environmental interests are in Dynamic Equilibrium is the challenge in India today. Such a balance will ensure 'Ananda Tandava', which India has taught the world over ages.

Alignment of a billion 'charged ions' in a Laser Head, needs application of a high voltage of Leadership Qualities of Truth, Integrity, Ethics, Humility, Inner Strength, Transcending of Self & Passion . . .

And once it happens it can LEAD to a Highly Powerful Laser Beam . . . !

While the Good Lord was probably 'born' with all Leadership skills, these can be surely developed in lesser mortals like us, to be able to leave the same kind of blazing trail. There are enough lessons from the expanding universe & the field of business too to learn from.

While the Universe continues to expand, it remains one unified whole. This 'oneness' ensures that there is

9

a 'commonality' of character in all its components. The purpose, mission, values of an organization also need to have a shared acceptance—the same energy flowing through all the divisions and subsidiaries. The Leader has to ensure that all elements of the organization are bonded together by a common energy, the gravitational pull that keeps the Universe as One. We don't have a 'breakaway' component of the Universe deciding to go its own way, creating its own 'New World'. The common nature of things, the characteristics & the gravitational attraction ensure that different parts operate in a huge cosmic show. Leaders in this show need to demonstrate Inner Strength & Maturity & hence transcend themselves. Tatas have demonstrated this again and again over their long history. In the recent past, companies like Microsoft, Google have given ample illustration of how organizations' can leap into globalization successfully and over relatively short periods. Scale does not matter then. In the absence of this bonding and shared purpose & values, the different parts of an organization will never be able to work as one organization. The implications of this are many. The case for a shared, all pervasive energy in the organization is so strong, that even at the cosmic level, scientists once believed in the presence of all-pervasive ether to carry electromagnetic radiation.

Another interesting lesson is that, the way the Universe is expanding, even though at tremendous speed, it actually moves out stage by stage. We have yet to learn of a part of the Universe jumping out ahead, beyond the edge of the Universe, into 'darker spaces' leaving the rest of the Universe behind to catch up. Really speaking, the principles of adjacency, related expansion, laying a foundation & then moving on further are relevant when globalizing. At each stage, knowledge of the market & having a global mindset are key. The Leader has to do a risk-return assessment while taking these calls. Lakshmi Mittal's expansion, while balancing & weighing these factors, is a classical example. Moving to adjacent domains, whether in terms of geographies or choosing which products to move with or with how much adaptation, all should be governed by the principles of adjacency, related & synergistic expansion. These principles come into play while making decisions on market entry through acquisitions, alliances or the Greenfield route. It definitely is more effective & efficient. Resources are always limited & a good judgment, in economic terms, is to allocate limited resources among unlimited demands.

The Strategic Choices are then based on a risk-return estimation. Needless to say, the principle of adjacency allows an efficient, effective, productive & low cost option. The more distant the next phase, the more energy & resources it will take. A question that needs to be answered is how much gain & at how much cost? The net has to be positive. The Universe, with all its so-called Unlimited Resources, still decides to expand out in adjacent, next outer domain!!

At each stage of expansion, The Leader has to be conscious of adapting the organization & its constituents to be ready to embrace the next phase, leading to a one whole again. There will be differences still, like different particles vibrating at different frequencies. With the global scale of operations, different particles, the subsidiaries may not vibrate at exactly the same frequency due to local situations. However, it is important to match & adjust frequencies to allow resonance to occur. Reading the pulse of the market & recalibrating are needed at all times. Skills at managing local teams across a global canvas are to be developed. Local leaders may have to be developed at various locations. While the subsidiaries should vibrate in total resonance within themselves, to have a high level of operational efficiency with minimum wastage of energy & resources, there has to be an all-pervasive wave engulfing all the subsidiaries, which has a uniform frequency. This is where the wave particle duality comes into play. If there is no wave engulfing all subsidiaries with a common frequency, they will move away like separate entities, the corporation becoming an agglomeration of particles doing their own dance, the only reason for staying together being like that of a portfolio of Mutual Funds, being managed for balancing financial returns. The organizational fabric withers away. The common purpose gets lost. This wave engulfing all subsidiaries with the same frequency is open, candid & continuous communication, leading to alignment of goals, cultivation of trust & clarity of team objectives while maximizing benefits of requisite grouping of differentiated knowledge, competence & skills. Group meetings, regular communication, collaborative efforts play an important role. Organizations get leaders from across the world to meet in offsite resorts, sometimes by rotation across subsidiaries to build this common bond. Familiarity builds, understanding &empathy increases. In the absence of such an unification, a higher level of entropy in the system can lead to chaos at the micro level, with the macro organization losing its appearance and character. No wonder one finds companies like Infosys, TCS, GE having a certain "character", wherever they operate across the world. This wave engulfing the entire organization helps to preserve the organizational DNA. At a subatomic level, the nucleus has a mass lesser than the sum of the particles that are bound together. This mass is converted into the energy that bonds the subatomic particles together & this is the energy that is unleashed in the explosion of a nuclear device. Not only internally, an energy exchange with the ecosystem external to the organization brings in the many benefits of networking.

To make it all happen The Leader has to ensure Empowerment, Accountability & Execution Excellence. There have to be certain immutable, unquestionable principles & norms of operation of the organization in place. Systems & processes have to be designed accordingly. These ensure that there is disciplined approach & thinking across the organization, while different parts operate smoothly, with the required autonomy & in line with organisational objectives. Measures and Rewards should be designed to encourage desired behavior of collaboration & knowledge sharing. Light has the same speed for all freely moving observers. The laws of nature appear the same for all freely moving observers. Only relative motion, which implies adjustments & adaptation due to local variances remain important.

While the Universe is many years old, light from our distant past is still reaching us. We need to tune into the right frequency to catch the microwave radiation just reaching us from those days. The spectrum of that radiation shows the characteristics of our heritage. So also, after the SME has tread on the path of globalization, values, DNA, culture, character & purpose should be passed on through folklore, anecdotes & documented learning's, to keep that energy of initial The Big Bang alive leading to Infectious Enthusiasm over the space-time continuum!!

## VISION—A GUIDING STAR

**How do you foresee your destiny? What are you aiming for?**

Vision statement provides a rallying point for an organization to march in a coordinated fashion towards its desired destiny like a guiding star.

Indian National Movement for freedom is a classic example of how a Vision statement properly worded, communicated and followed with right strategies could galvanize ordinary people to achieve improbable actions.

**"Swaraj is my birthright, and I shall have it"**, said Balagangadhar Tilak in the early part of 1900s.

Tilak was the first Indian nationalist to embrace Swaraj as the destiny of the nation.

In September 1920, Mohandas Karamchand Gandhi, known as the Father of the Indian nation prevailed upon congress to adopt 'Swaraj' as the vision for the organization.

The Vision of a Free Indian State, ignited the Indian masses in due course leading to the well know Indian Freedom movement and subsequent release of the subcontinent from the clutches of the British Rule.

INC took upon itself the mission of educating the masses through a series of activities and to sensitize them about the importance of freeing the country from the clutches of the empire.

While Gandhi used non-violence and non-cooperation as the strategy to evict the British rulers, what he used was a series of tactics and activities like Quit India Movement, Dandi March and a series of civil disobedience movements to galvanize the masses and keep up the momentum till the eventual end result are achieved.

In the same way, a Vision Statement that resonates with the stakeholders in an organization has got the ability to galvanize and motivate the members and provide a powerful unifying force that guides people at all levels to strive to achieve seemingly impossible things.

Vision Statement reflects the organization's wish for achievement for the long term. A clear vision could be broken down into a series of sub-visions that would lead to the development of mission and strategy of an organization. This should adequately capture the future position of an organization with respect its areas of operation, technology adaption, customers, stakeholders, business partners, vendors, products, services, positioning w.r.t competitors etc.

For example:

A vision statement for an Indian airline could be:

**To be the largest carrier of choice in Indian Subcontinent.**

Subsets to this could be:

- To delight the customers and be the airline of choice by a majority of air passengers

- To be a partner of choice to the travel agents across the country and hold a majority share of their earnings
- To be the most profitable of all the airline and reward the shareholders with more than Double the market rate of return
- To be the employer of choice and delight the employees through highest level of earnings and job satisfaction
- To be the partner of choice for all business associates like airports, banks, lenders and the like through consistent win-win transactions
- To be the best corporate in the country in the eyes of Government and society by complying with all the rules and regulations of the land, have highest contribution to society and the exchequer among all the airline companies.

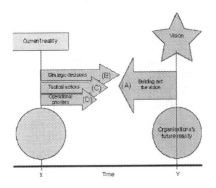

Once the vision is laid out, the company could lay out appropriate strategies, define the values, set up performance benchmarks along with corresponding timelines, reporting and reward structures to gradually inch towards the stated vision. This process of reaching the desirable future position as enunciated by the Vision statement becomes the mission of all the leaders of the organization at various levels.

The march of an organization towards its Vision will lead to implementation of strategic decisions, tactical actions, operational priorities at all levels. The vision statement should be sufficiently communicated and carried creating a number of leaders in the organization who are thoroughly convinced about the vision of the organization and carry the message through a systematic effort across various levels until the entire organization shares the vision & resonates with one goal, then the success indeed becomes probable!

In the case of Indian National Movement, a number of leaders like including C. Rajagopalachari, Jawaharlal Nehru, Vallabhbhai Patel, Subhash Chandra Bose and others—became the prominent voices of the Indian independence movement and carried the messages to the masses.

Leaders at various levels should strive to keep the entire organization focused on achieving the inspiring vision by excelling at their respective roles, which are designed as a part of the framework to work in synergy to achieve the overall goal while they achieve to strive their individual goals in a focused manner. This will ensure that there is an environment in which people are empowered to take ownership of their actions while the leaders perform the role of aligning the actions of various departments and ensure there are harmony, synergy and a shared sense of achievement.

**MISSION—A SENSE OF PURPOSE THAT ENERGISES AN ORGANISATION . . .** "One word comes to my mind. It is 'Mission Accomplished'. We believe we had the team to win and we achieved it!

—*Gautam Gambhir, Captain of Kolkatta KnightRiders, after winning IPL-5 in May 2012, from being mere pushovers in the earlier editions of the tournament.*

**Effective mission statements commonly clarify the organization's purpose and also ultimately seeks to justify the organization's reason for existing.**

—*Wikipedia.*

KKR team owned by the legendary Shahrukh Khan and captained by the astute & competent Gautam Gambhir, set out on a mission to outclass formidable competition from Delhi, Mumbai, Bangalore & Chennai who were much more star packed and seen as favorites to win the competition. The strategy formulated involved a number of elements some of the key ones highlighted could be:

a) Selection of a balanced team to strengthen the various departments through strong performers (not stars)

b) Disciplined and no nonsense approach, no talking to media, no revealing of game plans and strategies

c) Thorough study of the pitches and matching the team for each match with relevant players

d) Back key players and use them tactically in each match to keep the opposition guessing and unsettled

e) No undue emotional outbursts and excessive behavior on and off the pitch

f) An undue faith in the team members and in the Captain by the management, it is the collective strength of the team that counts and not individual brilliance

g) Garner strong home support through diplomatic handling and right words at right time h) Fight till the very end in each match and never give up and above all

h) Believe in themselves and never be intimidated by the more formidable opposition teams

It is indeed possible that every team that competed in the IPL have a mission statement exhorting them to go for the gold! But is it just enough to have a mission statement and not follow up with a clear strategy that accompanies a clear mission statement which the entire organization internalizes and swears to follow with their hearts?

It is a general practice for every professionally run organization to have a mission statement at the outset outlining three major aspects of the company's functioning namely:

The products and services provided, the target markets addressed and the distinctive benefits that they would strive to offer to their customers. By defining clearly, the purpose of the business, the mission statement should lead the organization to a strong and calculated strategy, instill the right values, set the guidelines to the business in the form of business rules and behavior of the members of the organization.

Eminently Successful Organizations, Spectacularly failed organizations and even moderately successful organizations have spent lot of top management time, money and effort to come out with inspiring mission statements with a firm eye on the Vision encompassing their organizations.

Let us examine some mission statements:

**Apple:** Apple is committed to bringing the best personal computing experience to students, educators, creative professionals and consumers around the world through its innovative hardware, software and Internet offerings

**Dell:** Dell's mission is to be the most successful computer company in the world at delivering the best customer experience in the markets we serve

**Facebook:** Facebook's mission is to give people the power to share and make the world more open and connected

**Google:** Google's mission is to organize the world's information and make it universally accessible and useful

**Microsoft:** Microsoft's mission is to enable people and businesses throughout the world to realize their full potential

**Skype:** Skype's mission is to be the fabric of real-time communication on the web

**Yahoo!:** Yahoo!'s mission is to be the most essential global Internet service for consumers and businesses

**YouTube:** YouTube's mission is to provide fast and easy video access and the ability to share videos frequently

**Walmart:** We save people money so they can live better"

A well-written mission statement most often explains the differentiation of the company's products and services with respect to the competition and creates a magnetic pull on the target customers.

While a good mission statement is simple to understand and causes the stakeholders to come together and energizes them, very often we see mission statements being too long, generic, disconnected with the sense of purpose, core strength and passions of the organization. Such statements confuse people and end up getting disconnected and lead to a lack lustre work environment and lead to eventual failure of organizations.

Let us look at mission statements of some failed companies:

**Lehman Brothers:** Our mission is to build unrivalled partnerships with and value for our clients, through the knowledge, creativity and dedication of our people, leading to superior results for our shareholders.

**Enron:** Respect, Integrity, Communication and Excellence.

While the mission statement of Enron is too general and non-communicative any specific goal or purpose, the one of Lehman Brothers seems reasonably well defined.

It shows that having a good Mission Statement is alone not enough, but the entire organization has to believe in it and resonate with the purpose defined as one entity for it show the desired results and this should continue for ever. The moment the organization and the top leadership gets out of sight of this, trouble is indeed round the corner.

# CULTURE—THE PERSONALITY THAT DEFINES AN ORGANIZATION

You can go as far as your culture takes you . . .

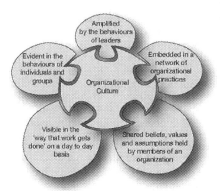

Organizations that have been most successful in recent times are those which have recognized the importance of creating an empowering, ethical, success driven, balanced work cultures and implemented this across their entities.

Culture impacts the way an organization is perceived in the eyes of its stakeholders, employees and the external environment and has a huge bearing on the valuation of companies as well.

Google, Tatas, Birlas, Godrej, TVS Group, Reliance, Infosys, HDFC, ICICI, Wipro, Apple etc are classic examples of companies that stand for well defined corporate culture that reflects in the form of a vision that they create in our minds.

The Organizational culture is one of the major factors that influence the ratings of the organizations among the best places to work for or study at etc. When most of the employers interview potential employees, the most critical thing they try to assess is whether the employee fits well into their organizational culture.

A number of times, wrong selections are made due to the lack of this very understanding. For example, having an individualistic and an introvert person in a team oriented or an autocratic boss in a participative decision making environment lead to divergence and disharmony at work places. It has been seen that brilliant employees get fired just because they were more focused on their own achievements instead of taking their teams along with them.

What is Organizational Culture?

Ravasi and Schultz (2006) state that organizational culture is a set of shared mental assumptions that guide interpretation and action in organizations by defining appropriate behavior for various situations. At the same time, although a company may have "own unique culture", in larger organizations, there are diverse and sometimes conflicting cultures that co-exist due to different characteristics of the management team. Deal and Kennedy (1982) defined organizational culture as the way things get done around here.

**We can say that Culture is the 'Consistently Used Language To Understand & Respond Every time, across the organization'.**

Culture, an intangible overhang on an organizational work environment, emanates from the promoters and the top management of the organization. It is communicated, reinforced and is consciously propagated across the organization through leadership at all levels represented through symbols, logos, tenets, stories and legends, standard operating practices, values, mission and vision statements written and posted across the work place etc.

While it is not possible to recruit and organize a work force with same set of cultural values, organizations try to create appropriate atmosphere, reward systems, and training to orient the employees towards the organizational culture.

**Google presents one of the finest examples of a Great Organizational Culture that has led to phenomenal success.** http://www.google.com/about/company/facts/culture/

'It's really the people that make Google the kind of company it is. We hire people who are smart and determined, and we favor ability over experience. Although Googlers share common goals and visions for the company, we hail from all walks of life and speak dozens of languages, reflecting the global audience that we serve. And when not at work, Googlers pursue interests ranging from cycling to beekeeping, from frisbee to foxtrot.

We strive to maintain the open culture often associated with startups, in which everyone is a hands-on contributor and feels comfortable sharing ideas and opinions. In our weekly all-hands ("TGIF") meetings— not to mention over email or in the cafe—Googlers ask questions directly to Larry, Sergey and other execs about any number of company issues. Our offices and cafes are designed to encourage interactions between Googlers within and across teams, and to spark conversation about work as well as play.

Google's 10-point philosophy constantly reinforces its culture and values across the organization constantly and consistently. http://www.google.com/intl/en/about/company/philosophy/

**Ten things we know to be true**

We first wrote these "10 things" when Google was just a few years old. From time to time we revisit this list to see if it still holds true. We hope it does—and you can hold us to that

- Focus on the user and all else will follow
- It's best to do one thing really, really well
- Fast is better than slowdemocracy on the web works
- You don't need to be at your desk to need an answer
- You can make money without doing evil
- There's always more information out there
- The need for information crosses all borders
- You can be serious without a suit
- Great just isn't good enough

Customer Centricity, focus on individual successes and for team accomplishments, ethical, informal, Innovation friendly, fun loving yet performance driven and endeavor to excel are some of the hallmarks of Google's corporate culture. Google recruits such employees that it feels, embody the company's values and also have an unlimited hunger for information, that drives the organization towards its mission. The healthy and robust organizational culture at Google enables the company to

- Have a Competitive edge derived from innovation and customer service
- Derive Consistent, efficient employee performance
- Have happy and satisfied employees and low employee turnover
- Create Team cohesiveness
- Achieve High employee morale
- Be a Strong company with complete organizational alignment towards goal achievement

In today's word of global work places, mergers and acquisitions, rapid change, defining, creating and maintaining a Culture across the organizations that constantly drive the enterprises to success, is indeed a challenge and inmost often neglected.

Very often the mergers and acquisitions are either not pursued or rejected at the advanced stages just because the organizations discover that the cultures do not match! There are also examples of lack of cultural fit has resulted in confusion and failure of merged entities. It is very important to consider the nuances of the country specific, race specific and regional specific cultures when we evaluate the case for mergers, acquisitions joint ventures, strategic partnerships and the like.

## DRIVEN TO GOALS THROUGH ENDURING VALUES . . .

> "Being Brilliant but having no 'Integrity' is like a police person with pistol wanting to randomly kill instead of protecting citizens against criminals . . ."
>
> —*Master Mentors . . .*

Organizational Values are the qualities that guide the people in an organization in their day-to-day behaviors while they execute the strategies to achieve the mission and the long-term vision of the organization. Values have an inextricable link to the organizational culture. A value driven culture in which there is a strong alignment between the Organizational values and the Personal values of most of the employees is the key to the success of any Organization.

While every organization is value driven, successful organizations consciously work on outlining and articulating the right values and align the organizations as per the same by ensuring that values are shared by all the employees and ingrained into their behavior. Most of the organizations drift along without a conscious effort, leading to sporadic success or failure or a mediocre performance that never stands out.

Some common examples of values are as follows:

Accomplishment, accountability, accuracy, achievement, ambition, balance, challenge, collaboration, compassion, competency, courage, credibility, dedication, dependability, dignity, diligence, discipline, diversity, efficiency, empathy, empowerment, enjoyment, environment-friendly, equality, excellence, flexibility, friendliness, fun, generosity, honesty, impartiality, improvement, independence, individuality, influence, innovativeness, integrity, learning, loyalty, optimism, persistence, professionalism, quality, questioning, responsibility, respect, security, service, sincerity, staff well-being, stewardship, teamwork, etc.

Like achievement, balance, diligence, empathy, honesty, impartiality, learning, professionalism are rated as the top personal values of a number of successful persons, accomplishment, dependability, empathy, excellence, honesty, impartiality, integrity, professionalism, respect, service and teamwork are highly rated by most of the successful organizations.

While personal values vary from person to person, Organisational values vary from entity to entity. Normally organizations define values at the highest level and take a number of actions to percolate them across the organization. Selection of employees with matching values, demonstration of values at the top level, reinforcement and reiteration of the values at every level and at possible occasions, reward systems to encourage right values and deterrent actions like demotions, transfers, suspensions, decrements etc. when an individual demonstrates undesirable values are some of the steps taken by the organizations to achieve a value fit and alignment across the entities.

In successful organizations, there is a high degree of co-relation between desired, stated and exhibited values across the organizations unlike in mediocre organizations where, the values espoused are mostly on paper and never propagated, exhibited and internalized.

Alignment of values in organizations thus enables successful organizations to achieve their vision through common norms of behavior across the organizations.

**WORKING WITHOUT A STRATEGY IN MIND IS LIKE TRYING TO CONSTRUCT A BUILDING WITHOUT A BLUE PRINT . . .**
*— Master Mentors . . .*

A strategy is defined as the road map chosen to achieve the end goals. Successful Organizations ensure that every action of theirs is a part of a strategy or a tactic, which is further a part of an overall grand plan to achieve their goals. Lack of Strategic approach leads to shooting in the dark or straying from the path of right direction leading to wastage of resources, suboptimal utilization of resources and ultimate failure. Strategic planning is applied to every element of functioning of successful organizations.

Strategic planning is an organization's process of defining its roadmap or direction, and making decisions on allocating its resources to pursue this strategy. In order to determine the direction of the organization, it is necessary to understand its current position and the possible avenues through which it can pursue a particular course of action. Generally, strategic planning deals with at least one of the three key questions:

1. "What do we do?"
2. "For whom do we do it?"
3. "How do we excel?"

In many organizations, this is viewed as a process for determining where an organization is going over the next year or—more typically—3 to 5 years (long term), although some extend their vision to 20 years.
(Source—Wikipedia).

Strategy also guides the organization in deciding "What not to do?" as this may distract the organization from the right path and from going after the goal set. The reason for failures at most organizations is the inability of the management or the persons responsible for achieving the goals, to choose the right strategy. Strategic thinking can be similar to the approach, a chess player adopts to win a chess game.

In chess every move made by a player is aimed at improving from the present position to capture the competitor's king. The players undertake a number of tactical moves depending on the situation to overcome the opposition. The tactical moves should not only keep in mind the immediate situation and the position surrounding the pieces moved, but also the overall position of all the pieces in the game of both sides and the emerging situation. Further, the players have to think 4-5 steps in advance by analyzing the likely responses of the competition to survive and stay ahead. Innovation, sacrificing short term gains for long term gains (gambits), choosing offensive or defensive strategies depending on the risk taking ability of the principals, trade off between own pieces versus competition depending on their importance are some more important features of chess that are relevant to strategic decision making. Further in Chess, all the resources need to act in tandem and the one who is able to harness their collective power to achieve the ultimate objective of capturing the competitor's king, wins the game.

Similarly in organization, it is imperative to focus the energies of all resources as per a set plan to achieve the ultimate goals.

A successful strategy should take into account:

I.   Goal to be achieved
II.  Resources in hand
III. Tactics to be adopted
IV.  Coordinated approach
V.   Likely response from the environment and other players in the system that may affect the execution and contingent response plan
VI.  Medium term, short term and long term nature of the goals and the corresponding time frames
VII. Cultural aspects of the people involved and
VIII.Risk bearing ability of the principals creating the strategy

Successful Organizations inculcate strategic thinking approach and a win-win approach to attain the objective of value creation, value capture, wealth maximization for their stakeholders, customers, vendors and the society, thus helping them to stay on track to attain their vision.

### BRILLIANT STRATEGY—EXCELLENT EXECUTION . . .

*—HCL Technologies . . .*

HCL Technologies a 4 Billion US$ Information Technology company and a part of the 6 Billion US$ HCL group, is an emerging Indian Transnational organization in the lines of Tata Motors, Tata Steel, Mahindra & Mahindra, Reliance Industries, Wipro, Asian Paints and the like.

At a time when the industry leaders are struggling to keep pace with the pressure to perform in the market place, HCL Technologies continues to exceed the performance estimates by seasoned analysts, coming out with stellar results quarter after quarter. In the words of its vice chairman and the CEO, Mr Vineet Nayar, In business, if you gloat over somebody else's poor show, you would become obsolete too. It is very important to compete with yourself.'

HCL Technologies is credited with a brilliant corporate strategy formulated by its top management to penetrate the global markets, achieve highest level of customer satisfaction leading to repeat business and good referrals, brilliant acquisition strategy to reach out to new product market & service segments and an aggressive on the ground execution strategy that never leaves anything to chance.

HCL Tech, led by the legendary Shiv Nadar, was falling into the trap of being a promoter driven organization, which limits the growth to the active lifetime of the promoters. But the business continuity strategy of the promoters led it to the appointment of competent professionals to take the organization into the 21st century in a robust manner.

Having transitioned from a promoter led group into a professional management led organization, HCL Technologies stands to join the ranks of global transnational organizations like Cisco and Samsung which have flourished even after the exit of their promoters from the business and are here to stay for generations.

At the outset, HCL Technologies, when faced with severe competition in its core business and the markets it operates in, set out to implement the blue ocean strategy of identifying to uncontested market spaces offering immense potential with a possibility of high value addition and high margin business. Its spread its tentacles deeper into global markets with much stronger presence in the Europe, America, Asia and the African markets. HCL acquired Axon technologies to cement its place in the higher end of the value chain of SAP consulting, globally.

With a strong presence across the globe, HCL Technologies is now a truly global organization of Indian origin.

Another aspect of HCL Tech's brilliant strategic thinking was revealed when, HCL Tech announced its intention to put 'Employees first and Customers second', which is different from the conventional logic of putting customers ahead of the employees as the most important pillars of the business.

As the information technology business is a manpower intensive business, focusing on the quality of the employees training them to be the best in what they do and keeping them motivated will ensure that they deliver the best results in front of the customers, thus dramatically improving the possibility of successful engagement.

HCL Tech has been consistently rated as one of the best employers in most of the countries it is present in and this has led to a delighted customer base that not only stick steadfastly with the organization but also helps in increasing the depth and breadth by engaging more & referring more business to the company.

A Brilliant Strategy which also added its own weight in achieving execution excellence by a company which is known to be the most enterprising of the Indian corporate spectrum, has set HCLT on a journey of transformation that has made it one of the fastest-growing and profitable global IT services companies in the world today. According to Business Week, HCL Tech is one of the twenty most influential companies in the world.

It can be safely said that HCL Tech is on an irreversible path of success, as its top management never believes in resting on the past laurels of the organization. In the words of Mr Vineet Nayar, 'Your downfall begins the day you start believing that you are invincible and that you are the god's greatest gift to mankind. At HCL, we do not allow that feeling to enter. We have done relatively better but we are more concerned about our future'.

**Every idea, every product or a service, every activity and every organization is subject to the phenomenon of lifecycle . . .**

*—Master Mentors . . .*

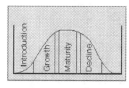

Understanding the lifecycle concept and applying the same to the day-to-day decision making process will lead us to take most appropriate decisions at any stage. Life cycle generally involves4 stages namely, birth, growth, maturity and death, of varying time frames.

The following are the examples of Lifecycle:

i.  **Idea:** Birth, buzz creation in a medium till critical strength in the form of the propagators, propagating rapidly and reaching a peak in interest levels and followers, decline in interest levels and finally disappearance

ii. Activity: Initiation, Preparation, Implementation and closure
iii. Tree: Seed, sprout, sapling, mature tree and sagi
iv. Animal: Birth, growth, adolescence, maturity, middle-age, old age and death
v. Product: Introduction, growth, maturity and decline
vi. Organization: Idea, formation, growth, maturity, decline and liquidation (can be challenged).

Resource and support requirements, issues faced for survival and growth, output levels are different in different stages, in all the above cases and hence it is imperative to know this when handling any situation.

Organizations, being non living organisms, exhibit complex life-cycle patterns compared to living organism. Each of their stages can vary in duration unlike in living organisms, where it is more or less constant, depending on the type of species.

While some organizations are quickly off the ground and grow large in no time, like Google, Facebook etc., some organizations like Citibank live for over 200 years and keep growing over time. Organizations like Apple computers passed through decline stage and came back with renewed vigour and accelerated growth, while rivals acquired organizations like Chrysler after a challenging period.

Unlike living organisms, organizations can be engineered and managed to survive eternally for generations through appropriate management and professional approach.

Life cycle of organizations that continuously reinvent themselves through innovation, adapting to the external environment and stay relevant to their target audience can look as shown above.

**Organizations life cycle issues could be described as follows:**

| STAGE OF LIFE CYCLE | KEY ACTIVITIES | REMARKS |
|---|---|---|
| FORMATION | Create Business Plan, Fixed investments, Strategy, Fine-tuning & Finalizing business proposition, Seed capital | Promoter focus is of paramount importance to get the idea off the ground and make the idea deliver as planned |
| GROWTH | Revenue growth, get people, processes and systems in place, Manage working capital, delivery to meet demand growth, innovative approaches to make most of limited approaches | Most of the businesses fail here as their resources are unable to keep pace with the growing needs and also lack of systems will lead to a building being raised on poor foundation leading to the crash. Also competition from established players will be a grave threat. |
| MATURITY | Steady state operation, growth plateaus, competition intensifies, focus on delivering the brand's promise consistently and ward off competition through trade promotion and brand investments. Aging manpower with growing salaries tend to get complacent | This is a consolidation phase. Profits generated during this phase should partly be reinvested to generate new avenues of growth by launching new products, services, brand extensions etc. to prolong the organization's lifecycle. Organizational issues due to power struggle, ego clashes, leadership issues start troubling the organization |

| DECLINE | Decline in volumes, profitability due to multiplicity of factors like changing consumer preferences, environmental issues, intense competition, new innovations changing market dynamics, alternate products, changing ownership or interest of owners, changing relationships with principals and business partners | Complacency and failure to adapt to the changing dynamics of the market will lead to the onset of the decline stage. Blame game de-motivates the staff. Re-orientation and training is a must in such a situation to survive decline |
| NEW GROWTH PHASE OR DEATH | Some organizations survive the decline phase and emerge victorious in the market shake out, reinventing themselves. Emergence of new growth trajectories from new launches starting fresh lifecycle and rejuvenation | Companies that adapt themselves and manage to survive the shakeouts through proactive approach undertaken during the maturity phase emerge stronger and start a new growth path |

Understanding the life cycle concept allows the leaders in an organization to adopt appropriate strategy, leadership style, employee orientation and adapt the organization by confronting any issues that arise to threaten the existence of organization appropriately, thus ensuring long term survival.

## PARANOIA+PASSION+POINTS OF INFLECTION = DISRUPTIVE GROWTH

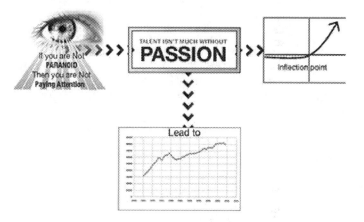

ORGANIZATIONS SOAR WHEN THEY FIND THEIR STRIDE

Successful organizations discover their fortune through perseverance, paranoia & passion, leading to continuous innovation, execution excellence. Theyconsistently stay ahead of their competition by riding the points of inflection. There is a fortune waiting behind the door for every organization borne with a purpose in mind.

**Organizations have to strive to find the right key to the door to their fortune of their life time . . .**

*—Master Mentors . . .*

Look around and we find thousands of organizations struggling to survive as they are unable to make profit despite investing lot of resources and toiling hard. They are termed as 'Busy Fools' who work hard only to make losses or at best, no money. They are unable to serve the stakeholders, employees and the society. On the other hand, we come across incredibly successful organizations that have hit the sweet spots in their business, again and again, leading to consistent growth and prosperity.

"Only the Paranoid Survive", quoted Andrew S. Grove, one of the Intel's founders and a legendary CEO. Intel is one of the most successful and ever growing companies of our times, which rode the points of inflection consistently in its growth curve, continuously reinventing itself, to be in tune with the customers' needs and leading the industry standards with more and more powerful processors.

In his book 'Only the Paranoid Survive', Andrew Grove discussed the concept of 'Strategic Inflexion Point'. "An inflection point occurs where the old strategic picture dissolves and gives way to the new", he said.

"There is at least one point in the history of any company when you have to change dramatically to rise to the next level of performance. Miss that moment, and you start to decline." *Andy Grove, Intel CEO.*

While it is never easy to find the inflection point and most of the companies are often blind sighted by this, the best companies are forever paranoid and are continuously innovating to keep themselves ahead of the curve.

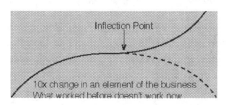

Some of the companies that dominated the world by riding the waves created by the inflection points through innovation, determination and passion in the recent history are:

**Google** — With its Search related products and services to capitalize on the rising need for 'Information services'

**Apple** — With iPod, iPhone and the iPad to capture the mobile consumers

**Dell** — Customized products to cater to the value for money conscious empowered customers

**RIM** — Black Berry phones for mobile enterprise customers

**Amazon** — E-commerce and Cloud computing platform to capture the sweeping changes in the service oriented architecture space

**FaceBook, Linkedin and Twitter**-Social media platforms to enabletoday's generation to express themselves, leverage their social networks, stay connected, share and validate experiences

**Nokia**—Telecom revolution with value for money feature ridden hand sets for brand conscious consumers

**Samsung**—With feature rich experience phones with multimedia experience etc.

It is important to note that some of the companies are unable to keep in tune with the fast changing market landscapes and are falling by the wayside losing their market share quickly.

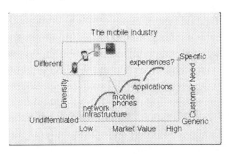

Nokia, Motorola, RIM, Myspace, Orkut faced trying situations to keep up their market shares as they miss the inflection points again and again.

While Nokia led the mobile market in its early stages and the application space, both of them are seen to be missing the bus in the era of 'experience' while Apple and Samsung are leading the pack. Apple and Samsung have been continuously unleashing cutting edge innovation to keep in tune with the multiple points of inflection occurring at smaller and smaller intervals.

Organizations, which are driven by passionate promoters, filled with employees who passionately lead the organization through the many curves of growth, take advantage of the points of inflection as they keep occurring. Such organizations are filled with competent professionals with positive attitude, purposefully and passionately driven towards a common vision with high motivation, leading to exceptional results consistently.

Apple Inc, Google, Microsoft, Dell, General Electric, Facebook are some such companies in the living history led by great promoters who have demonstrated an organization wide Paranoia along with Passion, infectious across the organizations which enabled them to conquer the Points of Inflection and take their organizations through phases of disruptive growth.

Companies like Polaroid, Xerox, Sega, Myspace, Orkut, Hindustan Motors, Kodak, Sony, Motorola are some of the numerous companies that have either lost their edge or got the soil under their feet completely washed off due to the tsunami caused by the points of inflection that occurred due to changing market places or disruptive innovations.

While there are Pots of Gold existing for thriving companies to explore and exploit, it is imperative for the successful companies to innovate and persistently try to find the keys to unlock the doors to their fortune.

# POWER OF FOCUS THAT PROPELS ORGANISATIONS

We observe is one of the single most attributes that has helped organizations and individuals achieve wonders and change the way we live. Focus is derived from a combination of inborn interest & passion, mixed with honed capabilities in the chosen direction combined with an unflinching concentration in the same direction. When all these synergize and resonate with each other, they produce earthshaking results that could change the performance of an individual or an organization.

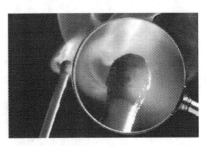

The sunlight, which is diffused over the entire surface, can at best cause a warm feeling on our bodies. But the same sunlight when it is focused on a point with the help of a magnifying glass can cause fire to be lit that can be used for hugely material benefits or damages.

This is a clear analogy from the nature as to what a focused mind or an effort could achieve. On the other hand we find a number of times, the organizations diffuse their energies in different directions, unable to choose one clear area of focus.

While the most desirable choice is to choose a right area of focus which is not only in line with the areas of core competency built over time, it is important to ensure that the organisational energies are synergized and aligned in the right direction to achieve the goals in the areas laid out. Indian National Freedom Movement is a classic example of the best results that a focused effort led by a magnetic leader would achieve while the World War-2 is the classic example of the destructive effects of wrongly focused efforts of satanic leader.

Some recent examples of companies built through focused efforts of pioneering promoters

| Google | Search engine technology for high quality experience of Information hungry surfers. |
| FaceBook | Social Networking among friends & acquaintances |
| Microsoft | Operating Systems & closely related technologies |
| Apple | Breakthrough Innovations in Technology |
| Walmart | Discount Retailing |

| Infosys | Trade Indian Technology expertise with earn in dollars, spend in Rupees approach leading to highly cost effective & high quality IT solutions to clients |
|---------|----------------------------------------------------------------------------------------------------|
| Dell | DM approach to Technology selling with active involvement of end user to cut costs and end with empowered, delighted customers |
| Linkedin | Business networking on the web for a better career & business growth |
| Twitter | Microblogging service for effortless, instant and speedy information sharing |

Interesting to note that all these organizations have offered some distinct benefit to their users and customers and always kept the customers at the centre of their universe.

While lack of sense of focus is clear reason for the limitations on growth achieved by a number of companies, loss of concentration on the core business and business models have led to steep losses or downfall of organizations.

Bausch & Lomb, the promoter of globally admired Ray-Ban Sunglasses, was the undisputed global leader for a long time, till it shifted its focus onto the Contact Lens Business. While the contact lenses and related products' grew, the lack of focus on one of the most admired brands in the world and BLI's claim to fame led to severe losses and ultimate sale of its Eyewear business to Luxottica, a global leader in Eyewear, which not only turned around the brand's performance but also took it to never before seen heights making it one of the most admired and profitable global brands.

In India, we find that companies like Tata Steel, Tata Motors and Bharti Airtel are growing bigger and bigger through strategic acquisitions in their domains of focus. However, care should be taken that companies do not take bets, which are much bigger than their capabilities that may lead to their sudden downfall. For example, when companies undertake acquisitions or green field investments in their areas of focus by leveraging their assets and borrowing heavily, they should take into account the fluctuating exchange rates, the variations in borrowing rates and the likely demand & competitive scenarios in the future that may drastically change the value propositions and business models of Indian companies.

## PRIORITIZATION—THE KEY PRODUCTIVITY DIFFERENTIATOR

**Successful Organizations invariably know the importance of prioritizing their actions to scale newer and newer heights of success**.

At every step of our day-to-day life, we are faced with a number of choices, but the resources that we have at our disposal are never infinite. The decisions we make and the choices we make determine the road ahead and lead to one's success or failure.

Theory of Constraints and Pareto's Principle are some of the most authoritative works in enabling an organization to prioritize their choices and undertake the best course of action in a given situation.

DrEliyahu Goldratt, the author of The Goal, the proponent of Theory of Constraints (TOC), and an Einstein of Management theory & practice, has once said, 'If you want me to condense all of TOC into one word, it would be FOCUS'.

But how do you decide in a given situation, what to focus on, because, focusing on everything is as good as focusing as nothing, when you are faced with limited resources like time, money, people, place and mindshare!

# YOU CAN DO ANYTHING, BUT NOT EVERYTHING.

-David Allen

80:20 rule proved and propagated by Pareto is one of the greatest insights that has attracted the attention of the mankind to the importance of prioritization in choosing the right strategy to spend the organisational or personal resources. It means, most of the time, 80% of the performance is dictated by 20% of the variables and focusing our resources in improving the performance associated with 20% of these variables will lead to a dramatic improvement in the productivity levels and leads us closer to our success.

Some examples we encounter in our day to day life being: 80% of the target market for our product or services could be found in 20% of the geographical area of operation or 80% of the sales coming from 20% of customers or 80% of the resources being consumed in 20% of the activities in the list or 80% of the salary bill in an organization being consumed by 20% of the manpower or 80% of the expenses in an organization being accounted by 20% of the account heads and so-on.

By doing what should be done for sure and minimizing the efforts on what need not be done, organizations could focus their efforts on 20% of the variables and could dramatically improve their productivity, profitability and hence performance levels.

Dr Eliyahu Godratt in his Theory of Constraints has gone further and discovered that in organizations, 0.1% of elements dictate 99% of the performance due to the variability of and interdependencies between the numerous elements that constitute the performance of an organization.

These elements manifest themselves as bottlenecks, synonymous with constraints limiting the performance of the system. Identifying these constraints, prioritizing this constraint in the order of priority to maximize throughput of the system and enhancing the constraint performance step by step, one after another, is a proven method to continuously improve the organizational performance.

We all know that a chain is as strong as its weakest link. Bolstering the rest of the chain while leaving the weakest link untouched is a sure way not only to waste resources, but also to get mislead into a false sense of security.

**Let's take the resources that we have, and prioritize, and manage, and focus our energy on just doing things that count—on real results . . .**
—*Phil Bredesen*

"we are what we repeated do.

Excellence is not an act but a habit"
— Aristotle

Excellence is achieved when you feel the 'Aha' feeling for a job well done, a target achieved and exceeded and a creation that exceeds your own expectations and stands out for being the best.

**"The minute you settle for less than you deserve, you get even less than you settled for"**
— *Maureen Dowd*

While achievement of excellence in every activity, creation and delivery of product or service is the goal of successful companies, they have a practical approach to delivery in their day-to-day work style.

The world's most admired ever technology company is undoubtedly, Apple Inc., under Steve Jobs. Steve

Jobs has the reputation of having a strong penchant for excellence and would never settle for anything but the best. The creations of Apple like its proprietary operating system, 'ilife', its products like MacBook, iPod, iPhone, iPad are creations of breakthrough innovations when they were launched and continuously changed the fortunes of the company to make it one of the most valued technology companies in the world.

Lets examine the following news articles:
Apple, AT&T mum on iPhone 3G issues — (http://goo.gl/dbF5q)
A month after the launch of the iPhone 3G, reception problems continue to plague owners with dropped calls, poor networking speeds, and frustrating customer service experiences. by CNET News staff August 11, 2008 4:00 AM PDT.

"The phone was a disappointment from the standpoint that it couldn't maintain a consistent connection with the 3G network . . . All the other features were fantastic," said Shaw, a sales professional living in a Cleveland suburb. But those other features weren't enough to prevent him from returning to Verizon and the BlackBerry after deciding the hassle just wasn't worth it.

Apple's iPad Woes Continue, Users Now Reporting 3G Connectivity Problems (http://goo.gl/YkjGf)

Brandon Hill (Blog) — April 6, 2012 11:34 AM
Apple announced its third generation iPad early last month, and customers began receiving their units soon after. Shortly after Apple's latest tablet was launched, there were complaints of the device getting much warmer than the iPad 2 during normal use and complaints that the larger internal battery resulted in much longer battery recharging times.
More recently, owners of Wi-Fi only iPads were reporting on connectivity issues (weak Wi-Fi signals,

slow download/upload speeds). Apple issued an internal Apple Care document instructing Apple team members to "capture" customer iPads that were brought in with this diagnosed problem.

What we notice by observing the above are:

a) Through the years 2008-2012, Apple launched new generation products, which faced problems in the market place and hence were not as perfect as the company intended them to be. Yet Apple continued the practice of launching such products the shortcoming of which must have been surely known to its brilliant engineers and product creators.

b) Apple's team continued to listen to the market, unfazed by the negative reports and on every occasion came out stronger to continue their growth momentum in the market place.

c) In one of the above cases, some of the users shifted to a rival phone company, which is struggling to survive today while Apple continues its growth unabatedly.

We find similar situations exist when we study the new product launches of the most successful companies in the world like Microsoft with its successive launches of Windows Operating System, Google with its various products and services, Facebook's platform and even the world's most admired companies in many fields.

What makes these companies continue to be the most preferred companies in their respective field and be the darlings of their target audience and their users?

Pursuit of excellence, that is a habit in such companies is supported by an unquenchable attitude of having their users at the centre of their universe and continuously strive to give them their best.

Successful companies believe in continuous innovation in the market place, making them either the pioneers due to their early-to-market effort or execution excellence that satisfies the needs of their audience in the most efficient manner. They have their eyes and ears firmly on the market place with their fingers on the customer pulse and commission instantaneous corrective actions. This leads to continuous improvements in their products' feature leading to launch of newer versions that take of the shortcomings unearthed. The way you step up your game is not to worry about the other guy in any situation, because you can't control the other guy. You only have control over yourself.—Oprah. http://goo.gl/FywSD

Pursuit of excellence is a habit that is firmly ingrained into the fabric of successful organizations who relentlessly push the limits of their own performance, even as they continue with their rapid strides in the market with not so perfect launches to start with.

It is the attitude to excel, appetite for better and better results, aptitude to figure out what stands out, that go to form the building blocks of the culture of excellence, that makes pursuit of excellence a routine act and thus a habit of great organizations.

# ETHICS & ENDURABILITY

**Ethics are the most important pillars on which an enduring corporation stands.**
— *Master Mentors*

Ethics is that part of the behavior of a human being or an entity that enables the person or the persons within the organization collectively to choose between the right and wrong actions. Ethical behavior forms the backbone of successful and progressive business.

Good corporate Ethics involve transparency of operation, responsibility towards employees, stakeholders, environment, customer, government and the society and keeps their well being in mind for any decision or action. Ethical approach is reflected in the way an organization chases its goals, makes credible and practical commitments & honors the same at any cost. Ethical approach follows sound practices with self-monitoring mechanisms rather than a response to enforced supervision. Ethical behavior has to do with the long-term approach of an organization, which is not bothered just about short-term profit maximization.

Ethical organizations meet the twin objectives of being on the right side of law and also work as per accepted principals of social justice. Ethics are moral values, which guide the mangers in an organization to undertake transparent behavior that is consistent with the interests of the organization as well as the society without compromising the profit motive.

Companies throwing ethical behavior to winds have been known to have undertaken short cuts to success for profit maximization like account fudging diverting money into the promoters' pockets and also manipulating share prices to hoodwink investors.

Companies following ethics benefit in the long run as their transparency and socially responsible behavior earn them a lot of goodwill leading to a good response from the shareholders, investors and customers. This will result in a higher business and also higher valuation in the stock markets increasing their financial power to raise resources when needed in an advantageous manner.

Companies following unethical behavior are always at risk of falling on the wrong side of law sometime or the other. History is replete with examples of such companies that have been mercilessly punished, leading to their bankruptcy or extinction. Enron and Satyam are some such companies which have borne the brunt of their unethical behaviour.

Organizations like Tata, Infosys and Wipro in India stand testimony to the fact that ethical behavior pays off in the long run and stands to be a key pillar of their endurance.

It is very important for organizations to realize that the ability to face the testing times during their growth period without succumbing to the temptations of achieving quick successes by following the shortcuts offered by the unnatural & unethical practices and approaches is one of the most important determinants of their long term viability of organizations, though it is easier said than done.

**"You have to withstand pressure, if you can't handle pressure you can't be a great or successful entrepreneur".**

—*Donald Trump*

The choice really is to live like a diamond that grows in value through the times or like an ephemeral cloud, whose life, no one knows, how long . . .

## BENCHMARK FOR BUSINESS ETHICS—INFOSYS & TATA GROUP

Infosys and the Tata enterprises are the living examples for highest level of ethical conduct and no compromise approach to integrity in the pursuit of corporate excellence.

### Infosys:

Infosys one of the pioneers in the Information technology industry in India, is a corporation which always stood for ethical and responsible approach to business. The customers, employees, society and the investor community have consistently viewed it as the most transparent and ethical organization. Infosys's founder and Chairman Emeritus, N.R.Narayanamurthy, has always been a great follower and advocate of ethics in business. Infosys's top management always championed the case of ethics in each and every one of its actions and messages, both within the company and outside as well.

> **"Professionalism and ethics are becoming more and more relevant in our quest to become better professionals, in our quest to make this country a better place and this world a better place. And that exactly is the background that we have set out with"**
> —*Narayana Murthy*

Narayanamurthy, through his simplicity, approach to business, honesty, integrity and professional excellence proved to the world that, ethical conduct, transparency and business acumen are not at variance with each other and are indeed interrelated. He along with his co-founders of Infosys, created perhaps the world's most ethical organization in the world with an incredible ascent on transparency, responsible behavior and ethical conduct. This has created an organization with a distinctive value system and culture focused on integrity, transparency and responsible approach while pursuing excellence.

While a number of organizations today are engaged in window dressing their accounts and also are trying to communicate a performance far better than the actual, with a view to inflating their valuation, Infosys always followed the policy of naked transparency in front of the investing community, through their 'When in doubt, disclose' approach.

In addition to complying to the laws of the land where ever it operates, Infosys ensures transparency and accountability through the adoption of a Code of Conduct and Ethics and a Whistle-blower policy. Infosys ensures that every one of the employees is thoroughly oriented with the code of ethical conduct, by incorporating orientation modules on the same in the employee induction programs and also regularly updates all the employees worldwide, through online and offline training & awareness programs through the 'Do you know your ethics' series of events.

Through the internal TV channel Infy TV, Sparsh the corporate intranet, direct lectures and training programs, the CEO & leaders at Infosys regularly talk to their employees about the importance of ethical conduct. An uncompromising stand on ethics is followed by strict actions are taken against the transgressors of the code of conduct, though they are few and far between. Infosys has been consistently rated at the highest level of CGR (Corporate Governance Rating) by all the rating organizations and agencies.

No wonder, Infosys has been consistently enjoying not only financial success but also a very high price-equity ratio that gives it an excellent valuation on the stock markets and a blue chip status.

**Tata Group:**
Tata's under the leadership of Ratan Tata have grown to be the largest corporate group operating out of India with a global presence. With an annual turnover of over US$80 Billion, dominating presence across the world in a number of businesses and millions of employees,

Tata Group is an epitome of success. Ratan Tata's uncompromising approach to bend to the whims and fancies of those in power and compromise on ethical business conduct may have won him a number of enemies. But, this is what has earned him and his group an amazing respect across the globe as Tatas spread their footprint in to the developed markets through strategic acquisitions of world leaders like Corus Steel, JLR etc. The high valuation of the Tata Group companies and the willingness of the financial firms to lend money to thegroup without any limitations, has its roots in the respectability Tatas earned through their ethical conduct. Ratan Tata and Narayana Murthy have established benchmark for ethical conduct and also proved unequivocally that long term business success and ethical behaviour are intertwined and inseparable.

# SUSTAINABLE GROWTH—THE 3BL APPROACH

**"Every action you take in business has two components: an impact onprofits and an impact on the world"**

*Quote from Triple Bottom Line by Andrew W Savitz and Karl Weber.*

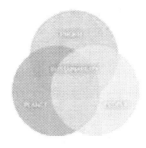

Image courtesy of Sustainability Partnership International

Triple Bottom line, abbreviated as **TBL** or **3BL**, and also known as **people (fairand equitable HR practices, planet (sustainable environmental practices), profit (economic value creation)** captures an expanded spectrum of values and criteria for measuring, assessing and reporting the economic, environmental and social success of organizations, corporations, projects or processes.

With the environmental degradation caused by the irreversible use of natural resources causing serious threat to the long-term viability of the planet, the net contribution of the carbon foot print is becoming an important measure of the corporate responsible approach to the survival of the planet and passing on a better life to our younger generations. Companies with focus on Triple Bottom Line understand that business success is not just measured by financial performance but also by the impact on the overall society.

A TBL focused company aims to limit the economic damage caused by the processes it undertakes to produce & deliver and also undertake necessary activities through the lifecycle of its products, services to minimize their carbon footprint.

Recycling of waste, use of renewable resources, conservation of natural resources, discouraging over exploitation of natural resources, reduction of consumption of products and services that lead to excess creation of environmentally hazardous waste, treatment of hazardous waste generated by them etc. are some of the activities necessarily undertaken by companies focused on Long term Sustainability.

Correspondingly the leading companies across the world now proactively disclose in their annual reports, the various steps and standing across various metrics relating to the company's efforts for a sustainable environment.

While it involves higher expenses and investments for organizations to follow such admirable processes, they indeed payoff in the long run as,

i.   Consumers across the globe are increasingly patronizing products and services of those organizations, which are demonstrating their commitment to the environmental preservation

ii.  Investors give higher valuation to companies committed to sustained development &

iii. It is also financially remunerative to be a negative carbon foot print company due to government subsidies, incentives and profits on sale of Carbon credits

Some of the actions taken by the world are leading companies

**Hewlett Packard—HP** owns and opens enormous "e-waste" recycling plants that shred discarded, obsolete computer products into raw materials that can be recycled into the industrial food chain. HP has also agreed to take back computer equipment of all brands, and has taken steps to ensure that its own products are 100% recyclable in the manner discussed above.

**TESCO:** This British grocery chain has enlisted its customer base in the fight to go green by offering savings to shoppers who bring reusable shopping bags to their stores. The company has also turned each of its stores into wind-powered, high-recycling, biodiesel truck delivered epicenters of environmental sustainability, running at such high efficiency Ralph Nader would be beside himself. In another major breakthrough, Tesco is aiming to estimate the "carbon costs" of each item it sells.

**Bank of America:** Internal recycling paper of over 30000 tones, incentivizing employees to buy hybrid vehicles.

**Starbucks:** With the company's decision to use coffee cup sleeves made of recycled paper saving over a lakh trees per year, Starbucks has also partnered up with many environmental organizations, from Conservation International to the Earth watch Institute, in efforts to do right by the communities it operates in.

**Walmart:** Committed to using its waste-eliminating corporate philosophy to make its own operations more eco-friendly; launched an ambitious long term plan to eventually power each of its stores use 100% renewable energy sources.

**Coca-cola:** Coca-Cola has narrowed down 3 environmental goals on which to focus their efforts: water stewardship, sustainable packaging, and climate & energy protection. Each of these initiatives is detailed and explained at their corporate website. Involved in community recycling programs and a complete, sustainability-focused overhaul of its packaging designs.

**Dell:** Through its "no computer should go to waste" recycling program, Dell allows customers to return any Dell-branded product back to the company for free. The company has even gone so far as to establish programs that accept computers, monitors, or printers from other companies for safe disposal, as well.

In India companies like Wipro, ITC Group, HCL Technologies, HDFC Bank, Suzlon, Hero Motors, Idea Cellular etc, are leading the group of 3BL focused organizations working towards a sustainable environment.

These are just some of the many cases of globally admired and eminently successful organizations leading the movement towards a sustainable environment. Many of these companies are undertaking humongous constructions to house their ever-growing staff. To ensure that they are following environmentally friendly practices, these companies follow the guidelines laid out by the LEED Rating system.

Developed by the U.S. Green Building Council (USGBC), and spearheaded by Robert K. Watson, Founding Chairman LEED Steering Committee from 1995 until 2006, LEED (Leadership in energy and environmental design) is intended to provide building owners and operators a concise framework for identifying and implementing practical and measurable green building design, construction, operations and maintenance solutions.

LEED 2009 is a third party certification system and a suite of rating system to assess the environmental impact of constructions. LEED-India Green Building Rating System is a nationally and internationally accepted benchmark for design, construction and operation of high performance green buildings.

In LEED 2009 there are 100 possible base points distributed across five major credit categories: Sustainable Sites, Water Efficiency, Energy and Atmosphere, Materials and Resources, Indoor Environmental Quality, plus an additional 6 points for Innovation in Design and an additional 4 points for Regional Priority. Buildings can qualify for four levels of certification:

**Certified:** 40-49 points
**Silver:** 50-59 points
**Gold:** 60-79 points
**Platinum:** 80 points and above The LEED for Homes rating system is different from LEED v3, with different point categories and thresholds that reward efficient residential design.

Points "based on the potential environmental impacts and human benefits of each credit" are distributed across major credit categories such as Sustainable Sites, Water Efficiency, Energy and Atmosphere, Materials and Resources, and Indoor Environmental Quality.

Infosys, which has undertaken some of the largest constructions in India, consistently achieved the level of 'Platinum ratings' for its buildings by Indian Green Building Council (IGBC). Infosys has over 3 buildings with a building area of 780,000 sq ft, as Platinum rated.

These are just some of the many cases of globally admired and eminently successful organizations leading the movement towards a sustainable environment.

## CHAMPION OF ENVIRONMENT—ITC (INDIA)
SUSTAINABILITY FOCUSED GROWTH . . .

ITC is a diversified Indian company with presence in FMCG (Fast Moving Consumer Goods), Hotels, Paperboards & Specialty Papers, Packaging, Agri-Business and Information Technology. ITC is one of the largest & most professionally run organizations in India. Established over 100 years back, ITC Limited, with a turnover close to US$ 7 Billion annually, net income close to US$ 3 billion and a market capitalization of over US $ 40 Billion, is undoubtedly one of the most successful brick and mortar companies grown out of Indian soil. ITC's efforts in Sustainable Development and Environmental preservation have been pioneering and exemplary. For championing the issues of environmental preservation through well executed and widely participated afforestation programs, ITC was conferred the World Business and Development Award 2012 at the historic Rio+20 United Nations Summit. By spearheading a low carbon growth strategy, ITC has achieved a number of milestones in the environmental and social dimensions.

i) ITC has been "carbon positive" for 7 consecutive years, sequestering twice its emissions

ii) It has been "water positive" for 10 years, having created freshwater potential that is more than twice its consumption

iii) ITC has been "solid waste recycling positive" for 5 years continuously

iv) More than 38% of ITC's vast energy requirements are met from renewable sources. More than a dozen ITC facilities including premium luxury hotels and factories in several locations as well as the ITC Infotech Park and the ITC R & D Centre in Bengaluru run more or less completely with renewable energy. Such a large footprint of renewable energy not only reduces demand for fossil fuels but also contributes to cost efficiency in the long-term

v) ITC Green Centre in Gurgaon has recently been re-certified as the world's highest rated Platinum certified green building by the US Green Building Council

vi) Several of ITC's factories have also received the Platinum Green Factory Building Rating

vii) ITC Hotels is the greenest hotel chain in the world with all the premium luxury hotels of the company being Platinum LEED certified.

ITC also undertakes several social development focused initiatives to provide sustainable livelihood opportunities to over 5 million rural & tribal people in India. Some of the popular programs ITC runs are:

a) Farmer empowerment program: ITC e-Choupal benefiting over 4million farmers from over 40000 villages

b) Social farming and Forestry Program: ITC has undertaken significant wasteland development and greening of over 125,000 hectares and uses renewable plantations from these areas enabling

ITC to offer the greenest products in the country such as Classmate notebooks and Paperkraft business and copier paper. c). Wealth out of Waste (WoW) programme: ITC's WoW initiative is supported by 3 million citizens, 500,000 school children, 350 corporates and over 1,000 commercial establishments. This in turn helps augment green cover, conserves energy and scarce natural resources, makes surroundings clean and healthy and creates livelihood opportunities.

With a number of well-crafted programs, ITC strategically follows a sustainable development model that has paid rich dividends to it as an organization as well. From a company suffering from a poor image of being a tobacco product maker once upon a time, ITC has transformed itself into a highly valuable and most respected enterprise, commanding a high price-equity ration for its stock in the Indian stock exchanges. This is one of the main reasons behind its soaring market valuation in excess of 40 Billion US Dollars, giving it a great financial strength to thrive in the extremely competitive environment of the 21st century.

ITC can be taken as a benchmark for the organizations aiming to achieve a fine balance of their Triple Bottom Line objectives, thus pursuing the Sustainable Development model of excellence.

## LEADERSHIP LESSONS FROM THE SPORTING WORLD . . .

Few teams in the world have so ruthlessly crushed their competition and dominated the international sports arena in the 21st century, as the Australian cricket team and the Spanish Football team. Spain has made a history in the recent times by winning three consecutive international titles, namely Euro 2008, World cup 2010 and Euro 2012, while Australia has continuously dominated all formats of the international cricket scene for an extended period of time, sporadically losing matches to over extending oppositions.

Spain are the current reigning World and European champions, having won the 2010 World Cup and the Euro 2012 as well as the Euro 2008. They are the first national team to win two consecutive European championships and a World Cup. In July 2008, Spain rose to the top of the FIFA World Rankings for the first time in the team's history, becoming the sixth nation to top this ranking, and the first nation to top the ranking without previously having won the World Cup. Between November 2006 and June 2009 Spain went undefeated for arecord-tying 35 consecutive matches before their loss to the United States, a record shared with Brazil, including a record 15-game winning streak and thus earning third place in the Confederations Cup.

Australia has played 752 ODI matches, winning 464, losing 256, tying eight and with 24 ending in no-result. They have led the ICC ODI Championship since its inception for all but a period of 48 days in 2007. Australia have made record six World Cup final appearances (1975, 1987, 1996, 1999, 2003 and 2007) and have won the World Cup a record four times in total; 1987 Cricket World Cup, 1999 Cricket World Cup, 2003 Cricket World Cup and 2007 Cricket World Cup. Australia is the first team to appear in 4 consecutiveWorld Cup finals (1996, 1999, 2003 and 2007), surpassing theold record of 3 consecutive World Cup appearances by West Indies (1975, 1979 and 1983). (Source—wikepedia)

A study of their success reveals interesting insights into an approach to building successful organizations:

Some of the lessons that can be learnt by studying these winning machines (at their peak) are:

A) Sustained hunger for victory despite continuous winning streak, making, going or success', an habit rather than a end in itself

B) Extremely competent leaders leading from the front with their performance. The performance records of Steve Waugh & Ricky Ponting in the case of Australian cricket team and that of Iker Casillas in the case of Spain were at their peak during the victorious runs of their respective teams

C) Emotionally balanced Leaders who are always accessible to their team members, urging them to give their best, mentoring them when required and stepping in to deliver outstanding results when needed, thus leading by example. With over 75 clean sheets and over 500 minutes without conceding a goal in an Euro, Iker Casilas has not only excelled in his own performance, but also, has a number of other feathers in his cap for excellence in his and his team's performance. Similarly, Steve Waugh and Ricky Ponting have often been rated as the best players of all time to have played the game of Cricket

D) No nonsense approach of an emotionally balanced leadership (coach, captain, board), allowing the individual members to excel without upsetting the team's sense of balance with their brilliance. At times, the pursuit of success is preceded by weeding out non-performers and those who spread toxicity in the system

E) A never say die attitude, which allows them to fight back even from toughest of situations and allows them to bounce back from unexpected adversities

F) Unflinching focus on the goal of winning the match by scoring maximum goals and conceding minimum goals to opponents & ruthless efficiency with highest ratio of goals/runs scored for versus goals/runs scored respectively

G) Extremely competent professionals always fighting for their place with strong reserve teams to back up H) Team spirit and partnership approach rather than focus on individual excellence

H) Focus on doing basics right consistently rather than go for sporadic excellence by taking unplanned and unwarranted risks. Spain has patronized and successfully exploited the efficiency of a simple strategy of football namely, 'Tiki-taka', a style of play characterized by short passing and movement, working the ball through various channels and maintaining possession, which is neutral to offensive and defensive techniques. This simple style has frustrated opponents and led them to success after success. Similarly, Australian Cricket's winning machines were characterized by simple, professional and efficient style that adapts to the requirement with a single objective of winning the game

I) Excellent succession planning and highly competent bench strength with systemic approach to nurture and develop excellence

J) Innovation and improvisation coupled with executing excellence

K) A thorough analysis of the competition teams that will help them pinpoint their strengths and weaknesses followed by thorough planning to take advantage of their knowledge

L) Success follows its own lifecycle, which gets extended when teams reinvent themselves continuously. Otherwise it fades away as the teams get aged, complacent or, are unable to keep pace with the changing circumstances &

m) When the goal of the team is to win, the ego issues take a back seat. This brings out the best of performances from all the team members as they support each other with a single most agenda of emerging victorious

For maintaining a consistent success record, one has to be relentless in pursuit of excellence, continuously reinventing themselves to push the bars higher and higher, keep an eye on the future firmly and cannot afford to relax as the competition is always trying to catch-up and waiting to have a go at the leadership slot ad the margin for error for a leader is extremely limited. Shortcomings in this very aspect have led to the consistent under-performance of greatest cricket teams like West Indies, the football teams like Brazil, Argentina, Italy and hockey teams like India. Recent drop in rankings of the Australian cricketing team's stature shows that success is never enduring and complacency can lead to downfall.

It would indeed be pertinent to note that, the drop in international ranking of Australia coincided with the compromising ethical standards of their captain Ricky Ponting in a game against India, which Australia won after Ricky Ponting claimed a false catch to get an Indian player out. This reveals that, while short term victories are assured when ethics are compromised, the longer-term implications of the drop in moral standards could be negative on the overall team environment and the resultant performance.

Dependence on a few brilliant individual players who overshadow the rest and also upset the team rhythm has never taken their teams far. Organizations could closely follow the reasons for success of the greatest sporting teams and learn from these experiences to create their own success stories.

The following are some of the commonalities of winning teams and Great Organizations:

1. Focus of the entire Organization on the Vision and Goals to be achieved
2. Team spirit to be inculcated as against individual brilliance, working as a lone force
3. Focus on achievement of objectives and not on individual relationships as a superior/subordinate etc

4. Thorough planning by taking into account complete SWOT of self versus competition and play as per the turf, suiting the style with the ground and taking the most out of any situation rather than trying to play own style on any ground

5. Competent leadership, leading from the front and letting the brilliance of individual players bloom without any hindrance. This happens when the organization selects the best and doesn't go for mediocre resources that will not challenge the leadership

6. Focus on doing basic things right with ruthless efficiency, rather than go for grand plans without corresponding output

7. Understand the life-cycle stage of the organization and adopt appropriate strategies at the same time reinvent themselves with appropriate steps to stay relevant and attractive to investors, customers and employees

8. Great leadership does not hesitate to fire non-performers and those who subscribe to mediocrity & spread toxicity among the employees. No body is indispensable in an organization pursuing success professionally, not even the leader

9. Trust and belief among the leaders and their team members is a hallmark of successful organizations. The true belief from within the heart of the leaders on their followers & the teams about their invincibility, most often acts like a self-fueling prophecy and leads to stupendous results

In a successful organization, great leaders ensure that the credit & fruits of success are well shared among the team members, reinforcing great performance and keeping the organization surging, towards its vision.

# OPERATIONAL EFFICIENCY THROUGH PEOPLE POWER

**Why Right People:**

An owner is fully conscious of his roles and responsibilities and why and how he has to do what he does. That is why we have a term called ownership. Hence, it is important to have The Right People at each level and what they should do to be like the owner himself, when it comes to key elements of customer service, continuous improvement, team work, integrity and passion!!

Organized Retail in India is clearly poised to grow. The last decade has seen the growth curve take a definite upward swing. With growth, come newer challenges and newer ways of looking at business. New players enter the market, as also, stakeholders from different domains, who, obviously, may not have been, or rather, definitely would not have been exposed to professional retail processes, considering the absence of opportunities to learn from . . . organized retail was not there and hence also, experienced professionals and education programs to offer know how.

Each stakeholder brings a background and knows how and definitely adds valuable contribution to the growth story. Each also has its own perspective and its own strategy on how to 'create value'. This diversity in skills and knowledge is definitely a good thing as it brings the much-needed basic skills and discussions to enable the evolution of a healthy new knowledge/skill base.

With multiplicity of players in retail, there will also be increased competition and that should be, for sure, good for the customer. Hence, Customer Value Offering will necessarily become extremely critical. Survival of the fittest will therefore be linked to whoever is able to master 'what the customer really wants' & 'what adds most value to the customer'.

Operational efficiency contributes a lot to customer's satisfaction in retail. Most products are sourced and hence, apart from a retailer's role in sourcing the right type, mix (after having studied customer preferences) and depth of inventory, the biggest value addition a retailer can do is through efficient operations i.e., serving according to customer preferences, efficiently. To a large extent, customer preferences at a macro aggregated level, can also be thrown up on an ongoing basis by an operationally efficient system, which 'tracks' the same accurately and hence, if the system is sensitive enough, records and adjusts inventory accordingly . . . very much like the dynamic equilibrium in nature, through an efficient feedback loop of an open system!!

And if there is a robust enough system, it can provide micro level individual customer preferences at the store . . . allowing the floor executive to mimic the 'intimate' understanding of customer preferences that an individual owner can do exceedingly well.

**What will Right People do:**

Strategically, a key differentiator that will emerge therefore, is operational efficiency . . . which includes cost, process efficiency, service cycle times, continuous improvement, width and depth of inventory etc . . . This will be an important input towards achieving high levels of customer service/satisfaction/delight.

Technology will be a key element and an accelerator in winning this game to cater to the huge mass of population. And for that matter, there is money to be made at all levels of the income hierarchy and geographic spread. But how does this get unlocked?

One point, which cannot get over-attention in this, is the importance of Right People and Right People Processes. It is people, across all stakeholders and across all domains, functions and levels, who fundamentally drive all the strategies, decisions and operations. Ability to select, develop, retain and grow The Right People will probably emerge as the single most important Success Factor. Many of the players in retail, definitely spend a large percentage of its revenue in people cost. This is probably the biggest expense in the P&L, after cost of goods . . . and just consider how much attention goes behind purchase of inanimate goods compared to selection, development, retention and growth of The Right People!!

Development of skills and talent, specific to retail itself, maybe an investment worth making in the business. This one activity could be the biggest value and profit enhancer, from the top end paying customer to a no frills outlet in rural areas, where also, as they say, there is a lot of fortune lying!!

It is people at all levels who will become critical to success.

Functional skills will and should vary to bring in diversity and different dimensions to the table/organization. However, a base level of skill sets and behavioral norms is a must and that should be ensured. The key lies in the owner (or Top Management?) to have confidence that the last person in the last store, will behave, act and serve customers as she would have done if she could be at all locations and with all customers all the time. Hence, is a base level 'cloning' good?

**Before you are a leader, success is all about growing yourself. When you become a leader, success is all about growing others.**
—*Jack Welch*

**How to get, retain, develop and grow Right People:**
However, having said that, there are ways to ensure that uniform levels of 'operational efficiency' are maintained. Processes, SOPs and continuous training are important elements. But all these are also decided and run by people/employees at all/different levels and locations

76

in the organization. Hence, also, what become important is evaluation norms that can be used at recruitment and development stages. The first things, which have to be checked (and which non negotiable), are alignment to organisational values, integrity and team work. Everything else follows.

**What then needs to be kept in mind, has three levels, to keep it simple at this point:**

1) Skill Set:
   Functional Skills
   Customer Orientation
   Coaching Ability
   Ability to take tough calls
   Adequate IQ level

But 1) above is a base qualification. It is a necessary but not sufficient condition. What are to be looked at, along with 1)?

2) Execution Excellence
3) Passion

**The guiding success equation is quite simple:**

1) = Base Condition
1)+2) = B grade
1)+3) = C grade
1)+2)+3) = A grade

It is only at that A grade that ownership, accountability, trust, customer orientation and motivation, all come into play naturally.

Leadership Challenge is to build bridges into the future . . . .

For those who think operational efficiency may not be as important, it may be appropriate to share here that **"Fielding, historically has been seen as a service function in cricket for too long, till Jonty Rhodes changed the game and showed that a 'Fielder' can win matches!!"**

## WHERE GOALS ARE THE BOSSES . . .

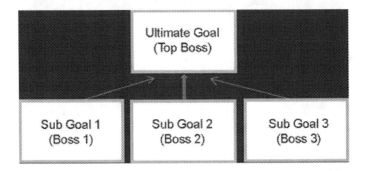

Achievement of goals set is the motivating factor for employees at all levels in a successful organization. In a successful organization, goals are set at every level depending on the functional area, level in the organization and the nature of work performed. The Balanced Score Card, one of the most widely followed corporate transformational strategies aims to analyze and set goals& benchmarks for the organization across 360 degrees of its performance across Financial, Customer, Internal Process and Learning perspectives. While the goals and benchmarks are set in line with the overall vision of the organization, these are set in such a way that the employees operate out of their comfort zones.

These goals then become the guiding stars for the employees. While there are various levels of hierarchy, the leadership at all levels is focused on the achievement of the set goals for the respective departments with an eye on the achievement of the ultimate goal set for the organization.

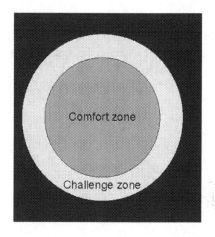

Thus there is no space for individual egos, idiosyncrasies, personal likes and dislikes, emotions to play a role in the performance of the employees at various levels. Animated discussions between the superiors and the subordinates have only objective, that is to create conditions and support performance towards achievement of the objectives at all levels. Every boss will thus try and act as the ideal boss to work for and this behaviour is encouraged.

Where the employees are motivated by the achievement of their individual goals and the overall goals of the organization, and where the goals at various levels across all the departments are in line and in harmony with the goals of the organization the performance of the organization has only one way to go, that is to soar higher and higher.

Teamwork is the ability to work together toward a common vision. The ability to direct individual accomplishments toward organizational objectives. It is the fuel that allows common people to attain uncommon results."

**Individual commitment to a group effort—that is what makes teamwork, a company work, a society work, a civilization work.**

*—Vince Lombardi*

Shahrukh Khan's Gautam Gambhir lead KKR cricket team, and pulled off one of the most stunning performances ever seen in the recent history in the IPL-V championship in May 2012. Starting from hopeless performances in the earlier versions of the championship and starting as a distinctly underrated team, KKR team lifted the cup by beating the reigning champs CSK team. Team spirit and team performance as against the individualistic brilliance has been behind many successes in the corporate history.

Successful organizations organize teams, inculcate team spirit, and encourage healthy competition among the teams to aim for higher and higher performance. Celebrations and Rewards, cups and mementoes keep up with the excitement and carry forward the moments of excitement as mementoes. TEAMBLI at Baucsh & Lomb India, the founder of RayBan Sunglasses' is one ofthe finest examples of a team spirit that has resulted in excellent performance consistently over a period of time to result in the successful turnaround of the organizations in a matter of 3 years between 1996 and 1999.

TEAM BLI' pioneered the first organized sector entry into the eye care products market. Industry standards had to be re-framed. Capacity utilization was low. The start-up was burdened with high leverage and perceptions of low quality/ high price.

Ray-Ban sunglasses launch in India had to overcome quality perceptions of a locally manufactured product, as well as successfully establish the value-proposition in line with purchasing power. Intense brainstorming and honest debates cleared the way forward. Thanks to the '100% DO IT (Delivery with Ownership through Interdependent Teams) credo; cross-functional teams came together seamlessly to pull as one. Accelerated learning curves and Execution Excellence in every sphere became the name of the game. An 'open' culture rated organization climate amongst the best companies of the world. The organization structure was realigned to bring in clear accountability.

As a result, India became a 'Top 10' Global market for Ray-Ban sunglasses within 3 years. Despite all the challenges the entity broke even in a record time becoming one of the very few successful entries into the India market in those times.

While Team BLI was one team comprising all members of the organization working in unison to achieve the vision set in front of the organization by the visionary Jaspal Bajwa, the company was organized into various functional teams and regional teams which competed among themselves to not only exceed their performance objectives that were set out in front them in line with goals of the organizations, but also be the best amongst all in terms of every parameter.

Innovative target setting ensured that the targets kept in mind not only, quantitative parameters like sales and receivables, but also the performance of the teams in terms of being within their means in incurring their capital expenses and operational expenses budgeted versus actual.

Innovative competitions like the Golden Baton Trophy, which measured the performance of teams in various functions in terms of their service levels to their internal customers and delivering on their performance goals, made the entire organization reverberate with a sense of healthy competition and sheer excitement as they together cracked one goal after another leading to the final vision of being not only a profitable entity but also an undisputed leader in its businesses in India, admired by consumers, dealers, distributors and all stakeholders.

Even today after 12 years, after a smooth transition into 2 different entities following global acquisition, demerger etc, TEAMBLI members continues to resonate with each other and share the good times of success and relive their moments of excitement.

## STRETCH & RAISE THE BAR—PUSHING PERFORMANCE LIMITS

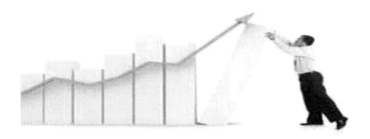

**This world wouldn't be what we are today and what we will be tomorrow, but for the excellence of brilliant individuals, scientists, business persons, politicians, organizations who continuously perform at their 100% level, stretch themselves to give their best every time and continuously raise the bar to deliver better and better . . .**

*—Master Mentors Advisory*

Successful organizations are continuously pushing the barriers of performance. Intel coming out with faster chips, Apple Inc coming out with a newer version of iPhone every time, Microsoft coming with a better and cheaper version of Windows and the rapidly falling prices of every expanding memory chips are a very few of the examples we see and experience in our every day life, that is symbolic of Great Organizations.

Stretching the Limits and Raising the bar every time is woven into the fabric of thriving organizations. While ordinary organizations wait for emergency and respond to extremely challenging situations as a fire fighting measure to stretch the performance of their systems and people, vibrant and thriving organizations challenge their human resources to continuously go for and deliver excellence. This leads not only to operational excellence, but also results in the organization remaining competitive and profitable like Apple Inc, while those who continued to burn money and resources at the same pace or were not prepared, perished.

Stretching the performance in organizations starts by setting SMART goals. Normally—SMART is read as Specific, Measurable, Achievable, Realistic and Time-bound, in thriving organizations it is read as SPECIFIC, MEASURABLE, AMBITIOUS, REALISTIC & TIME-BOUND.

The idea is to challenge the status quo and mediocrity and keep the system dynamic and fast paced leading to a high intensity and performance. The management not only takes extreme care in recruiting the employees with the right attitude and mind set to aim for excellence, but also keeps the system continuously oiled by regular orientation and training programs or re-skilling exercises that will help them to be prepared for the renewed challenges to the organization from its own approaches, competition and external environment.

The management and the team in thriving organization never take the ambitious goals to be unachievable or something that are for paper. The belief that they have in themselves that turns into a 'Self Fulfilling Prophecy' is a hallmark of vibrant and eminently successful teams. While it is easier to achieve ambitious targets in a benign and high growth environment, in challenging environments and failing demand scenarios, the real caliber of the teams and their companies are truly tested separating the men from the boys.

'When the going gets tough, the tough gets going'. This is truly believed and implemented in thriving organizations.

Margin for error and in-efficiency is nil or almost negligible in thriving organizations. The quest for execution excellence and a disdain for failure or mediocrity leads the teams and individuals to success and enables them to surpass the ambitious goals set.

Once the goals are reached, the time comes for raising the bar to continue the path of excellence. Successful organizations realize that the benchmark for success is a dynamic parameter. What is ambitious today may become mediocre in the near future. Hence, unless we continuously improve and raise the bar every time we achieve the set goals, it is possible to start falling behind the competition and fail to survive.

# RAISE
# the Bar

This is truly one of the key secrets behind the gaining momentum and repeated delivery of excellent performance at thriving organizations.

## SOARING ORGANISATIONS SELDOM STOP . . .

'If you really want to succeed, you'll have to go for it every day like I do'
— *Donald Trump*

Successful Organizations are like juggernauts moving from one success to another without halting to savor their success over long breaks. They continuously raise the bar for themselves and their teams to go for higher and higher performance objectives leading to better performance everyday. This is because of the passion to achieve the long term vision of the organization which has been internalized and bought into, never let's them take a wink and loose sight of their goals.

One of the biggest & most inspiring success stories of recent times in India has been the growth of Nokia Mobile phones in India through its Sales and Distribution Partner, HCL Infosystems, the leading hardware and system integration services company in India.

Under the dynamic leadership of its Chairman, HCL Info, grew the sales of its telecom business from under Rs 1000 crores per annum to over Rs 10000 crores per annum in a matter 4 years. While the organization had very good support from the Principal, M/s Nokia, a global leader in mobile phones, the real indicator of the success was the fact that, while globally Nokia mobile phones was enjoying 40% market share, Indian subsidiary reached a market share of over 80% virtually annihilating the competition.

How was this achieved?
     HCL infosystems organized a competent sales team through careful selection procedure under an efficient leadership team. Relationships with Nokia were managed superbly and the two organizations planned for a soaring growth through a series of marketing and sales strategies.
     While HCL infosystems was fired up with the vision of becoming an undisputed leader in the telecom, hardware and system integration business, the teams were set aggressive performance objectives and were persistently challenged with constructive competition among the regional teams at the same time they were motivated to go for aggressive collective goals in line with the spirit of the organizations.

Setting Targets to operate out of the comfort zone:

HCL Info, being aggressive sales organizations' realizes that the best results are achieved when the teams operate out of their comfort zones. When competent teams are inspired with a goal and challenged to achieve aggressive targets and constructive competition among the teams, magic happens.

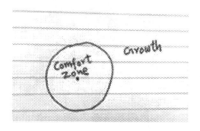

Reward performance: HCL Info understood the importance of motivating the sales teams for achieving the aggressive performance objectives through innovative collective and individual reward systems designed to extract excellence with all the members of the organization stretching the limits of excellence.

While month after month the teams achieved bigger and bigger successes, which looked seemingly impossible when they were set, the celebrations were chaired by the top management and rewarded with money, but also honors, mementoes, parties, individual and team recognitions.

**Team and Individual rewards**

**Team celebrations**

While the celebrations never halted the organizations, they were followed by the charged up teams going back to the field with renewed vigor to keep up the momentum and stretch them to achieve the overall goal of the organization.

In the words of the inspiring chairman, '**The team should celebrate the success by closing their eyes for a few minutes, savoring the fruits of the success and move on towards the next goals**.' Stopping for too much of a time, pondering too much and resting on past laurels will develop complacency in the organization and it requires more effort to gather back the momentum lost.

**"Celebrate what you've accomplished, but raise the bar a little higher each time you succeed."** Mia Hmm

Just as the Earth never stops rotating around itself and revolving around the sun and the Banyan tree never stops growing. Soaring organizations never stop their march, setting higher and higher goal & reinventing themselves to remain contemporary, ever relevant and forever growing.

In a matter of 2 years from June 2004—December to May 2006, HCL Infosystems grew rapidly from around 6 lakh units per month to over 25 lakh units per month and became an undisputed leader in the Indian cellular market with over 75% share in quantity terms, far higher than the 35% share it enjoyed globally.

**'Success is never a never a stop and failure is never final".**

*—Master Mentors . . .*

There are any number of cases in front of our eyes, where organizations have continuously reinvented themselves to become bigger and bigger by becoming an indispensible part of the lives of their consumers. Microsoft, Apple, Unilever, Procter & Gamble, Coca Cola, Pepsico, Mc Donalds are some such companies which have tirelessly and relentlessly reinvented themselves and applied themselves to the cause of creating value to their consumers and stake holders thus becoming evergreen corporations in the process. History is also replete with examples of those where success has been ephemeral and they have fallen by the way side unable to build on their successes and go from strength to strength.

Tirelessly working towards the goal by continuously reliving the passion with which one starts is the hallmark of soaring organizations.

## BACKUP PLAN THAT ENSURES CONTINUITY

While insurance for all critical assets could provide a backup for loss of such assets, backup plans provide ongoing contingency measures to keep the projects and the organization moving forward without loss of time and profits.

While it is comforting to have a backup plan for every plan put in place, it is important to ensure that over slack is minimized to reduce redundancies in the system that could increase idle time of under utilized resources and thus reduce return on over all investments.

### SUCCESSION PLANNING & LEADERSHIP PIPELINE . . .

Successful Organizations survive for ages. There are over 60 organizations in the world today that are more than 100 years old and thriving, contributing to over US$5 trillion revenue to the global economy.

While initially the passion from the promoters takes forward the organization and sets in a growth path, it is not possible for the promoters to be with the organizations for ever. Hence to survive and thrive for a long period of time, the organizations need to find new leaders who may not be from the family of founders many a time.

In 1985, Apple Computers, after 9 years of existence, threw out its promoter Steve Jobs and brought in a new management under John Sculley. But the new leadership that has come from outside the company could not resonate with the original vision of the promoters and the dynamics of the market place and drove the company to disaster. This led to the recall of the original founders who led the company to unprecedented heights till the death of Steve Jobs in October 2011. What followed this time was a totally different scenario. The company carried forward the legacy with many more successes in the market place and became the most valued companies globally with a market capitalization of over 500 Billion US Dollars, far ahead of the 2nd best in the word. This was possible due to well-crated and executed succession plan.

Cisco, one of the finest companies in the world flourished after the exit of the promoters due to well crafted succession plan. John Chambers, the current chairman of Cisco who has taken the company from a small organization to a global leader with 40 Billion US Dollars is a product of an excellently executed succession planning effort at Cisco that aimed to create a pipeline of leaders for the future.

In some family led companies the scions of the promoters take forward the agenda of the promoters successfully, provided they are well groomed to lead the business into the future. Classic examples like that of Reliance Industries (Mukesh Ambani & Anil Ambani taking forward the mantel from Dhirubhai Ambani), Bajaj Auto (Sanjeev Bajaj and Rajiv Bajaj taking over from Rahul Bajaj) and Kumara Mangalam Birla (taking over from Aditya Vikram Birla) are excellent cases of successful transition of leadership to the next generation of the family ahead, separate the promoters from the leadership and carve out an succession planning strategy leading to the creation of a pipeline of leaders for the future.

Multinational organizations like Unilever, Infosys, Wipro, Tata Group, ICICI have in place well planned and managed programs to develop the leaders to take over the mantle, whenever any gaps arise or when the organizations experience growth.

HCL group successfully transitioned the executive leadership from its charismatic promoters to professional leadership successfully that future proofs its business and ensures continuity.

Developing a well crafted Succession planning an creation of a strong pipeline of capable leaders who re oriented well to take the organization into the future is a must for the 21st century organizations who wish to last for ever.

### DIE – DELEGATION – INTRAPRENEURSHIP – EMPOWERMENT

Successful Organization takes extreme care in selecting the right candidates for the job and grooms them to a position of responsibility. The employees are empowered to handle the responsibility and deliver on their accountabilities successfully at the same time enjoying their work.

Positioning right persons in right jobs by matching their unique skills, competencies, experiences and above all their passions will enable the organizations to let their employees handle responsibility to yield the desired results in line with the overall vision of the organization. Competent employees enjoy work when they are trusted, given authority with responsibility and rewarded appropriately.

Organizations destined for greatness encourage
A) **Delegation**, B) **Intrapreneurship** and C) **Empowerment** at all levels. Selecting the right person with the right competence is the key to successful delegation.

This will enable all the employees to focus most on their key deliverables while the rest of the organization works on the other elements of the execution with due diligence. While delegation is an extremely useful and important aspect of an organizational effectiveness, delegating the work to wrong employee and delegating without periodic supervision is a sure path to failure in most cases

Delegating managerial tasks to a secretary without necessary skills and relaxing totally by taking eyes off — too dramatic but a symbolic representation of a wrong type of delegation.

Successful Organizations encourage Intrapreneurship at all levels. Gifford Pinchot III introduced the word intraprenership in 1985, a term that marries the spirit of an entrepreneur with the resources of a large corporation. They want employees at all levels to work with spirit of ownership like an entrepreneur within the organization. This will enable the organization to deliver extraordinary result, as it is akin to a train running with many more engine, instead of one engine pulling all the passenger compartments.

**A 100 Coach Goods train pulled by a 3 Engine front.**

Having more engines work in same direction will help a train pull heavier loads with ease.

Having a number of leaders in the organization acting like an entrepreneur in his own sphere of work and contributing to the organization in line with the overall goals, objectives and vision of the organization will catalyze the growth of the organization and reach its vision faster than planned.

In many organizations, apart from challenging work environment and delegation of authority, organizations implement a number of programs to encourage intrapreneurship. These include:

a) Encouraging innovation by continuously inviting ideas from all the employees and consider them with full regard

b) Back the employees with chosen ideas by offering them mentoring to let them evolve into viable businesses

c) Support the employees with innovative ideas and a sound business model with resources at their disposal while their regular needs are taken case through fixed salaries and perks

d) Review periodically to ensure that the intrapreneur get due support and are on the track planned out

e) Encourage the intrapreneurs and back them to the hilt in times of failure and motivate them to take risks, learning from failures

f) Give lion's share of the benefit derived from the success of intrapreneurs to the concerned employee and motivate them to achieve more and more

This will foster an intrapreneurial culture where more and more employees will be motivated to think and act like entrepreneurs that will help the organization to keep up with the spirit that has helped to be conceived in the first place. Sometimes the intrapreneurs end up coming out with radically different business models or areas of growth, which need to spin off as separate companies with the idea champion at the helm. Google, Microsoft, Infosys are some such companies which have always encouraged intrapreneurship and enabled the employees get the double benefit of being an employee and an entrepreneur.

Google encourages intrapreneurship through its 'Innovation Time off' project enabling the employees to explore and work in the areas of their passion, 20% of their time. This has led to launch of a number of innovative programs. Successful companies have a significant budget for incubating ideas of their intrapreneurs.

With the increasing trend towards entrepreneurship in the recent past, encouraging 'Intrapreneurship' is a sure shot way for great companies to retain, motivate and reward top talent and keep up the growth momentum.

## EMPOWERMENT

It is indeed surprising to find that many organizations today want to manage their employees by setting them objectives to be achieved but, back them with little resources.

Successful organizations are the one who let the employees go after and achieve much more than their objectives by offering them the right work environment, powers to take decisions within their own spheres that will help them in deploying the appropriate resources to achieve the set objectives and reward them when the objectives are achieved.

While the environment is meritocratic, the healthy competition and the urge on the part of the employees to live up to the management's expectations, draws out the best from the employees and make them a motivated lot.

A company that empowers its employees, delegate's responsibility and fosters an entrepreneurial culture by a formal process of encouraging intrapreneurship is on the right path to success in the 21st century.

Working hard without working smart is working hardly. Promoting work-life balance of employees, promotes smart working . . . .

*—Master Mentors*

Successful companies recognize the rights of their employees to have a balance between the time spent at their work and the time they have to spend on other aspects of their life like, family, hobbies, passions, recreation, religious pursuits, self care and a need for proper rest.

Leaders of great organizations like Infosys; Coco-cola have consistently been ambassadors of the employee's approach to achieving a work life balance. In many family owned and not so professional companies, employees are judged by the number of hours an employee works as against his/her standard working hours. It is a taboo in a number of organizations to go home while the boss is still around in the office. This encourages a rat race among the employees to stay for more hours than their colleagues to get better chance for increments and promotions.

**Work expands so as to fill the time available for its completion**
*—Parkinson's law*

Great companies hold the employees responsible for their performance against goals as against the number of hours they work. While as a matter of discipline, employees are expected to stick to the work timings, standard number of hours at work etc., the performance of the employees in these hours spent on official work that counts. This encourages smart work and not just working hard. Quality and not Quantity is more important for success. Some organizations frown at their employees when they are seen to be working over time and they treat this as a matter of inefficiency on the part of employees, rather than the urge on the part of the employee to contribute more.

a) Encouraging the employees to work within the boundaries of their work timings is a smart and successful habit by great organizations because: i) Employees will stay focused on their job during their office hours leading to fewer distractions to others
b) Employees stay refreshed and energetic every day, as too much of work may lead to burnouts and severe stress, having a bearing on the performance
c) Organization need not incur higher operating expenses to take care of electricity, food, maintenance expenses, safety while travelling by employees during late hours etc.

d) Organizations can attract smart employees at competitive salaries if they are known to encourage employees to work smartly

e) Avoid financial losses due to inefficiency creeping in because of stress at work

## FLEXIBLE YET FIRM. . .
## ENABLING LONG TERM SURVIVAL . . .

But for the ability to sway, most of the trees in the world would have been broken . . .

Successful Organizations realize the importance of being flexible yet firmly rooted to their core values. Ability to withstand extreme circumstances increases rapidly, when you take necessary steps to adjust to the dynamic external environment without compromising on the principles you stand for. Flexibility allows the organizations to adapt themselves to the circumstances and stay relevant at all times. This is very much required by the organizations to survive.

**"Be firm on principle but flexible on method".**
— *Zig Ziglar*

The case of Tata-Singur project in West Bengal, India, highlights the outlook of great organizations to be flexible when required to diffuse complex situations and stop value depreciation for the company and the society. Tata Motors, one of the finest Indian companies, set-up its factory in 2008 at Singur, to manufacture the path breaking US$ 2500 Nano cars. Despite incurring huge expenditure and having undertaken heavy investments, faced with a severe opposition from the ex-landowners and surrounding people led by politicians, Tata Motors decided to move out the factory from Singur to Gujarat in October 2008.

This has helped Tata Motors to not only avoid any more controversy, but also have a great new partner in the form of Gujarat Government and a far more favorable industrial climate that has let it expand the business rapidly. The flexibility on the part of Tata Motors, helped in salvaging the situation and weather the storm that was looking increasingly unmanageable.

Too much flexibility indicates spinelessness and lack of firm grounding in a set of core values that will guide the organization towards its vision at the same time earning respect from all the stakeholders and the society. Flexibility also helps organizations not only weather the storm, but also adapt to the rapidly changing customer tastes and preferences and sometimes lead the way in the market place.

Lack of flexibility on the part of Nokia in moving towards the smart phone revolution, has led to its loosing market share rapidly. Similarly, failure on the part of Research in Motion in understanding the changing trends of the market and adapting to the same with better products with more features has caused a massive loss to its position in the market.

The key is to be very strict in adhering to the core guidelines like Vision, Mission, Values and Goals while being flexible in the methods being adopted to achieve the goals. Methods could be tailored to the changing circumstances, ensuring that the progress is made in the direction of goal achievement and long-term value creation objectives are achieved.

# KEY PERSONAL ATTRIBUTES OF EMPLOYEES OF SUCCESSFUL ORGANIZATIONS.

When Passion is in the game, work becomes a play and earnings become the bye product.

Successful organizations strive to perfect the art of recruiting the right people for the right job. The employees carefully handpicked, trained and placed on respective jobs by successful organizations have to necessarily possess the following qualities, while Integrity at work is taken for granted:

A) Passion to work in the chosen field
B) Being a self starter
C) Pro-active nature and
D) Have fire in the belly, a hunger to achieve more

These are together, reflected as a spark they find in the interviewee when they interact during their interview.

Jennifer White in her bestselling book, 'Work Less, Make More: Stop Working So Hard and Create the Life You Really Want!' helped thousands of people to lead more fulfilling lives by discovering passions and unlock their hidden potential to enable them lead more successful and fulfilling lives!

Imagine what would happen if Sachin Tendulkar were to focus on acting in movies and advertisements, instead of concentrating on his game of Cricket! His game would take a back seat and earnings would also tumble in due course.

Following one's passions, not only makes the job easy as a breeze and a pleasurable affair, but also the expertise one gains in being an absolute specialist in a given area, results in the ability being recognized by the world thus leading to increased earnings as well!

It is indeed surprising to note that, when you observe the world around, most of the people land up in their careers not by choice but by sheer chance. Their lives are shaped by their circumstances and not by the power of their will. Their lives continue that way and they continue till the end living a life of dissatisfaction forever trying to escape from the clutches of boredom inflicted by the drudgery of work, which never entertained them.

It is also unfortunate to see individuals who reach their zenith in the area of their passion, lose focus, and get distracted by the fruits and paraphernalia that surround their success.

Every individual is born with an inherent talent, which is waiting to be discovered, nurtured and focused upon, which seldom happens. Amir Khan famously enunciates this in an Indian film, 'Taare Zameen Par' in which he helps a child discover her true passion and reach up to his potential.

Though it happens in a story, it still has a lot of lessons for the entire humanity and especially the parents, who shape up the lives and careers of their children.

What following one's passions could do to the life of a person, could be studied by reading the biographies of great achievers like Einstein, Srinivasa Ramanujam, Billgates, Steve Jobs, Magic Johnson, Amitabh Bachan, Shahrukh Khan, Sunil Gavaskar, Sachin Tendulkar, Kapil Dev and many more who have managed to overcome insurmountable difficulties to achieve phenomenal success in their lives.

**Magic is who I am on the basketball court. Earvin is who I am".**

*—Magic Johnson*

Figure out what triggers you, Focus on it, Follow it through the life and achieve not only financial success but also a life filled with happiness. Successful organizations are good at figuring out what are the areas of work that resonate with their respective employees, ensure a match that leads to high levels of productivity resulting in joyous work places.

# LEARNING & DEVELOPMENT an INTEGRAL PART OF EVOLUTION.

Learning and Growth are invariably linked to each other.

A human being continuously learns as he grows. Learning is at a rapid pace in the early stages of life, when the person learns to communicate, express oneself before going through a structured learning program till mid-life, when he starts to earn. Learning is at a varied pace for different individuals. Typically, the learning prospects are linked to the nature, quality and amount one learns.

Persons, who stop learning in their life, reach a plateau and fail to keep pace with their rapidly changing external environment, where newer skills are required to leverage the evolving tools and technologies. Their productivity levels fall and they end up and becoming unemployable and unworthy. In other words, while experience can add value to ones life if properly leveraged, without continuous learning, it cannot make the human being more prosperous.

Organizations, while they start with the collective learning's, experiences and expertise of their promoters, they encounter lot of experiences during their journey and evolution. They learn from their experiences, fine tune their strategies and continue to evolve by putting their learning into practice. As they continue to grow, they take more and more employees who need to be integrated into the culture of the organization. They have to ensure that everyone is working for the same vision with perfect harmony and in alignment with the rest of the organization.

An evolving organization has to undergo the following learning activities at different stages:

A) Learning as an Organization through own experiences to fine tune strategies

B) Learning of the employees starting their careers to adapt themselves to the organization

C) Learning of the employees in different levels and different functions as they undertake new areas of work and take up higher/different positions which involve acquiring functional skills, managerial skills etc.

D) Learning as an organization from listening to customer and user needs and their experiences with its products and services

E) Learning as an organization to benchmark with the best in the world and continuously improve themselves and set new standards

F) Learning of the employees to close skill gaps w.r.t their job profiles identified through performance appraisals, acquire new skills to master new technologies or the upgrades of the older versions through on the job training and also from internal and external workshops

G) Targeted learning aimed to overcome problems that may arise out of the complexity resulting from the growth (For example, the interpersonal problems, ego clashes, politics, lack of team spirit etc., need to be continuously tackled)

H) Learning as an organization to achieve the standards and certifications (for example CMMi Level 5, ISO 27001 etc.) that will enable them to institutionalize the best practices and so on

The external environment is changing skills, knowledge of its employees and itself as an entity. This needs to be harnessed. An Organization's learning is the collective learning of all the skills and knowledge of its employees and itself as an entity and this needs to be harnessed through effective knowledge management systems to be able to be leveraged effectively. Successful organizations, not only have excellent knowledge management systems but also have put in place rigorous systems of knowledge management, rigorous systems of evaluation of their employees learning through institutionalized approach to facilitation of learning process and testing of the wisdom gained, which goes into the employees' performance records.

As the world evolves and a number of brilliant minds work to continuously evolve new technologies and new methodologies, older approaches to work are becoming a liability.

For example, Digital Marketing, Social Media, Mobile Applications, Customer/User Experience Management and Sustainable growth (3BL) are the buzzwords of the 21st century and those organizations that are unable to adapt themselves to these new trends in their respective fields will rapidly loose ground to their new born and nimble competitors and loose their ground to become extinct in no time.

Industry and Academia interactions, Executive and Management development programs by premier management institutions, workshops developed and conducted by world class training organizations, internal infrastructure and facilities developed by the organizations and programs by world class trainers in their respective fields will rapidly lose ground to their new born and nimble competitors.

While knowledge and skills are important, without the right attitude and good habits, employees cannot put them to good use. Hence successful organizations focus on ensuring that the knowledge and skills are acquired, but also ensure that the right attitude and habits are developed, nurtured, incentivized and harnessed. This will lead to all round excellence, and their successful evolution into thriving entities.

## KNOWLEDGE ATTITUDE SKILLS HABITS—KASH FOR PERFORMANCE AT WINNING ORGANIZATIONS . . .

Habit is what we repeatedly do and is what truly defines our capability to perform. Positive attitude and Good habits of the employees are invariably the reason behind the performance of Great Organizations.

Success Model

| Knowldege | Attitude |
| Skills | Habits |

While most of the organizations focus on selecting employees based on the knowledge and the skills they possess, successful companies differentiate themselves by focusing not only on the Knowledge and Skills possessed by their employees which are more defined by the left side of the brain, but also on those soft aspects of the personality that are defined by the right side of the brain, namely the Attitude and the Habits.

Knowledge is sum total of learning, theoretical and practical, that an individual acquires over a period of time and is a building block for the competence and success of a person in his career and corporate life. Knowledge of the subject, environment, general matter etc form the building blocks for the ability to understand, internalize and deliver on the performance objectives.

Skills are those capabilities and competencies that are gained through experience and learnt through practice. Technical skills, Communication skills, Analytical skills, Presentation skills are some such skills that will help the employees in their communication and delivery of performance.

While K&S are important, the ability to put them to use is defined by the Attitude of the professionals who possess them. Attitude is the outlook and a perspective that an individual develops that will help the individual in leveraging his knowledge and skills and perform in the work place.

**Attitude determines the Altitude . . .**

*— Anonymous*

A negative attitude will result in the professional not only unable to deliver his performance but also come in the way of those around and the organization overall, as a cascading effect. A positive attitude helps the individuals to galvanize themselves and those around, to give their best and maximize their performance.

Habits are those aspects of our behavior, that reflects what we do repeatedly and believes deep within. Successful Organizations want 'Winning' to be their habit. Success is a product of doing the right and desirable things repeatedly. This happens when the employees are habituated to work hard, work smart, work systematically and perform consistently.

Successful organizations realize that, it is the negative attitudes and wrong habits of the employees are mostly the reasons behind the failures and not lack of knowledge or skills.

| Most organizations and people spend their time and money developing the left half of the kashbox. | **K** Knowledge | **A** Attitudes | Most terminations and business failures are due to weakness in the right half of the kashbox. |
| | **S** Skills | **H** Habits | |

Training programs at successful organizations are focused on improving all the four aspects of the employees and in fine tuning them, to enable the employees develop a healthy attitude and get habituated with desirable traits by the use of various forms of motivation and reward systems, apart from a periodic assessment and up-gradation of knowledge and skills.

When the older companies were set up, the workforce—both "labor" and "management" were from similar socio-economic backgrounds. An employee is slotted as 'manager' or 'managed', based on his/her education/knowledge and skills alone, as the attitude and habits were more similar than diverse. Hence culture got built more easily in older companies in the yester years. It is more difficult today.

Attitude and Habits differ based on the socio economic backgrounds of people.

Habits are usually very difficult to break and a smart organization leverages on the habits of effective people to make it an organization habit and later on, it becomes the culture of an organization. A great example can be seen in Asian Paints, one of the top 10 paint companies in the world and it is totally Indian. It is Asian Paints culture to take detailed notes in all meetings whether with dealers or otherwise. The action points are clearly highlighted and the same is reviewed in the next meeting. This is a habit and now is a part of the culture of the company. The culture is one of being mindful of even the smallest detail and hence the company is just and plain efficient and therefore dominant in its operations!!

Attitude is a more individualized trait and is even more difficult to leverage on, for creating a successful organization. Asian Paints recruits over 200 fresh graduates from top management and engineering schools as trainees every year. To ensure that the individual's attitude "gels" with the overall company's culture without affecting his individuality, Asian Paints has a training program for a year whereby every trainee starts off at the lowest level in the function he is assigned to. For example, a sales management trainee starts off as a salesman in one territory where, he is an under study to the regular sales officer. He travels by the same conveyance, eats the same food and stays at the same hotel as the sales officer. This is generally meant to "grinds all inflated egos to the ground", generates an attitude to help others and understand the real "market". Later on, when the trainee manages the sales teams, he knows their issues and problems and is able to take effective decisions without any "false" attitude. Anybody who does not make the "cut" is clearly reassigned or eased out after the first round of promotions. This has created a culture of friendliness, apolitical approach that has made Asian Paints, what it is today.

# REWARD SYSTEMS THAT REINFORCES SUCCESS . . .

Rewards, not Punishment, bring out the best from employees and motivate them to be achievers . . .

Organizations raise resources mainly from 3 different sources:

> Investors,
> Employees and
> Customers.

Employees contribute to their organizations by delivering much more value than what they are paid.

It is imperative for today's organizations to attract right talent at the right price, get the best out of the employees and retain them. Inability to retain good employees will results in not only a gap to be filled, thus losing time and productivity, but also at times result in plugging the positions again by paying much more to new employees. Apart from a negative impact on profitability, this also has an impact on the morale of the rest of the employees who end up feeling that, they are being taken for granted and paid lower salaries for being loyal.

Employees who receive bonuses for their efforts will work even harder, increasing productivity and potentially bolstering profits. But those subjected to penalties tend to distrust the supervisor and, because of that, work less hard' says, Karen Sedatole, associate professor of accounting in Michigan State University's Broad College of Business who authored the study with Margaret Christ of the University of Georgia and Kristy Towry of Emory University.

Rewards for employees can be for Individual or Team performance in the form of Financial or Psychological incentives. While the rewards could be offered in the form of an increment or a performance bonus (cash or equivalent), this takes into account, individual or teamwork approach, encouraged by the company.

While most of the companies make the practice of recognizing the employees' contribution (program oriented and transactional), by offering gifts, certificates and mementoes, exemplary companies encourage the employees through spontaneous programs and special mentions in public. These activities build the self-esteem of the employees and inculcate a sense of feel good and motivation to achieve more, among the employees. Such programs increase the bond of the employees with the organization and encourage them to be ambassadors of the company.

Employees value the recognition given by the organizations in the form of awards, promotions, special mentions in public in addition to the certificates and mementoes that go with them. Successful organizations use a right mix of transactional and relational recognition programs. Transparency in reward and recognition is the most important aspect of the programs at companies known for being the best places to work at.

Companies like Citibank, Unilever, Procter and Gamble, Cisco Systems, IBM, Infosys Technologies, Wipro, Tatas, Bharti Airtel, Idea, Godrej etc. enjoy some of the lowest employee turnovers as they encourage, recognize and reward brilliance at work places. They keep the employees charged up consistently by giving them challenging roles that match their competencies.

Transparent, fair and performance oriented reward systems that take into account both financial and psychological angles, in tune with the organizational culture and professional HR Practices are the hallmarks of Successful Organizations. This is what, that motivates the employees to stick to their organizations and give their best, consistently for life.

## Process Excellence for sustained outperformance

Increasing competition, dealing with uncertainty and chaotic business cycles and an insane customer promiscuity are putting a never before pressure on business performance to reduce costs, improve revenues and enhance service. Very often, CEO's of Airlines say that their industry is no longer profitable. But what makes South West Airlines deliver profits quarter after quarter for over 60 quarters now?

What makes such companies so different to stand out? Well, Process Excellence to say the least. Over time, approaches to business improvement have also undergone substantial evolution. In the 70's and 80's the buzzword was Total Quality Management and Business Process Improvement, which focused on service. The 90's saw the growing popularity of Six Sigma and Lean based approaches, which added a cost element to service. As we are now galloping in the 21st century, Business Process management came into being which added the third dimension of revenue. And the last 2 years, to embrace the current business challenges, we have seen the emergence of Customer Experience management. The current focus has clearly shifted from managing processes for outperformance to managing outcomes for the customer through use of technology as differentiators

| | 70's & 80's | 90's | First 10 years of 21st Century | Last 2 yrs |
|---|---|---|---|---|
| Service | TQM & BPI | Six Sigma & Lean Methods | Business Excellence Management | Customer Experience Management |
| Technology | | | | |

## Which of these is best for my business?

Pressure to perform has never been greater at both personal and professional levels than it is today. Each of the approaches have clear merits and are a step more complex than the previous approach. Depending on the stage of the life cycle of the company and the challenge faced and complexity of operations, you can choose the right mix of tools for your business.

The recent researches are however increasingly pointing to players who dominate their markets and industry and those achieving what I would say a hat trick plus in terms of service, cost and revenue excellence are increasingly utilizing methods and approaches which fall into the Customer Experience management domain. It is for this very reason that when you look around at say the original pioneers of earlier successful approaches like Toyota and Lean, General Electric and Six Sigma, you find that they have been on a continuous process journey and are amongst the first to imbibe and internalize concepts of Customer Experience Management (CEM) along with companies like Amazon, Best Buy, Flip kart, Virgin Group, FedEx, Citibank, Ryan Air etc.

As the economic storm battering confidence across the globe looks set to continue into 2013, business leaders who focused primarily on short-term exigencies can no longer afford to be disengaged from longer-term strategic issues and process excellence is therefore a must part of the survival kit While there are unknown elements in the future, many of which will be challenging, the trick today lies in looking at the exciting opportunities from factors such as: 'the Cloud'; new enabling technologies; new working patterns; new contact channels; capabilities being developed around "Big Data" all of which are enablers to laying strong foundations to business in the evolution towards Customer Experience management

## How can I get on the Process Excellence Path?

Process Excellence is a journey. A fine blend of certifications and best process methods need to be created to lay the foundations of process excellence in an organization. Process Excellence Governance Model is the backbone to align to strategic objectives. It starts with incremental innovations through methods impacting one of the business deliverables of service, cost or revenue and then adding to the list through methods like TQM, Kaizen, Six Sigma and then as the organization matures moves over to quantum leaps through business analytics, business excellence management to ultimately winning hearts through innovative and long lasting Customer Experience Delivery. Process Excellence is a journey. Loyalty is a destination.

## CEM—What are the common themes and current challenges?

The philosophy of CEM stresses on identifying parameters that are most valued by customers, emphasizes on implementing an approach that is customer centered and all processes developed around the core customer expectation. Employees play the biggest role in delivery and delivering experiences starts at home, focusing first with own employees. Common themes are an "outside in" perspective, alignment to exceeding employee and then customer expectations, knowledge management through best experience sharing and replication across employees, constant stretch to delivering innovative and successful customer experience outcomes and relentless focus on business success through reduced costs, enhanced revenue and enhanced service

The skills needed to successfully run a multi-channel; multi-site, multi-partner operation is becoming more and more challenging. With customers increasingly use intuitive technologies such as smart phones, tablets etc and getting more and more interactive and freely expressing views on social media like facebook and twitter, the challenges are becoming more and more complex with every passing day. Mixed-model operations are hugely important and are becoming increasing recognized by boards globally, particularly where mergers and acquisitions are becoming the norm. Big Data is the emerging new trend in Process Excellence implementation, which has the potential to outstrip competition for, sustained performance just like six sigma did a few years back for companies like Motorola and General Electric. Harvard Business Review reported that companies have collected more information from customers since 2007 than was ever collected prior to that date.

Process Excellence is quite simply, a better way to do work and stay ahead in the minds for the 21st century's successful corporations!

## BENCHMARK FOR PROCESS EXCELLENCE— TOYOTA . . .

TOYOTA MOTOR CORPORATION:
TOYOTA = OPERATIONAL EXCELLENCE

The largest automobile company in the world today is Toyota. With over 255 Billion US Dollar in annual revenue and having manufactured over 200 million automobiles, Toyota is an iconic organization that has revolutionized an entire industry with its revolutionary practices aimed at operational excellence. Incorporated in 1937, Toyota today manufactures a huge range of cars, Sports utility vehicles and Luxury sedans across a wide price band through its factories across the globe.

Toyota pioneered the efforts to create process management models and methodologies to achieve operational excellence like "Lean Manufacturing" and Just In Time Production that significantly improve productivity and profitability. Today, Lean Manufacturing and JIT methodologies are increasingly adapted by global manufacturing organizations to cut down their operational expenses and drive down the manufacturing cost, thus increasing productivity drastically.

Toyota has become the global benchmark for best practices aimed at process & operational excellence. The Toyota Way, a set of principles and guidelines developed by the company embodies the outlook to be developed by global leader.

Two main pillars support the Toyota Way:

a) Respect for people and
b) Continuous Improvement.

Together, they define how the people of Toyota treat others and how they perform their work in order to deliver the company's values to customers, shareholders, associates, business partners, and the global community.

Toyota way, summarizes its values and guidelines as follows:

**Respect for People: Respect**—We make every effort to understand each other, take responsibility and build mutual trust **Teamwork**— We stimulate personal and professional growth, share development opportunities, and maximize individual and team performance.

**Continuous Improvement: Challenge**— Long-term vision, meet challenges with courage and creativity to realize the dream

**Kaizen**—Improve business operations continuously, always drive innovation and evolution

**Genchi genbutsu**—Go to the source to find the facts, make correct decisions, build consensus, and achieve goals at best speed.

These principles have led Toyota to be and be known as a true leader in Manufacturing Processes and Production techniques and Methodologies across the world. Known for its proactive concern for Environmental Preservation, Toyota has been a leader in environmentally friendly vehicle technologies. Toyota's R&D engineers are consistently focused on improving the performance of Toyota's products on various aspects like fuel efficiency, emissions and noise during vehicle use, the disposal recovery rate, the reduction of substances of environmental concern, and $CO_2$ emissions throughout the life cycle of the vehicle from production to disposal.

The United States EPA has awarded Toyota Motor Engineering & Manufacturing North America, Inc (TEMA) with a ENERGY STAR Sustained Excellence Award in 2007, 2008 and 2009.

Toyota has proved to the world, the positive impact of being an environmentally friendly ethical corporate with sound manufacturing methodologies and process excellence.

# PROCESS EXCELLENCE—QUALITY MODEL

The Golden saying "Customer is King" is truer today than ever before. As the quality of life improves, demand an expectation all over the world for Consistent services & products is turning out to be the order of the day.

Quality plays a major role in the survival of any business today. Quality is given equal importance, irrespective of whether it is manufacturing set up, services or any other enterprise. Quality is an outcome of the organization's understandings of the fundamental inter-connectedness of structure, processes and outcome.

An organization needs to design excellent processes to achieve high quality of product or service.

Success in the 21st Century is all about performing with passion & perfection, leading to excellence in all processes that we undertake.

Any business entity has three key functions, namely, Marketing, Operations and Finance. Managers & Leaders have challenging goals particularly, in operations.

Operational excellence in terms of Productivity and Customer delight are the drivers to sustained outperformance. To achieve excellence in operations, there are certain proven tools techniques methodologies and systems such as:

- Standardization and simplification
- Reliability and redundancy
- Value engineering
- Ergonomic considerations
- JIT
- Group Technology
- Work measurement & Time study

- Work sampling
- Learning curves
- Total productive maintenance
- 5 S concept
- Quality circles
- Management systems (ISO9001, EMS 14001, ISMS 27001 CMMI, OHSAS18001)
- Process management coupled with PDCA
- 7 QC TOOLS
- FMEA

5S is Japanese technique comprising the following five steps—Seiri (sorting), Seiton (Straightening or orderly arrangement), Seiso (Shining & cleaning machines and work place), Seiketsu (Standardizing & personal upkeep) & Shitsuke. (Sustaining the practice).

**Seven Wastes**—These are sometimes are called as 7 deadly disease which an organization must avoid.

Overproduction: reduce by producing only what is needed as & when it is needed

- Waiting: synchronize the workflow
- Transportation: minimize transport with better layouts
- Processing: "Why do we need this process at all?"
- Stock: reduce inventories
- Motion: reduce wasted employee motions

—Product defect: Focus on doing it right first time By avoiding the above, productivity and operational excellence would certainly improve on sustainable basis.

**TPM** (Total productive maintenance)—To prevent equipment related losses viz.,

- Break down loss
- Set up and adjustment loss
- Speed loss
- Defective work loss

**7QC TOOLS**—The QC tools are techniques in QC activities for discovering problems, organizing information, generating ideas, analyzing causes, taking action, effecting improvements and establishing controls to improve performance.

The seven tools used for, Generation of ideas, Decision making, Data presentation, Data collection, Analysis are:

- Cause-and-effect or Ishikawa diagrams
- Check sheet
- Control chart
- Histogram
- Pareto chart
- Scatter diagram
- Stratification (alternately, flow chart or run chart)

**Statistical Process Control** (SPC)

- A quantitative method for determining whether a particular process is in or out of control
- Application of this tool ensures the predictability and process out stability and avoid inspection

**Kaizen**: Kaizen is the Japanese philosophy of continuous improvement by all the employees in an organization, so that they perform their tasks a little better each day. It is a never-ending journey centered on the concept of starting new each day with the principle that the methods can always be improved.

**FMEA**: FEMA (Failure Modes and Effects Analysis) is a structured analysis for identifying ways & methods in which the product or processes can fail and then plan to prevent those failures. FMEA is a proactive tool for reducing defects and non-conformities.

**Quality circles**: Quality circle is a small group of voluntary members under the leadership of their supervisor, trained to identify, analyze and solve work-related problems and present their solutions to management, to improve the performance of the organization.

Globally, there are a number of awards and recognitions provided by different programs and organizations to encourage the organizations to focus on quality and excellence in processes.

Some of them are:

## BALDRIDGE NATIONAL QUALITY PROGRAM—USA
The award is given by the president of USA in areas of manufacturing, education, and health care to recognize the quality and excellence in US firms based on the following criteria: leadership; strategic planning; customer and market focus; measurement, analysis, and knowledge management; human resource focus; process management; and business results.

## EUROPEAN FOUNDATION OF QUALITY MANAGEMENT —EUROPE
The European Foundation of Quality Management is an organization that provides businesses in Europe a model wherein they could gain efficiency, effectiveness and competitive advantage. (2007) The excellence award is given to organizations that have effectively implemented the EFQM Excellence Model on their operations.

### Japan Quality Award
Japan Quality Award is provided by the Japan Productivity Center for Socio-Economic Development (JPC-SED) to encourage innovation and the transformation of management systems in Japan into customer-oriented structures.

## ASIA-PACIFIC QUALITY ORGANIZATION (APQO)
APQO awards is for the businesses and companies in Asia and the surrounding countries in the Pacific Rim to promote the development in the quality of the goods services as well as the quality of life of people on an international scale.

SRINIVAAS M.

## AUSTRALIAN ORGANIZATION FOR QUALITY

The Australian Organization gives the Gold Award for Quality by assessing the quality management principles of the nominees on the dimensions of learning; positivity; achievement; leadership; sustainability.

In India we have many National awards for quality excellence sponsored by pioneering organizations. Some of the popular National Quality Awards are:

### Golden Peacock Awards:

Golden Peacock Awards, instituted by Institute of Directors in 1992, are now regarded as holy grail of Corporate Excellence worldwide. The Award applications are assessed at 3 three levels by independent assessors and finally by a grand Jury. A Jury headed by Dr. Ola Ullsten, former Prime Minister of Sweden, finalizes the Global Awards. The Awards are bestowed annually and are designed to encourage total improvement in each sector of our business. All institutions whether public, private, non-profit, government, business, manufacturing and service sector are eligible to apply. Leadership Awards are determined through nomination. They provide not only worldwide recognition and prestige but also a competitive advantage in driving business in this tumultuous world under Golden Peacock Award models.

### The Rajiv Gandhi National Quality Award;

The Bureau of Indian Standards instituted Rajiv Gandhi National Quality Award in 1991, with a view to encouraging Indian manufacturing and service organizations to strive for excellence and giving special recognition to those who are considered to be the leaders of quality movement in India. This award is intended to generate interest and involvement of Indian Industry in quality programs, drive our products and services to higher levels of quality and equip our Industry to meet the challenges of domestic and International markets.

## IMC Ramakrishna Bajaj National Quality Award.

The IMC Ramakrishna Bajaj National Quality Awards was instituted in 1996 to give special recognition to excellence in organizations. The Award Criteria emphasize: openness and transparency in governance and ethics: the need to create value for customers and the businesses: and the challenges of rapid innovation and capitalizing on your knowledge assets. Whether a business is small or large, is involved in service, manufacturing, health care, education, or has one office or multiple sites across the globe, the criteria provide a valuable framework that can help the organization, plan in an uncertain environment. The criteria can also help in aligning resources and approaches such as ISO 9000, Six Sigma, Lean Enterprise System and International Quality Maturity Model, improve communication, productivity, quality, effectiveness and customer satisfaction; and achieve strategic goals on the journey to the vision.

## CII-EXIM Model for Business Excellence

CII and Export Import Bank of India have, in 1994, jointly established the CII-EXIM Bank Award for Business Excellence, with the aim of enhancing the competitiveness of India Inc. The Award is based on the internationally recognized EFQM Excellence Model.

Essentially the model tells us that, "Excellent results with respect to performance, customers, people and society are achieved through leadership driving policy and strategy, people, partnerships resources, and processes." Organizations are assessed on their standing with respect to the above model and the best organization in the respective category wins this prestigious award.

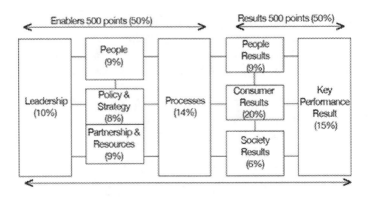

These Quality Awards go a long way in encouraging the organizations in aiming for excellence in their processes and deliverables and stay ahead of their competition. Apart from their urge to provide the best to their customers in a standardized manner, these awards when achieved, improve the image of the organizations dramatically. Even otherwise, trying for these awards needs criteria of framework that would enable them to measure their sincerely throws up the weakness areas to be rectified and improved upon thus resulting in long term benefits to the organizations.

There are many approaches to achieving excellence in organizations. However the top management on their journey to achieving excellence performance. This framework should be universally acceptable, objectively measure performance, be easily understandable and indicate the quality of management so that the gaps in the achievements can be identified and suitable actions initiated. But, whatever be the framework or model, some elements remain fundamental in relation to performance to excellence in organizations.

Process excellence comes by way of:

- Challenging the status quo and effecting change by using learning to create innovation and improvement opportunities

- Maximizing the contribution of employees through their development and involvement
- Managing the organization through a set of interdependent and interrelated systems, processes and facts &
- A leadership that is focused on pursuit of excellence as a strategy.

## INSTITUTIONALISING & INTERNALISING PROCESS EXCELLENCE—ISO & CMMI

A high level of product or service quality is a necessity for any successful organization. It is important to benchmark, the quality of product/service produced and also the processes to be followed to achieve the same. Following ISO standards or CMMI methodologies and getting accredited with the corresponding certifications, enables organizations to, not only reach high level of productivity by bench-marking themselves to global best practices, but also improves their performance potential in the market place, by providing their customers with a comfort level of being a quality player.

While ISO standards are evolved in consultation with the users as the minimum standards to be met by products/services across the globe, CMMI levels are the reflection of the capability and maturity levels of the organization in following processes, bench-marked to global best as developed by soft ware Engineering Institute—Carnegie Mellon, USA along with US government and industry officials.

It is important for organizations to adhere to these standards and methodologies in spirit and not just for the sake of doing it. Normal organizations revert back to old way of doing things upon achieving the certifications resulting in poor quality and cost overruns due to inefficiencies.

**International Standards Organization (ISO)**— Founded in the year 1947 and based in Geneva, Switzerland, ISO (International Organization for Standardization), a global network of country level standards organizations, is the world's largest developer of voluntary International Standards, a set of state of the art specifications for products, services and good practices. These standards are meant to achieve better co-ordination among organizations globally thus breaking down barriers for international trade. This is done to help the industry more efficient and effective. There are more than 19000 ISO standards covering all aspects of technology and manufacturing. ISO 9000 series focuses on the quality management systems at organizations, where quality management consists of all activities aimed at a) Quality Measurement, b) Quality Assurance, c) Quality control & d) Quality improvement. A quality management system (QMS) can be expressed as the organizational structure, procedures, processes and resources needed to implement quality management. (Source—Wikipedia)

## SEI (Software Engineering Institute, Carnegie-Mellon) promoted CMMI

(Capability Maturity Model Integrated) provides model process improvement methodology organizations with a defined structure and practice. CMMI is an improvised version of the process maturity measurement system, CMM launched in 1988 by the efforts of Watts Humphrey at Carnegie-Mellon's Institute, as an approach demonstrating that organization's processes mature in stages based upon problems they must solve. It provides the organizations with the essential elements of effective processes, which will improve their performance. CMMI based process improvement aims to eliminate weaknesses and convert them into strengths.

First published in 2000 and replacing CMM at the end of 2002, CMMI, according to Software Engineering Institute (SEI), "helps integrate traditionally separate organizational functions, set process improvement goals and priorities, provide guidance for quality processes, and provide a point of reference for appraising current processes"

CMMI is generally intended for application to the area of software engineering, system engineering, product development, supplier sourcing and does not address the issues related to IT operation, for example, human resource management, security, configuration and change management, and incident response.

CMMI has two representations, namely Staged (CMMI 1-5) and Continuous (0-4 across 22 process areas out of which company can choose those which are strategically important to reach its vision).An organization being appraised for CMMI successfully will be used a maturity level rating and not a certificate.

**ISO standards:**

Experts in consultation develop ISO International Standards with the people who need them so as to ensure that products and services are safe, reliable and of good quality. For business, they are strategic tools that reduce costs by minimizing waste and errors and increasing productivity. They help companies to access new markets, level the playing field for developing countries and facilitate free and fair global trade. The following table gives the summary of some of the key ISO standards that are widely used. ISO 9001 specifies the quality standards that will enable the organizations, what to do, so that the customer and regulatory requirements are met. It enables the company to document and undertake its own process and methodology to achieve the goal, as along it is consistently done

| ISO standard | Description | Benefits S | Strengths | Limitations |
|---|---|---|---|---|
| ISO 9001: 2008 | **Quality Management System** for any servicer manufacturing company, that allows the company to develop well-documented set of processes and procedures that are followed consistently. | Demonstrates supplier's capability of providing adequate product quality, and enhanced performance. Improves efficiency of operations and enhances profitability, Increases eligibility to quote against customer requirements and also gives competitive advantage in tenders. Improves image of companies following the certification. | International standard providing assurance to customers and hence focusing on their wellbeing & satisfaction Flexibility to adapt to wide range of industries& functional areas. | Too general and hence a little confusing to companies in different industries. Doesn't focus on continuous Improvement like ISO 9004-1 & 9004-4. |
| ISO 14001 | **Environmental Management System** A framework for organizations to: a) Minimize harmful effects on the environment caused by their activities, b) Meet regulatory requirements, | Assists companies' to identify the areas within their operations where they can improve their environmental performance. This leads to a better image in front of the customers, society and other partners leading to higher acceptance. Improves. | International standards focusing on decreasing the environmental impacts and improving its use of raw materials and recycling. Increased awareness among global community regarding the need for this will help in tremendous goodwill and | Being a new area, there is a shortage of resources working on this and hence is difficult to implement for most of the smaller companies, while at the same time there is an urgent need to comply to retain image in the market place. |

| | | energy efficiency, cost savings and better environmental compliance. Increased acceptance of products in the global markets | also revenues in the form of carbon credits etc. | |
|---|---|---|---|---|
| OHSAS 18001 | **Health and Safety Assurance System** is the part of the overall management system which is involved in developing, implementing, achieving, reviewing and maintaining the OHS policy and so managing the risks associated with the business of the organization. | Helps avoid damages due to illness, injuries to employees at workplace. Legal compliance is taken care. Ensures all employees are aware of the health and wellness related issues. A healthy workforce is an asset as it will improve productivity. | Improves the image of the company as legally compliant entity. Can help the image of the company in the eyes of the employees for taking care of their health and safety. | For best benefits, needs to be implemented along with ISO9001. Hence requires more organizational resources and continuous commitment. |
| ISO 22000: 2005 | **Food Safety Management System** focuses on the total food chain—farming, processing, manufacturing, wholesale, retail food service and also on the interested parties— customers, suppliers, public authorities, etc | Adopting FSMS ISO22000: 2005 helps reach global standards, demonstrate compliance to Regulations/ Customer requirements besides providing safer food devoid of chemical contaminations. | Increases global acceptance of products and hence help boost export potential. | For best benefits, needs to be implemented along with ISO9001. Hence requires more organizational resources and continuous commitment |

| ISO 27001 | **Information Security Management System**ISO/ IEC 27001 aims tonsure that adequate controls addressing confidentiality, integrity and availability of information are in place to safeguard the information of interested parties. These include customers, employees, trading partners and the needs of society in general. | Helps companies adopt appropriate procedures to ward off threats such as computer-assisted fraud, sabotage and viruses, from internal or external, accidental or malicious sources. | Helps make a public statement of capability without revealing security processes, and minimizes business risk by ensuring controls is in place. Reduces the risk of security threats and avoids system weaknesses being exploited. Improves confidence of business partners leading to competitive advantage. | For best benefits, needs to be implemented along with ISO9001. Hence requires more organizational resources and continuous commitment |

Similarly, other important ISO Standards are, Supply chain security (ISO28000), Energy management (ISO 50001), Road traffic safety management (ISO 39001) and Risk Management (ISO31000).

**Process of acquiring the ISO certification:**
A company wanting to acquire ISO Certification undertakes the following:

- Identify the ISO standard to apply for and get organizational commitment for the same
- Identify an internal champion and/or an external consultant to go through the process till the certification is achieved
- Identify the gaps in the existing standards and the desired standards as per the ISO requirements

- Identify the new processes required to achieve the desired standards, document the same and put them into action
- Conduct an internal audit, once the desired level of performance is achieved
- Invite an external auditor representing a 3rd party certification organization like BVQi, TUV-Nord etc and go through a thorough review of the systems, processes in action w.r.t the documentation done
- In case the external auditor is satisfied with the compliance, get the ISO certification

If not, repeat the process.

Generally the PDCA (Plan, do, check, act) or PDSA (Plan do study Act) are the steps undertaken to complete this process.

Once this certification is done, there will be a periodic review of the company's systems in action w.r.t its documentation, to ensure that there is continuity of the quality assurance cycle being implemented by the company and the certification is renewed.

## CMMI

CMMI is used to evaluate the process maturity of an organization, typically in the technology domain. CMMI currently addresses three areas of interest:

- Product and service development—CMMI for Development (CMMI-DEV),
- Service establishment, management, and delivery—CMMI for Services (CMMI-SVC), and
- Product and service acquisition—CMMI for Acquisition (CMMI—ACQ)

Applying the processes, methods, tools, and technologies of the Software Engineering Institute throughout the Product and service development, Service establishment, management, and delivery, acquisition cycle of any product/service from vendors, helps the organizations to meet complex challenges and achieve their goals. CMMI applies to teams, work groups, projects, divisions, and entire organizations CMMI models are collections of best practices that help organizations to dramatically improve effectiveness, efficiency, and quality. These products, or CMMI solutions, consist of practices. Practices cover topics that include causal analysis; configuration management; quality assurance; verification and validation; risk management; requirements management; supplier management; project management; interface compatibility; make, buy, or reuse analysis; capacity management; availability management; disaster recovery, data collection, process performance; and more.

## CHARACTERISTICS OF THE MATURITY LEVELS

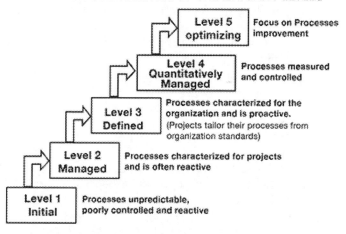

## CHARACTERISTICS OF THE MATURITY LEVELS

CMMI's latest version 1.3, lists 22 core process areas, present across 5 staged models. There are generic and specific goals for each area for which assessment is conducting for awarding the level. The five stages of CMMI in the staged model are given in the adjoining figure (Source—Wikipedia).

Achievement of levels by a company is a step-by-step process and a company cannot skip any levels in its journey from level 1 to level 5.

The organizations going for the continuous CMMI model identify any of the 22 processes listed as per CMMI and go for the level they intend to.

The Software Engineering Institute's (SEI) Team Software Process methodology and the use of CMMI models can be used to raise the maturity level. A new product called Accelerated Improvement Method (AIM) combines the use of CMMI and the TS.

Technology Companies get themselves appraised for CMMI, as it enables them to

- Improve on their process excellence by identifying and plugging the gaps w.r.t the best practices as per CMMI
- Achieve substantial improvement in productivity & profitability &
- To showcase their capabilities favorably to potential clients, employees, partners etc.

A number of times, only organizations which are assessed at CMMI level 5 are eligible to quote against large tenders.

While ISO 9001: 2008 and CMMI are different in their scope, methodology and approach, organizations tend to start with ISO 9001:2008 certification process, as it is an inexpensive and much quicker approach to improve their productivity levels at the same time helps them to project themselves better externally. Subsequently, they try to gradually move into the higher CMMI levels.

Top companies choose to adopt the best practices of both by integrating them, to achieve highest levels of process excellence and productivity gains that takes them to much higher echelons of growth in revenues and profitability.

# PROJECT MANAGEMENT APPROACH TO PRODUCTIVITY MAXIMIZATION . . .

**Operations keep the lights on, strategy provides a light at the end of the tunnel, but project management is the train engine that moves the organization forward.**

*—Joy Gumz*

One of the most under-rated and under-stressed aspects of the management of an organization is the importance of managing its projects successfully. There-in lies the secret of great organizations that have taken great strides and overwhelmed their followers and investors with their sheer ability to pull off large projects successfully.

Reliance Industries Ltd., one of the largest private organizations emerging out of independent India, has built its organization from the scratch with its amazing ability to commission large scale projects of world class that have given it economies of scale to become global leader in the manufacturing of number of petrochemical, textile and plastic products.

Why is efficient project management, the most important aspect for any organization?

When a business unit is started or an expansion undertaken or the conversion of an idea into a product or service is put in action, the first step to execution is the creation of a project proposal and a business plan. The business plan underlines the investments to be undertaken and the milestones to be achieved in various stages.

**All things are created twice; first mentally; then physically. The key to creativity is to begin with the end in mind, with a vision and a blue print of the desired result."**

*— Stephen Covey*

Successful execution of the projects planned will have a favorable impact on the cash flows reducing capital related interest expenses and operational expenses This will lead to higher profitability and increased interest levels in the investors who not only help raise more resources for growth required in the future, but also will repose their faith in funding more projects of the organization.

Similarly, delay in execution projects if not rectified can snowball into big losses for the company and sometimes lead to bankruptcy if the project is too big and important.

Lets examine the case of a spectacular project failure to understand the essential aspects to be taken care while executing a project:

**Spectacular failure at UK's 20 Billion Pound IT project of NHS (National Health Scheme):**

*£20bn NHS computer system 'doomed to fail'12:01AM GMT13Feb 2007http://goo.gl/CVGT3*

Labour's multi-billion-pound project to create the NHS's first ever national computer system "isn't working and isn't going to work", a senior insider has warned.

The damning verdict on the ambitious £20 billion plans to store patients' records, and allow people to book hospital appointments, on a central computer network has been delivered by a top executive at one of the system's main suppliers.

Andrew Rollerson, the health-care consultancy practice lead at the computer giant Fujitsu, warned that there was a risk that firms involved in the project would end up delivering "a camel and not the racehorse that we might try to produce".

'£12bn NHS computer system is scrapped . . . and it's all YOUR money that Labour poured down the drain' UPDATED: 17:08 GMT, 22 September 2011 http://goo.gl/QOTTE

Sum would pay 60,000 nurses' salaries for a decade
Scheme replaced with cheaper regional alternatives
Decision comes after report said IT system was not fit for the NHS

The reasons analyzed for the failure of the project were given as follows:

a) No clear vision envisaged for the massive project on how the health service can make best use of new technology.

**"No matter how good the team or how efficient the methodology, if we're not solving the right problem, the project fails."**

*—Woody Williams*

b) Users were not consulted while drawing up the complex project
c) Too many incompatible vendors working together with frequent fights among themselves
d) No visionary leadership that would integrate all the aspects of the project together and lead the project to a logical end. The project manager is expected to integrate all aspects of the project, ensure that the proper knowledge and resources are available when and where needed, and above all, ensure that the expected results are produced in a timely, cost-effective manner."—Meredith and Mantel
e) Lack of proper accountability for public money
f) Lack of adequate competency that would help execute such a large project
g) Lack of periodic reviews and adequate information flow that help monitor the project

of such a large scale and keep it on track for successful completion

**"The project manager must be able to develop a fully integrated information and control system to plan, instruct, monitor and control large amounts of data, quickly and accurately to facilitate the problem-solving and decision-making process."**

*—Rory Burke and above all,*

h) Despite adequate warnings from various quarters, no turnaround could be attempted over a 5-year period, which is astonishing. This also indicates a complete breakdown of communications between various executing parties and lack of review mechanisms that would put the project on the right track.

**I have witnessed boards that continued to waste money on doomed projects because no one was prepared to admit they were failures, take the blame and switch course. Smaller outfits are more willing to admit mistakes and dump bad ideas.**

*—Luke Johnson*

From such failures, we can outline some of the important steps required to run successful projects:

**Step 1:**
Outline clear objectives and deliverables for the project:

**The single best payoff in terms of project success comes from having good project definition early.**

*—RAND CORPORATION*

Key success indicators of the project should be clearly determined. They could be, the deadline goals, increase in key rations, increase in market shares, reduction in turnaround times and any such qualitative & quantitative factors

Care should be taken that the organization does not over-commit and under-deliver. The negotiations should be transparent and clarity should be established to avoid any misunderstandings leading to breakdown in the future

## Step 2:
Plan for the 4 aspects of the project namely Performance, Cost, Time-lines and Scope very clearly.

**Project management is like juggling three balls— time, cost and quality. Program management is like a troupe of circus performers standing in a circle, each juggling-three balls and swapping balls from time to time."**

*—G. Reiss*

- Project launch & release criteria should be clearly determined. What makes the product ready for the final release should be clearly identified and agreed upon between the constituents
- There should be perfect clarity between the project sponsor, client and the organization managing the project regarding the budget for the project, qualitative aspects of the project meant to be achieved, deadlines to be met and delivery schedule to be adhered
- The scope of the project and the exclusions also should be clear

## Step 3:
Plan for all the likely risks along with the corresponding backup plans and risk mitigation strategies to ensure that unforeseen events do not sink the project

easily and there is adequate safeguard that will allow the system to respond to minimize deviation or loss.

**Step 4:**

Breakdown the project into a series of steps, some running one after another and some running concurrently to come out with an accurate schedule and also understand the constraints affecting the project within which the project team must deliver.

> **Running a project without a WBS is like going to a strange land without a roadmap.**
>
> —*J. Phillips*

The steps should form constituents of stages of the project along with corresponding time-lines that must be met. Care should be taken that each step should have strict deadlines and also a reasonable buffer at the overall level to make-up for any delays in anyone of the steps.

**Step 5:**

Assemble the right team with appropriate competencies, complementing each other. The team leader has to have clear vision about the project's progress and expectations with the end clearly in the mind.

> **"Project managers function as bandleaders who pull together their players each a specialist with individual score and internal rhythm. Under the leader's direction, they all respond to the same beat."**
>
> —*L.R. Sayles*

**Step 6:**

Create a set of guiding practices in line with the guiding vision for the project and ensure that the team sticks to the same.

**Step 7:**

Organize clear communication channels among the team members and across levels to enable excellent coordination and also periodic review to update and monitor progress. Daily updates, weekly progress reports, deviation reports and action taken reports and any course corrections required should be clearly discussed in the meetings. This will enable the project to stay on rails throughout the execution stage.

**Step 8:**

Incorporate a right mix of control mechanism and self guiding principles to be adhered to by the team members individually and as a team to ensure, not only an objective monitoring of the project but also a urge on the part of all the members of the team to be motivated to take initiative and deliver on the deadlines on their own will.

Quality assurance rather than quality control is more useful in optimizing the project functioning, as prevention is better than cure. At every stage, there should be adequate checks and balances to ensure that the deviations from the desirable results should be analyzed and action taken to correct the same so that they do not exaggerate at the end when it is too late to rectify the situation.

At any time, if there is any shortage of expertise, necessary expertise should be brought in immediately or the project personnel trained to handle the situation instead of trying to fix the situation with available team members.

**Step 9:**

Close the Project once completed and the desired objectives are met. Sometimes, a decision is taken to extend the project to give more time for completion or a next phase is launched taking advantage of the success, to milk for more benefits. Some time, prudence results in scrapping the project and limiting the losses if it is not found viable to continue further.

As and when the project is completed, the results and the execution should completely be documented and analyzed. Communication with all the stakeholders should be recorded and the project closed. The satisfaction levels of the project beneficiaries should be well documented and also lessons learnt from them should be carried forward to enable better execution of future projects.

Transparency between the project sponsors, team members, clients and all the stake holders will ensure that the deviations are minimized and the project is always ahead of the expectations leading to successful execution.

A number of times, the projects do not go as planned due to a number of internal and external factors. Dispassionate analysis and decision making to ensure good money is not thrown after bad money frees up valuable resources that could be deployed elsewhere profitably and losses are minimized.

Successful companies follow the Project Management Methodologies rigorously and ensure that their money is put to good use and ROI maximized.

# THROUGH THE PRODUCTIVITY PRISM

Every organization is in search for ways to enhance productivity. With ever increasing competition, costs and complexities, only the fittest survive. Hence, the demand for higher productivity from all resources—people, material, time, money.

'Cost cutting' ends up becoming the favored buzz words (with the recent recession, probably rightly placed too) in almost all organizations. 'Do more with less' kind of slogans finding a prominent place in corporate presentations. There is absolutely nothing wrong with these as guiding principles for operations. However, neither of them yields the best outcomes without an understanding of the organisational context. Hence, for example, while 'frivolous' expenses are definitely not desirable, cost cutting can add to productivity only to the extent that it cuts flab. Beyond a limit, you 'cannot cost cut your way to glory' for productivity.

> **Economics is the science/art, which studies human behavior as relationship between ends and scarce means, which have alternative, uses**
>
> —*Lord Robbins.*

This is probably the most useful and practical principle that can help in productivity increase, if understood well. The subtle meaning captured in this definition throws open the spectrum of possible ways in which organizational resources can create an impact. Along with the following statement by Archimedes, it provides a robust model for productivity increase.

**Give me a lever long enough and a fulcrum on which to place it, and I shall move the world**
— *Archimedes.*

Productivity, in its very simple mathematical/scientific form, is a ratio of output over input. Or in business context, Return on Investment. This can be depicted as a product of (A) Profit/Sales & (B) Sales/Investment. These ratios dance in a colorful spectrum when viewed through the prism of organisational context!! Robbins and Archimedes together provide the canvas and brushes respectively, with which to paint organisational success.

A statement like 'Do more with less', breaks up into multiple hues, when passed through The Productivity Prism of organisational context. These are:

1) Do less with much less
2) Do same with less
3) Do more with same
4) Do much more with more

On the spectrum from 1) to 4) are choices available to organizations operating in different situations. a shrinking/contracting scenario, holding ground, marginal growth or a high growth environment needing investments respectively!!

In situation 1) above, if input is reduced in a manner that output is not reduced to the same extent, the resulting ratio of productivity still ends up being better. The same 'mathematical' logic applies to the other three cases as well.

However, in the absence of human intervention, these are 'passive' mathematical ratios. In business, as in life, there is available the option of 'managerial' discretion and 'free will'. This can influence the way these ratios behave, rather than being handed over in a 'fatalistic' take it or leave it manner. Understanding and picking the Right 'shade' can make all the difference. The palette thus exposed by The Productivity Prism can be used suitably to come out with flying colors'!!

Robbins helps when you try to understand the 'Core Customer Deliverable' and 'what in the Value Chain adds most Value to The Customer'. It is such help in the allocation of scarce means (with alternative uses; and mind you, organizations always have finite resources) for an optimal outcome.

Archimedes helps by pointing out that unless the 'leverage ratio' is calibrated and fixed well, movement at the other end of the organisational 'lever' will be sub-optimal.

Robbins and Archimedes provide the canvass and brush. The palette is made available through The Productivity Prism. The only thing that one now needs is a 'thinner' to dilute the paint to the right consistency, so as to be able to get the 'Right Flow and Application'.

Organizations can gain through external expert help here. There are tools available for understanding cause-effect relationships between various parameters, risk analysis and prioritization of issues. Such tools can provide the right 'consistency' to enable decision making with Optimal Innovative Solutions.

Theory of Constraints, Lean & JIT manufacturing and Kaizen (continuous improvement) are some of the tools available for today's managers to continuously improve their productivity leading to a phenomenal improvement in profitability.

**Theory of Constraints:**

The theory of constraints (TOC), introduced by Eliyahu M. Goldratt in his 1984 book titled The Goal, adopts the common idiom "A chain is no stronger than its weakest link" as a new management paradigm. This means that processes, organizations, etc., are vulnerable because the weakest person or part can always damage or break them or at least adversely affect the outcome.

The analytic approach with TOC comes from the contention that any manageable system is limited in achieving more of its goals by a very small number of constraints, and that there is always at least one constraint. Hence the TOC process seeks to identify the constraint and restructure the rest of the organization around it, through the use of five focusing steps. Assuming the goal of a system has been articulated and its measurements defined, the steps are:

- Identify the system's constraint(s) (that which prevents the organization from obtaining more of the goal in a unit of time)
- Decide how to exploit the system's constraint(s) (how to get the most out of the constraint)
- Subordinate everything else to above decision (align the whole system or organization to support the decision made above)
- Elevate the system's constraint(s) (make other major changes needed to break the constraint)
- If in the previous steps a constraint has been broken, go back to step 1, but do not allow inertia to cause a system's constraint.

The goal of a commercial organization is: "Make money now and in the future", and its measurements are given by throughput accounting as: throughput, investment, and operating expenses.

The five focusing steps aim to ensure ongoing improvement efforts are centered around the organization's constraint(s). In the TOC literature, this is referred to as the process of ongoing improvement (POOGI)—(Source Wikipedia)

**TOC:** enables the organizations to substantially increase their output by understanding the constraints that are blocking them to increase output, focus their resources on surmounting those constraints, thus maximizing the output using existing resources thus leading to increase in productivity.

**LEAN**: Lean is a practice in production of a product or a service that focuses on eliminating wasteful expenditure that does not create any value for the customer or those who consume the product or the service. The Lean Approach is a generic process management philosophy derived mostly from the Toyota Production System (TPS), which was aimed at eliminating the 7 highest contributors to wastes that reduce value delivered to the customers, and also from other sources

**TQM:** Widely used in Manufacturing and Service industries, TQM or Total Quality Management is an organizational strategy aimed at improving productivity by encouraging Quality Consciousness across the organization by focusing on doing it right first time, thus eliminating waste due to duplication of processes to produce output within specification. In particular, processes that operate with six-sigma quality produce at defect levels below 3.4 defects per (one) million opportunities (DPMO). Six Sigma's implicit goal is to improve all processes to that level of quality or better.

**JIT:** Just in Time (JIT), is a production strategy that involves, minimizing the in-process inventory and

carrying costs involved in the manufacturing of a product or a service.

**Kaizen**—Kaizen or continuous improvement is a process used by organizations to evolve continuously by systematically improving the output per unit of input.

Conscious use of strategies like TOC, Lean, TQM, Six Sigma, Kaizen, JIT can multiply the productivity and efficiency of an organization leading to an unending growth with increased profitability and enduring success.

**"I truly believe that going forward 'lean, mean and hungry' is the best way to thrive"**
— **Vineet Nayar,** *CEO, HCL Technologies*

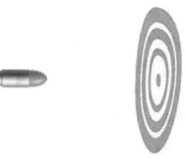

A Lean, Mean and Hungry Luxottica SPA., Italy took over the world's finest sunglasses brand, Ray Ban from its fat and comfortable rival, Bausch & Lomb Inc, USA, and turned it into a profitable business in no time.

In today's competitive world, the success of a business is viewed more by their ability to survive and sustain over the long term at the same time delivering the promised ROI to the investors and on their commitments to the society.

Any business that survives on wafer-thin margins, high burn rates that result in spends more than the revenue generated, risk the problem of running into operational losses, working capital squeeze and devalued creditworthiness.

Companies that work on low capital but high value added through service related efforts have a natural ability to sustain over long period as they let their ammunition much longer than those who spend away their surpluses or run up cash losses.

Those companies that are lean, mean and hungry end up agile, adaptive and flexible to fine-tune their strategies and remain efficient and effective.

A bullet moving fast towards a focused target, is million times more dangerous than a huge boulder moving towards a much bigger target (hence easier to reach).

A 13-member team (read Instagram) creating a 1 Billion USD valuation in just under 2 years is no more unthinkable in today's IT enabled full of enterprising businesspersons.

Instagram's success has opened the eyes of the world to the need of being a lean, mean and hungry operation that leverages the power of breakthrough idea, followed with sustained passion and focused efforts to create a unforeseen valuations in a short time.

It is a nightmare for today's companies to face lean, mean and hungry competitors with low overheads, rapid market action that could take the ground off their feet, eating into their market shares.

Nirma, once a virtually unknown brand of detergent powder, created a rapid dent in the market share of the Market Leader, Surf, with its low overhead, low priced, high volume strategy that shook the Unilever's marketing might, till Unilever responded with Wheel detergent powder. High family running expenses, huge wastage in the economy, low saving rates are some of the problems that have led US economy down a few notches during the recent recession, while countries like India and China managed to keep their head above the water with much superior growth rates while the western economies struggled. This is because of the very low survival needs of a typical Indian and Chinese family, that would ensure them to live comfortably with much smaller incomes.

A fatter and a comfortable enemy is the wish for any company, as it would mean that the competitor does not have the necessary hunger to go after the business growth and also is pulled down by the weight of the bureaucracy with in.

Today's successful organizations are taking every possible step to keep the operations lean, profitable and enterprising by inculcating an entrepreneurial culture across the organization, by encouraging the employees to take ownership of their sphere of operation, take calculated risks, think innovatively and take responsibility with accountability for their performance.

To fully realize its innovation potential, Google encourages all of its employees to think and act like entrepreneurs. Cutting down layers in an organization, encouraging networking among employees and enabling them to work in flat networked structure rather than in hierarchical structure, focus on brilliance and competence rather than on age and experience alone, cutting down inefficiencies and excess flab in the system, that does not add value to the customer and the ultimate consumer are some of the strategies followed by the companies to remain lean and agile in today's competitive world to outwit competition and sustain a long term growth trajectory.

## LEAN MEAN & HUNGRY—GENERAL ELECTRIC

Lean Mean, Hungry and Agile at 120.

Lean, Mean and Hungry is the motto at GE, one of the finest brick and mortar businesses of the world.

Founded as Edison General Electric by Thomas Edison and later evolving into, General Electric by the 1892 merger of Edison General Electric of Schenectady, New York and Thomson-Houston Electric Company of Lynn, Massachusetts GE went on to become a Transnational Conglomerate, operating through four segments: Energy, Technology Infrastructure, Capital Finance and Consumer & Industrial.

Through a series of acquisitions, mergers, reorganizations and divestitures, General Electric became an industrial behemoth with a nine layered management structure which was slow to respond to the market dynamic.

GE made a phenomenal progress under Jack Welch who took over the reins of the company as its youngest Chairman and CEO in 1981.Jack Welch delayer the organization, made it into a lean and hungry machine with an insatiable appetite for leader ship. He took a stand that; GE will operate in only those businesses, where GE is wither the 1st or the 2nd in market share. He rewarded the employees who figured in the top 20% of the performance list and fired those who were in the bottom 10%. His carrot and stick policy of driving performance gave him the nick name of 'Neutron Jack' named after the Neutron Bomb, which destroys lives without damaging the structure of the buildings they are housed in. Nevertheless, his leadership style kept the organization on its toes, nurtured execution excellence and led to the achievement of a phenomenal growth of 4000% during his tenure spanning 20 years.

Today, GE, under the leadership of Jeffrey Immelt, is one of the largest corporations in the world, with a turnover of over 147 Billion US Dollar and a net income of over 14Billion US dollar, employing over 3 lakh employees.

# LEVERAGING TECHNOLOGY FOR COMPETITIVE EDGE . . .

## TECHNOLOGY—A CRITICAL LEVER FOR GROWTH AND COMPETITIVE EDGE . . .

**Give me a lever long enough and a fulcrum on which to place it, and I shall move the world**
— *Archimedes*

Successful organizations have learnt to leverage the Power of Technology to the hilt and continue to stay ahead in the race for leadership by innovative and effective use of Technology.

Growth of the use of Technology in Communication, Banking, E-Commerce, Travel, Enterprise Resource Planning, Automating various facets of the company, Marketing have led to tremendous improvements in productivity & profitability for the companies and high value for money for the customers.

While the mobility of the workforce is empowered by the use of mail on the move, tele-presence, live video connectivity and ERP lets organizations manage and enhance productivity in resource utilization most effectively, the most critical use of Technology has been in the field of studying the customers, users, maximizing the life time value of the customers, providing enhanced user experience and marketing efficiently to the customers by leveraging the digital media.

The advent of Cloud Computing and Service Oriented Architecture has put the power of technology in the hands of small companies and also reduced the resource requirement for creating new products and services in the technological domain.

Today small enterprises are able to rapidly develop and test their ideas with limited resources while large organizations are able to quickly deploy IT services within their organizations with a limited investment in hardware and complex applications', thanks to the advantages provided by the Cloud Computing.

Some of the trends in the use of Technology by the thriving companies are as follows:

i) **Automation:** Automating various aspects of the operations like manufacturing, service delivery, campaign management, especially the routine and repetitive operations that do not require customer interface will help in reducing operating expenses, enhancing precision and in improving predictability & productivity.

Enterprise Resource planning enables the organizations to leverage technology for most productive management of all resources.

ii) **Studying & Analyzing Customers:** Technology empowers the organizations with its ability to crunch large amounts of data and make sense for enhancing user experience, getting right products in the right place, improvements required in the delivery of the proposition, cross selling opportunities to enhance life time value of the customers.

With the explosion in the Social media space there has been tremendous increase in the user-generated data globally. The task for today's organizations is not only to keep track of the data but also to make sense of it and get most value from the business point of view and stay ahead of the competition. BIG DATA ANALYTICS is the upcoming area of information processing and knowledge management that is being leveraged the thriving companies in the race for leadership. Big Data Analytics helps organizations in crunching large set of data in a limited time to make sense of it for productive use. This will help them in studying the customers and operational information at frequent intervals and more widely across the organization ranging from offices, places to plant to customers and also segment and target customers with precision in a more customized manner. This will help the organizations in attaining dramatic improvements in productivity and profitability by helping them to save wasteful expenditure, develop new products as per customer needs at a faster pace, enable cross selling to mine the customers better, enhance customer service levels, increase efficiency and quality of operations by acting on feedback etc. Keeping track of customers who visit your websites and increasing conversions out of abandoned shopping carts, fans and followers is greatly enhanced by the use of data mining and analysis.

iii) **Engaging with the users and the customers:** Technology empowers the organizations to engage one on one with their customers and users. Through websites, social media channels, one to one advertising, the organizations are able to reach out to their customers to tailor make their products and services as per the needs of the consumers. Today, tablets are being used at the retail level to give a better idea about the menus to customers and explaining the technical details better at auto showrooms in a comprehensive manner.

Augmented reality is being used to leverage multimedia in enhancing visual experience for a better feel of the products and services to the customers. Technology is surely a very big lever in enhancing user experience through innovative engagement techniques.

iv) **Marketing and Reaching out to Customers:**
Technological advances and innovative organizations have enabled marketers and advertisers to precisely segment and target the individual consumers with measured responses that has dramatically improved the effectiveness of advertising and marketing investments. As companies and publishers collect important information like demographics, tastes and preferences, psycho-graphic details through the online behavioral patterns, about their users, members and web site visitors, the marketers and advertisers are able to deliver targeted campaigns.

Techniques like Email marketing, Affiliate Marketing, Search Engine Marketing Targeted Banner Advertising, Pay per click, Pay per action, Social Media Marketing, On-line Public relations, Video advertising, mobile advertising through the web to targeted customers.

Use of mobile applications to engage with the customers and reach out to them through location based advertising and services have led to micro targeting opportunities.

Affiliate marketing is effectively used by large e-commerce organizations like Amazon to rapidly scale operations across the globe.

Thus the most innovative and technologically pro-active companies are able to converse, engage, empower, and entertain their customers on the web thus enhancing their lifetime value for the business.

Technology has empowered the creation of viral buzz that allows good words or bad words to travel fast through reviews, recommendations, mentions in social media, blogs and in media sites. This instantaneous transmission of information and multiplication has helped in creating huge business opportunities and also huge failures. The power of the viral buzz on social media could be gauged by the fact that, this is supposed to have helped Barack Obama in gaining edge in US Presidential Election Campaign-2008 and also in the fall of powerful and autocratic rulers in the Middle Eastern countries like Egypt.

Organizations can also earn substantial additional income by monetizing the traffic that they get on their websites through ad placements, cross promotions etc.

On-line Reputation Management is actively pursued by the successful organizations of the 21st century who monitor the reputation of the company across the important on-line platforms and take action for speedy resolutions of complaints and negative mentions wherever and when ever they occur. The increasing pervasiveness of technology in today's operations has also brought along with it, threats related to information security, virus attacks, confidentiality and the need to create backups and safeguards to ward against such lapses. Further inefficient use of technology also brings in duplication of efforts and wastage of valuable resources including time and money.

Hence it is indeed a challenge for today's organizations to manage their digital presence and also to leverage technology to the hilt in making best of the opportunity presented by the ever-changing technology landscape. This requires the dedication of the top most management and also high quality resources at the senior levels.

Thriving organizations have managed to be always ahead in this aspect of 'Leveraging Technology' for maximum benefit and gaining consumer affinity, across the important on-line platforms and take action for speedy resolutions of complaints and negative mentions where-ever and when ever they occur.

## MICROSOFT — DOMINATING THE TECHNOLOGY LANDSCAPE . . .

MICROSOFT — Dictating the Technology agenda for the 21st Century organizations.

The technology story of the world would never be complete without the mention of Microsoft. Bill Gates and Paul Allen started Microsoft in 1975. Microsoft is the largest software company in the world with an annual turnover of over US$ 68 billions.

Microsoft started with the audacious vision of the founders to have a 'computer at every desk and every home'. Microsoft windows are now more or less an integral part of people's computer related work. Bill Gates and Paul Allen studied together in high school. In Lakeside Prep School, they had their first interaction with computers. Both of them were hooked. They loved programming and spent hours working in front of the computer.

The turning point for them came when Allen brought a magazine where they came across an article about Altair 8000, a mini computer. The duo approached the manufacturer to launch a programming language for Altair, even though they did not have any exposure of Altair. The manufacturer was busy and gave them 8 weeks for the demonstration. In these 8 weeks, Gates and Allen developed the interpreter. The interpreter worked at the demonstration and MITS agreed to distribute Altair BASIC. This was the start of many achievements that shaped Microsoft and the computing industry.

Here is a list of things that make Microsoft the most successful software company on the planet.

**Vision**

Vision statements for general guidance guide the teams. They have the freedom to implement things their ways keeping in mind the objectives of the company. The focus is on the essentials but with a vision towards the future.

**Smart people**

Bill Gates has always advocated working with the best professionals to build the best products. The most important factor for building products is the quality of people involved. Microsoft has been built around the best people.

**Bet Your Life**

Since its inception, the DNA of the company has been to put everything into the projects. The projects are reported on a regular basis to the higher management to avoid any last moment surprises. The focus is on the results and addressing the issues at the earliest through proper communication.

**Early Mover Advantage**

Microsoft has shown the ability to be the first, or early, to enter a market, find and build mass markets, don't wait for perfect products but build incrementally better products in the direction of the market.

**Solution rather than problem**

Excuses don't work, solutions do. The teams at Microsoft are often small and focused on achieving their results. They are primarily focused on delivering quality products and do everything possible to fix the problem.

**Focus**

At Microsoft, the employees are focused on one task or project. This helps them to keep away from the distractions and help them stay focused with increased productivity.

**Market Dominance**

The windows operating system accounts for nearly 90% of the PC market. Microsoft completely dominates markets in which it competes. Go for 100% of every market you are in. Market share is the key to success.

**Results rather than Rules**

The focus is on the results and not on rules. Microsoft believes that employees' time should not be wasted on irrelevant rules and processes. Empower the employee and they will make reasonable choices and make them accountable for the results.

SRINIVAAS M.

## Ruthless Competitor

Microsoft almost missed the opportunity provided by Internet browser. However, once Microsoft had realized Internet's potential, the company not only rapidly caught up but also overtook all its competitors. In 1995 Netscape Navigator was the leading the market share with approximately 90% market share, but Microsoft soon took over using its monopoly in the operating system market. They started bundling Internet explorer with the operating system and regained the lost ground. Users no longer needed to install Netscape navigator and Internet explorer dominated the market.

## An eye on the future

The leaders at Microsoft keep an eye on the changing market dynamics. They do whatever is necessary to shape future opportunities in the market, and capitalize on them for Microsoft. Microsoft has now trained its eyes on the exploding market of Cloud services with the launch of Microsoft Azure. With an aggressive strategy, it is rapidly penetrating the small and medium enterprise segment and is empowering lakhs of businesses to leverage the power of the cloud. This enables them to reduce their infrastructure requirements to take their products and services to market and hence reduces the cost of running their businesses. With more productivity of their scarce resources and investments, small businesses have a much higher chance of success, thanks to Microsoft.

## RAISING CAPITAL FOR BUSINESS GROWTH . . .

As an organization starts taking shape, it requires funds for consolidating its achievements and start growing rapidly.

While the promoter/company brings to the table,

- Unique, scale-able customer value proposition with strong business potential
- Passion to drive the business
- Thorough domain expertise
- Deep execution competence & management bandwidth
- 100% commitment levels
- Transparency
- An urge to grow business and multiply value for all stake holders

Investors bring to the table,

- Financial bandwidth
- Validation of the business idea
- Network of people to support the business to grow
- System driven approach with guiding & monitoring capability to ensure that the progress is on track
- Experience gained from investing in different sectors over a varied time period and
- Strong business instinct coupled with acumen to help the business grow

When both the Promoters and Investors, join hands to pool in their best efforts together and complement each other well, the foundations for take-off of great organizations are firmly put in place.

It is very important to understand that, the type of funding is very much dependent on the risk associated at the time of raising the fund. In the initial stages, the business is very much in the form of an idea and the risks associated with the execution of the business plan and the development of the business are very high. The investors understand that the capital invested may not surely result in a successful business creation and hence the money may be completely lost and the capital wiped out. The capital that goes to fund the business with the maximum risk is generally funded by the funds from the entrepreneur or the close relatives of the entrepreneur who are ready to bear the loss.

A number of times, businesses are started by loan funds, A loan fund entails compulsory outflow of principal and interest even if it is after a small period of moratorium and becomes a noose around the neck of the entrepreneur. Should the business fail or if there is a delay or failure in raising money from the business, this will lead to mounting negative cash flows that may adversely affect the working capital and the financial position of the business leading to a high probability of business failure.

Any company raises resources and capital from the following sources:

- Promoters, Investors and shareholders who put their money in the form of cash and kind including time spent to grow the business
- Customers who patronize the company's products and services
- Banks, Financial service institutions and others who lend money to the company as loans an debentures
- Employees who work for the company and deliver much more value than what they are paid by the company
- Government and other supporting agencies that provide subsidies, grants and other concessions

As the company starts, the capital required for its establishment come mainly from the promoters and early stage investors. As the company starts rolling out its products, the company starts generating revenues from customers and the overall contribution from employees in the form of profit per employee starts growing. In the maturity stage, the company is at steady state earns enough money to pay for its expenses and have surplus to be paid as dividends to investors and/or invest in assets, unless it commissions big projects aimed at furthering the growth. The capital raised by the company through the various stages is as follows:

| STAGE OF COMPANY | KEY ACTIVITIES | FUNDING REQUIREMENTS & REMARKS |
|---|---|---|
| IDEATION | Define the problems and pain-points of the target customers to be addressed. Define the size of the market planned to be addressed, shortcomings of the existing players. ZERO-IN on the area of focus after identifying core strengths of self, organization and partners to be leveraged for the business. Prepare a Business plan giving details of the opportunity, fund requirements, growth plans, market structure, | Initially minimal and mostly restricted to meetings, secondary research and reports. In case of subsidiaries, the parent company, as a part of its expansion, new Venture creation will spend the same by leveraging its existing resources, to be capitalized later. |

| | | |
|---|---|---|
| | and differentiators to enable success, return of investments, payback period and exit options. | |
| **START UP/ EARLY** | The top management team is in place. Initial work place and basic office and amenities are setup. Brainstorming of the idea with potential investors. Clients, partners and employees is undertaken to fine-tune the product/service strategy with clear focus on what to-do and what not to do. High levels of focus from the promoters are required to ensure that the foundations are laid strongly for a good future. Proof of concept is established. Go or no go decision is taken. Focus on customer acquisition to iron out the business value proposition and establish viability. | Funding is essentially from the promoters and close associates. Angel investors and HNIs co-invest along with the promoters in the form of Series A round of investment. Series A refers to the class of preferred stock sold to investors in exchange for their investment. It is usually the first series of stock after the common stock and common stock options issued to company founders, employees, friends and family, angel investors, etc. |
| **PRODUCT/ SERVICE DEVELOPMENT** | Focus on ironing out technical glitches; scale up product/service creation capability. Key focus on getting paying customers and iron out the value-price equation for optimal profitability and growth. Increase employee base at both backend and customer facing levels. | Venture capital funds, Angel funds and Strategic partners interested in taking advantage of high growth potential and subsequent possibility of a higher multiplier effect on investments, provide the much needed capital in the form of Series A round of investment. Series A refers to the class of preferred stock sold to investors in exchange for their investment. It is usually the first series |

| | | |
|---|---|---|
| | | of stock after initial investors. Money also starts rolling in from paying customers and subscribers. |
| **GO TO MARKET GROWTH** | Start by penetrating pilot markets and tries to gain prominence through concentration of limited resources. Once this is achieved, fine-tune Go-to-Market strategies for a larger scale expansion. Growth requires huge working capital investments | Series B round is used to fund the growth stage and follows Series A round of funding from Venture Capital firms and Angel funds and is linked to achievement of certain milestones. |
| **EXPANSION** | Rapid growth phase, where the company grows in size, geographical reach, employee base, number of customers. Growth in the revenue is matched by the expenses and need for further investments aimed at infrastructure development, investment in new projects, marketing activities and net customer receivables & market credit. | Series C & mezzanine fund to finance the rapid growth and also the need for short term capital. Heavy dependence of short term and long term borrowing, Private equity investments, Public issue offering of shares, convertible and non convertible debentures, suppliers credit etc. |
| **MATURITY & STEADY STATE** | Stable growth period, revenues from sales much higher than expenses and returns to investors in the form of dividends and also investment in projects aimed at future growth from available surplus being generated. | Long term secured loans, short term bank loans for working capital etc are raised from banks on a routine basis. Lookout mergers, acquisitions and takeovers during this period for inorganic growth opportunities. |

| DECLINE | Inability to keep pace with the market place, unable to compete with the competitor or shrinking margins lead to rapid loss of market share and eventual death or sale of the company | Stripping of assets, sale of businesses to private equity funds or potential suitors or eventual liquidation to pay off the loans and shareholder if any. |
|---|---|---|

To summarize, When a company wants to raise equity capital, there are many options available like

Faith capital
Angel Capital
Venture Capital
Private Equity capital

Let us define characteristics of each of the above sources:

**Faith capital**
Faith capital is usually from friends, immediate family members and unsuspecting individuals. They believe 100% in what you are doing and do not mind loosing the money, if you fail!

**Angel Capital**
Usually angels are individuals with solid experience in your field of operation/technology and/or HNIs with deep pockets. The usual sources are angel networks like Mumbai Angels, Hyderabad Angels, and Indian Angels Network etc. Their typical investment is usually less than Rs. 2.5-3 crores.

Positive aspects of angel investment are

- Faster Decision making (Gut feeling)
- Quick cycle—cash in the bank
- Value addition possibilities

Negative aspects of angel investment are

- Hidden agenda of angel(s)
- Likely day-to-day interference
- Negative Network effect (Club)
- Take a large chunk (%)of your company at a low valuation.

## Venture Capital (VC)

VCs are large organized institutional investors from both domestic and international (Including corporate VCs) lineage. Their typical investment size ranges between Rs. 2.50 crores and Rs. 50 crore. Your company should be generating revenues with reference able customers and ideally should be EBIDTA +ve for attracting VC investment.

- Positive aspects of VC investment are
- Institutional investors bring lots of credibility to company,
- Large appetite for investment (2/3 rounds),
- Better valuation,
- Value addition—network effect/strategic partnerships,
- Due diligence of investee companies possible

Negative aspects of VC investment are

- Value addition by VC is sometimes a myth,
- Lucky to get like minded and progressive board nominee from VC.

## Private Equity (PE) capital

PE investors are large institutional investors both domestic and international. Their typical investment size is between Rs. 25 crores to Rs. 500 crores. Your company should have sizeable market share and revenues of at least Rs. 30-40 crores with good growth track record in revenues and profitability.

Positive aspects on PE investment are

- Institutional investors bring lot of credibility to company (especially, for IPO),
- High corporate governance levels,
- Large appetite for investment,
- Valuation discovery,
- Value addition—network effect/strategic partnerships,
- Due diligence of investee companies of PEs is possible

Negative aspects of PE investment are

- Mismatch of aspirations
- Mid course correction
- Exit pressures

Any of the above options depends upon stage of the company like

> Stage 1: Idea/Seed
> Stage 2: Early
> Stage 3: Mid
> Stage 4: Late

Though fund raising is not a must activity for every company, the funds raised apart from providing cash for fuelling growth, can also benefit the company from the experience and wisdom of the venture capital firms who, upon becoming the stake holders, lend their helping hand in growing the business by putting their investees, clients and network to work.

Fundraising is an exhaustive process that may take 6 to 9 months on an average if everything works out.

While Venture capital firms and funds are on the lookout for excellent firms to invest money and provide excellent return to their partners/investees, the

Companies aiming to raise funds have to knock on an average of over 20doors before they can raise funds.

The companies aiming to raise funds successfully and provide excellent return to their investors should have the following traits:

- Aim to build a company for the long term by focusing on genuine market opportunity mapped to core competencies of the founding team and management. They should focus on building products/services that customers would be willing to buy at a price profitable to the organization
- 100% focus and single minded commitment of the top management
- Clear cut business plan with a crisp executive summary and an elevator pitch to explain the market opportunity to busy fund managers bombarded with too many requests than what they could manage at any time
- Cultivate and showcase satisfied customers
- Have practical business plans backed by believable, factual and substantiated financial projections
- Have a clear milestone backed project delivery schedule backed by a clear exit plan

Usually VCs invest in any company using one or combination of following instruments

- Equity @premium
- Optionally/Compulsorily Convertible Preference shares/Debentures.

The conversion linked to performance of next year or next 2-3 years They are open on performance based "Claw back" provisions for promoters (usually 2-3% of company)/Options/MSOPs (Usually 5-15% of company)

**Various modes of investment are**

**I. Primary — Investment in company for:**

- Product development (Salaries — R&D staff, Product Proto-types etc.)
- Marketing expenses (Salaries, Advertisement, Branding, Conference expenses, Travel etc.)
- Reasonable CAPEX — commensurate with your project plan
- OPEX (Till you become EBIDTA +ve)
- Transaction expenses (Due diligence, ROC costs, Intermediary fees)

**II. Secondary — Buy-out of existing shareholders**
(Money does not go to company)

* Promoters (Part time/Sleeping Partners)
* Other minority shareholders (3 Fs)

Funds assess the potential of Market attractiveness, team competence, the uniqueness of the product/service and the entry barriers an enterprise can create in the market place along with the attractiveness of its financials to decide whether to consider investing or not. Next comes the valuation. Valuation is based on one or multiple methods like

- Revenue multiple
- EBIDTA multiple
- Price Earning Multiple (PECV)
- Discounted Cash Flow Method

Ultimately valuation is that value that is negotiated and agreed upon between the investor(s) and the promoters seeking investment, which may take the above as a guideline, but not necessarily stick the value thrown out by the above calculations.

Negotiation of valuation and required shareholders' rights is more an Art than Science. It depends upon exceptional negotiating capability of promoters & investors and also compulsions of promoters/founders to raise capital to execute the plan. It is a Give and Take principle of the promoters, which will get the money to the organization. One has to appreciate the desire of the investors to make money at the time of exit. It is desirable to approach multiple investors to evaluate your plan and negotiate hard with interested investor(s) to get best deal for the company.

Organizations seeking investment have to hire a good corporate lawyer who will advice them on various legal terms and implications of them on the company. Lawyer's fees (usually high) will be worth an investment to avoid confusion and anxiety later.

Once the investor(s) and the company arrive at a common understanding regarding the valuation at which the investment is to be made, the following steps are undertaken:

- Draw up a Term Sheet, which forms the basis for a detailed legally binding agreement later. A Term sheet is drawn depicting the terms at which the VC fund agrees to invest funds in the company. The key aspects of the term sheet include amount of investment, price per share, pre-money valuation, liquidation preferences, percentage stake sought, anti-dilution provisions, registration rights, Drag along rights, operational issues & exclusivity regarding investment, usually for a period of 90 days.

- Undertake due diligence to check authenticity of information and compatibility of the promoters and investors Due diligence involves going into details of the project, projected financials, assumptions underlying projections, past financials (at least 3 years), Statutory registers like Minute of meetings, share holder's register, fixed asset registers, legal documents/contracts, project deliverables, credentials of founders/

promoters/management team, reference checks, market visits and other issues legal and non legal that may have a bearing on the performance of the company. For successful completion of the due diligence process, a team of founder(s), CFO, statutory auditor, company secretary, lawyer and the company's own support staff to collate the data and understand complexity of assessing the data.

- Once the due diligence is completed, sign the Shareholders agreement with all the shareholders, investor(s). Funds are transferred as per the schedules drawn and the modalities planned i.e. after meeting conditions & precedents.

## Some of Do's for raising venture capital

- Emphasize of team's experience & company track record
- Be clear about roles & responsibilities of each team member
- Be upfront about failures in previous jobs/earlier ventures
- Clearly specify the market opportunity with your Go to Market strategy
- What are the target customers presently doing to solve problem?
- Rigorously study the competitive landscape
- Be open to criticism & discuss assumptions for financial projections.
- Appreciate Investors' investment strategy
- Be aware about background of person you are meeting with, in the Venture Fund
- Talk with a few investee companies of target investor about "Value Addition"
- Clearly define exit strategy for the investors
- End meetings on positive note and line up definite 'next steps' with timelines (minute the meetings!)

**Some Don'ts for raising venture capital—**

- Show desperation for capital infusion
- Approach investors directly (mostly references work!)
- Critical of investors' investment strategy/failures
- Go unprepared for the meeting w. r. t. Growth Strategy, Industry/competition data-vagueness/ no source/gut feel, Financial data & assumptions for projections/fund raise, Any other critical issues which affect your business
- Not business like personal appearance
- Lie/bluff about strategy/data
- Unnecessary arguments over trivial issues (incl. amongst team members)
- One upmanship—No-nonsense/I am always right attitude!
- Attempt to bribe the investors/IC/Board members
- Use the capital raised for personal gains/ buying personal assets

It is important for the company receiving funds to maintain transparency of reporting utilization, take utmost care to utilize the funds as per the project plan and strive to exceed the expectations of the investors. This will help build the trust and sound partnerships that will enable the company grow steadily with ability to raise more funds as and when required.

## INNOVATION AND MARKETING—THE CRITICAL SUCCESS FACTORS FOR TODAY'S ORGANIZATIONS

*"Because the purpose of business is to create a customer, the business enterprise has two— and only two—basic functions: marketing and innovation.*

**"Marketing and innovation produce results; all the rest are costs. Marketing is the distinguishing, unique function of the business"**
*—PeterDrucker*

We are living in an ever changing and ever evolving world. Only those organizations survive, that have continuously adapted themselves to this change and have consistently reinvented themselves to be in vogue with the times. This is possible through a process of innovation that leads to disruptive products, services and processes. There was a time when we used to communicate through post and travel in animal pulled carts.

**"Electricity and Internet, products of some of the greatest innovative minds, are two earthshaking inventions that have changed the life of human beings on this planet earth".**

Today, we communicate through instant mails, video chats on mobile devices and travel in high speed motored vehicles. Whatever happened to the ubiquitous Ambassador car and the once favorite Bajaj Scooter on the Indian roads?

The never changing design of the ambassador car & Premier Padmini has led to the downfall of once an undisputed market leader the Hindustan Motors &Premier, while companies like Maruti, Tata Motors, Toyota, Honda, Hyundai continuously innovated and came out with new products to stay with the times and continue on their growth path.

While there are many examples of continuous innovations that could be given, the continuous evolution of a classic brand has led to its survival and continuous growth over the years, despite strong competition that has marked its domain. Successful organizations have continuous stream of new products to replace old products that are continuously phased.

Intel, Microsoft, Samsung and Apple are famous examples of organizations that consistently come out with superior products through innovation and replace the old products with newer products and newer versions.

## New Products provide the Lifeline for the organizations and Innovation provides the Oxygen . . .

New Product development is not the only area in Marketing that is affected by innovation. While Google encourages every employee to think about new ideas one day every week, Starbuck's CEO pushed all his key managers to come out with new ideas to recreate customer experience. Steve Jobs, the immortal ex-CEO of Apple Inc known as the most innovative technologist on the planet commissioned, 'The Crazy Ones' a video that features Einstein, Edison, Branson who changed the world with their thoughts, to commission his 'Think Different Campaign'.

3M is one of the most innovation driven companies in the world that inspired a number of successful companies to monitor the contribution of new products and services to the annual sales. Successful organizations continuously look for opportunities to cannibalize old and outdated products, replacing them with far superior products in line with the customers changing tastes or sometimes, even lead the change.

Innovation can dramatically effect every aspect of marketing.

For example:

Digital Marketing has allowed tremendous innovation in targeting customers leading to amazing increase in the productivity of marketing budgets. Market research is conducted by Media, agencies and organizations themselves by using mobile applications, sms forms and interactive TV and web-based services unlike person-to-person interviews earlier.

Product and service level innovations have led to customized products and services based on individual tastes. Dell allows its customers to configure their computers while textile companies allow their companies to choose their designs and fittings based on individual tastes. Pricing innovations have allowed the companies to offer tailor made pricing, bid their prices, Innovation in advertising systems has allowed advertisers to choose their target audience, daily budgets and bidding rates while publicity can be done by directly updating the media through web.

Innovation in supply chain coupled with collection methods from customers for products has allowed extensive use of direct to home delivery and a rapid growth of e-commerce business in India. Innovation in packaging has helped in longer shelf lives of perishable goods and flexible product propositions to customers. Innovations in creating new stories, music, production techniques, use of multimedia technology, 3D technology etc. have kept the cinema audience continuously entertained and growing a trillion dollar industry across the globe. Bollywood and the rest of Indian cinema industry creates hundreds of movies and thousands of unique songs that drive the Indian public to the cinema theatres resulting in an ever-growing entertainment industry in India.

It is imperative for today's marketers to keep their product propositions attractive, interesting and continuously relevant to the ever-changing tastes and profiles of target audience through innovation in their marketing, strategies and tactics.

Behind every organization's success is an outstanding culture of innovation and a great marketing effort. Such Organizations will continuously stay ahead of their competition and will keep growing forever.

## INNOVATION LED GROWTH. @ 3M
3M = INNOVATION

]If there is one company in the word that personifies innovation in the world, it is 3M. Started as Minnesota Mining and Manufacturing company in USA in1902, 3M, came to be strongly associated as one of the pioneers of innovation catalysts in the world today. With a turnover of 29 Billion US Dollar in 2011 and a net income of over 4 Billion US Dollars, 3M has shown that innovation pays rich dividends in establishing a highly profitable global enterprises, while allowing it to touch the lives of people it serves in a number of ways, very fondly.

Started as an unsuccessful stone mining company, 3M encouraged its employees to come out with new ideas by offering its employees to spend 15% of their time at work to come out with innovative products. The products developed through this strategy, have now become the core of its product portfolio. Known globally for its Post-It Note, a revolutionary, yet simple product that has generated huge sales, 3M today has over 55,000 products, including adhesives, abrasives, laminates, passive fire protection, dental products, electronic materials, medical products, car care products (such as sun films, polish, wax, car shampoo, treatment for the exterior, interior and the under chassis rust protection), electronic circuits and optical films.3M aims to achieve 33% of its turnover from new launches every year and all its innovations that have been taken to market, are showcased in its corporate office at Minnesota.

3M don't believe in innovation for innovation sake. It believes in operational zing innovation through efficient and profitable manufacturing, leading to launch of unique products that positively impact the lives of its target audience.

3M is truly a global company with its products being available in over 200 companies. It has manufacturing operations and innovation laboratories in over 60 countries, employing over 80000 people, mostly local residents of respective countries.

## DECODING INNOVATION

We are ourselves creation of God and by being creative, we further continue the process set forth by Him. Not only is it in our nature to be creative, but by doing so, we give back to The Creator, in our own specific ways, His gift of creativity to us. Creation, in its very basic meaning, is a process of 'causing to exist'. Life has, inherent in its nature, an element of creating 'newness' and 'novelty'. The continuous cycle of Creation, Preservation and Destruction is The Cosmic Cycle of Brahma, Vishnu & Shiva. When we are creative, we harness the universality around us and make it flow through us. Hence, creativity is life; it is opening oneself to GOD (Good Orderly Direction). When we refuse to be creative, it maybe self will, but contrary to our true nature, leading to things becoming static/still/dead.

Nature continuously plays out and demonstrates its tendency to create novelty. The process of evolution is one of the ways in which nature expresses it's creativity. Evolution generally refers to the gradual process of development that we see in nature. This process has been going on for billions of years, from the time the first simple single cells were formed, through all the stages as life evolved into forms with higher complexity and order. The key routes to evolution were random mutation (once in millions of cells), trading of genetic pools (bacteria had access to a vast pool of genes, through which they passed traits in a powerful and efficient global exchange) and symbiogenesis (this is the key route of evolution for all higher organisms, in which there is creation of new forms of life through permanent symbiotic arrangements). The latter two are demonstrations of the powerful effects

183

of collaboration, co-creation and co-evolution that exist in nature and these were then fine tuned and honed by natural selection. It seems that there is a grand design where collective memories and energies (without any regard to size, caste, colour and hierarchies) are at play to create 'innovative evolution' in an interconnected Dance of Life!!

Innovation stands for a new way, technique or method to do things. By definition, then, it is a creative process. Evolutionary history of life is full of examples of 'innovative evolution'. Breathing and photosynthesis are excellent examples of this. When bacteria expanded, their energy needs led to shortage of hydrogen. Photosynthesis was an innovation to break water molecules using sunlight, to release hydrogen and oxygen. While hydrogen was used to build sugar and carbohydrates, oxygen was emitted into the atmosphere, leading to an oxygen crisis. Free oxygen is toxic as it produces free radicals and also causes combustion and corrosion. Breathing was the next innovation!!

Whether there have been challenges of the kind where an oxygen crisis was looming large, or whether the processes of mutation, gene trading and symbiosis were in any case running continuously, followed by natural selection, what is important in all these is that nature has its own ways of creativity. We can call it 'Evolutionary Innovation' or 'innovative Evolution', but this concept of 'Creative Evolutionary innovation' has elements of sharing knowledge, competition and collaboration, co-existing, adapting and growing. But 'who collaborates with whom?' and 'who adapts to what?' The species have interplay with each other and also with the environment and the ecosystem, shaping and adapting to each other and the environment itself, thus creating an Innovative Co-Evolutionary Dance. Nature's creativity is boundless!!

Organizations can learn a lot from this process. Each organization itself is an ecosystem or an organism and has inter-relationships within and outside. Every function/ department/location within an organization is also an ecosystem or an organism with such inter-relationships within themselves, with other functions/departments/ locations, with the overall organization and with the external world. Such similarities with the way ecosystems and organisms are organized and behave in nature, cause organizations also to mimic the patterns and behavior of species and ecosystems. Especially useful is the observation and learning attained through the processes of 'Creative Evolutionary Innovation' in Nature, no matter what the size of the organization. As is the case in nature, where size of the organisms is immaterial for this process to propagate; the smallest single cell organism or an amoeba or bacteria all played this game with equal adeptness, provided they followed the rules well!!

In organizations, or more so in the corporate world, innovation has to play a more practical and commercial role. It cannot be just a 'nice to have initiative' without any observable impact. Organizations exist to 1) add value for the customer and2) create ROI for the investors.

Both these can happen, **ONLY IF ALL THE STAKEHOLDERS IN THE VALUE CHAIN, COLLECTIVELY STRIVE TO ACHIEVE** them, by creating a Differential and/ or Cost Advantage in a WIN-WIN situation for all. If this basic premise is accepted and understood, the parallel drawn till now can make sense. Otherwise the organization and this discussion both can become extinct.

Creativity can be a lone/solo process and we have heard about many creative people who operate alone and do end up creating masterpieces. However, there are also the creative masters like Edison, who actually had the benefit of learning's of a whole team with him. There definitely are stories of creative geniuses who worked alone, but we are talking here of common people and minds, working in day-to-day operations in closer to ground organizations. How do they bring alive creativity in their work? A streak of genius happens once in a million, like random mutations in nature. Rest of the story of evolution is about the other two avenues of gene trading and symbiosis, honed by natural selection.

What then, could organizations do? Draw on learning's from nature and life. The simplest life forms could have Creative Evolutionary Innovation. Organizations will not achieve it only by the chance stroke of a brilliant idea that occurs to an employee in romantic environs on a Sunday afternoon, relaxing on a hammock in the sun, glass of beer in one hand and cigarette in the other . . . . He can probably keep waiting for that once in a million random mutations to strike. Or can organizations actually engineer the creative process proactively by drawing on the know how encoded in the gene pool of the system and using symbiotic relationships to collaborate and co-evolve innovative solutions, taking the organization to the next level of growth and existence.

The fact is that every organization has tremendous information encoded in its DNA and the irony is that managers think that they know everything and do not need help. Even if I know that I do not know something, how can I be seen as admitting it in public? It was this ego that the primitive species did not have and hence continued to collaborate and evolve. And mind you, this was not only collaborating with other members of the same species, butat times with species competing for the same resources, to create a dynamic balance with win for all. While bacteria are associated with disease, they are also vital for our survival. The story of evolution of life on our planet is one of cohabitation and co-evolution, rather than of combat and rivalry!!

Creativity, evolution, growth, learning and innovation are the lifeblood of any dynamic organization. Continuous learning and improvement are the hallmark of an adaptive organization. These organizations keep trying various things/doing things differently, some work some don't. Very much like natural selection. But the key element is their continuous effort to stimulate progress. They keep evolving and growing.

What is required here is a process and mindset, which further reinforces and structures the same. This not only supports evolutionary growth, but also, in the way we look at innovation in more practical terms in our day to parlance. Breakthrough growth as well. The process involves bringing together all the knowledge bearers (genes) together, to place their understanding on a common plate (symbiosis), look at the same from different perspectives and evolve combinations and solutions that are innovative. This is not just a brainstorming exercise, but can involve techniques and expertise that make this seemingly simple process very effective. Selection of the right people to contribute their learning's, framing the right objectives, asking the right questions are some critical skills which can be facilitated if organizations are willing to take this journey. The expertise lies in making the complex looking process simple and structured. To engineer innovation rather than hoping that it will happen one day. And experience says that it can be engineered!!

At a critical phase in the lifecycle of one business, profitability and hence survival was a big issue. A team comprising people from manufacturing, materials, marketing, finance and maintenance, including shop floor workers who are closest to action, worked together. Within six months they came up with actual, permanent, annualized cost savings to the tune of 4% of revenue. Engineered innovation achieved through facilitation with the right people, posing the right questions and using the right approach made all the difference for this organization. Between extinction and thriving growth towards industry leadership!!

In another situation, a business was faced with the challenge of a competitive launch within one week. Competition had guarded the news very well and hence there was no time for preparing defense. A team of key people was brought together. Facilitation through a structured innovation process brought out a creative plan within one hour. The result was that the competitive launch was totally blunted and in spite of all the preparation, they could never gather the confidence and put their act together again to gain any respectable market share.

There was yet another organization with issues related to ROCE. Gene pool trading and symbiotic facilitation process led to a restructuring of P&L lines and asset turns to yield an increase of 7%. Examples abound, of the ways we have been able to utilize this mechanism in strategy, manufacturing, sales, problem solving, decision making, business processes, marketing etc. with equal success.

The process starts with divergence of thoughts (gene trading and symbiosis) followed by convergence (natural selection), which includes perspectives, analysis, combinations, risk analysis and action planning. All in a structured process. The attempt is not to just leave innovation to chance, but to be able to engineer and determine our destinies to the extent we possibly can. Loss of information in black holes reduces our ability to predict the future. But at least we should not end up creating organizational black holes ourselves, to be sucked up under the pull of organizational gravity itself. The idea is to have an organizational dance to release positive energy for Thriving Growth and Prosperity!!

## INNOVATION & MARKETING EXCELLENCE AT ITS BEST . . .
### BENCHMARK FOR BRILLIANCE . . .

Samsung is the finest organization in the world to combine brilliant innovation, marketing and execution excellence for a transnational dominance in its areas of operation.

**'Samsung Electronics' future is not guaranteed because most of our flagship products will be obsolete in 10 years from now. . . . .**
*Lee Kun-hee, Chairman, Samsung Electronics.*

The above statement by Samsung's chairman reflects the restlessness of the organizations in continuously reinventing the future with breathtaking innovation & excellence in go-to market strategies. With a group turnover of US$248 Billion and a company annual turnover of US$ 149 Billion & a net income of over US$ 12 Billion in the year 2011, if there is one company in the world which is the most successful across the spectrum of its operations in Consumer Electronics, Technology hardware. Mobile Phones and Consumer Appliances, it is Samsung Electronics. Known for an incredible picture quality in all its products including digital cameras, mobile phones, colour televisions, LCD screens etc., Samsung always strives to offer the best experience to its consumers.

Setting itself with a mission of overtaking the Japanese in its area of operation in the early 2000s, Samsung achieved its first mission aimed at the dominance of the world's global markets in 2005 by overtaking Sony.

Today Samsung achieved the following:

#   World's largest information technology company measured by 2011 revenue, far ahead of Apple (109 Billion US$ and Hewlett Packard 128 Bullion US$).

#   World leader in Memory Chips and the world's 2nd largest in Semiconductor technology after Intel.

#   World's largest Mobile Phone company by selling 92 million Mobile phones in the 1st Quarter of 2012 as against Nokia's 83 million.

\# World's largest seller of Smart phones devices ahead of Apple, with its Galaxy range of products.

\# World leader in Flat panel televisions based on LCD & LED technologies.

\# Best Value for Money Technology Brand combining the best in technology, features with a the most competitive price in each of its category of products.

\# Largest seller of 3D Range of televisions in the world and the first company in the industry to have the full line of 3D offerings, including 3D television, 3D Blu-ray play, 3D content, 3D Home Theater and 3D glasses.

**What are the factors behinds the success of Samsung?**

Focus on Innovation as a core strategy: Samsung is consistently ranked in the list of Most Innovative organizations in the world by every leading publication in the world. Innovation, which has-been emphasized as its core strategy since the early 200 has once again been highlighted as its main stay in its Vision 2020 strategy document, where Samsung has outlined plans to reach a turnover of over US$ 400 Billions. Samsung has consistently been one of the largest investors in R&D along with Google and Apple, with over 20 state of the art research and development centers across the world. This has allowed to be a continuous stream of Cutting edge technologies for the world. Samsung has also a sharp attitude of keeping itself abreast of latest technology developments happening its domain of operations and adapting to the same through alliances, strategic partnerships and rapid product development.

**Focus on Marketing:**

Samsung has invested heavily in marketing right from the late 1990s, to create very strong brand awareness.

By sponsoring some of the biggest sporting events across all the games, Samsung has leveraged the high patronage of sports to create a strong association with fitness, excellence and leadership across the world.

**Focus on Quality:**

Samsung has invariably come out with the finest quality products with excellent value for money built in, at the same time. This enables it to not only to develop its own branded products, but also to sell to other global brands as OEM Products. Samsung is perhaps the largest brand company in the world that sells parts, components and products to its competitors. This is not possible unless it focuses on producing flawless quality.

**Focus on Global markets:**

By penetrating into all the major markets in the world, Samsung has overcome the limitation of a small domestic market and exploited the vast size of target markets globally. It has set up subsidiary companies and branches across the world, ingrained itself into the local fabric of all the countries it is present in and developed ones the best selling infrastructures. It attracts the best of manpower locally across its various division and consistently invests in training them to keep their skills sharpened. This is unmatched by any technology company in the world. This will give Samsung, a strong of products in April 2010.

With over 90% of its products achieving the global Eco-label, Samsung is ranked as the world's number-one company in terms of the number of products meeting Global Ecolabel standards. Through its well-acclaimed voluntary "Samsung Recycling Direct" program is accelerating its efforts to recover and recycle electronic wastes in a number of companies across the world.

The insecurity feeling that Samsung imposes on itself, acts as a spring board to keep leaping ahead and ahead, not from competition, from its existing status of indisputable leadership as the organization never rests on its past laurels.

Samsung is undoubtedly the company to watch for and benchmarked against, for the companies aiming for success in the 21st century.

# DECODING VALUATION & VALUE CREATION

Business is philosophy, an approach, a mindset and does not just follow the empirical rules of mathematics. While in Math, 1+1 = 2, in business it can be anything but true, mostly. It was quite obvious all over. Practical observations confirmed the validity of such a phenomena. Management Gurus & literature continued to reinforce the effects of synergistic operations. Related expansion and diversification made sense. Unrelated diversification would naturally tend to be less efficient as there would be consumption of effort, resources, and time energy towards keeping the unrelated parts of an enterprise together. different particles (?) to be held together by the application of external energy. Unless each particle or business in this case, of its own volition, gives up some of its own energy and contributes to The Bonding Energy!! But this 'contributory' Bonding Energy or Force never really happens without the so-called 'Common Thread, Knitting, Synergy or Interest, that can lead to A Clear Differential Advantage' and gain for all units. If The kinetic energy of each unit is higher than the bonding energy, they would tend to move apart releasing this energy into the environment, somewhat like in a nuclear 'fission' reaction. However, if The contributory Bonding Energy is higher, due to a 'common interest or desire to stay' together, you get a unified organization where 'Whole is greater than the Sum of Parts'!!

Primarily, organizations exist only for two reasons 1) To create Value for The Customers & 2) To create Return on Investment for the Owners. And in that order, in social organizations also these remain valid, but maybe expressed as 1) To create Value for the Beneficiaries & 2) To create a 'Surplus' through efficiencies.

The world is one continuum of energy, represented by different frequencies manifesting as particles. The higher the frequency of a 'wave particle', higher is its mass as manifested in the 'particle'. Business units also replicate such energy continuums and particle duality in a similar way. When they resonate with the same frequency they are one particle of existence. Different frequencies will have them vibrating as separate particles, obviously connected by a weak energy flow, which exits in the cosmos in any case, between diverse entities as well. What then is the purpose of 'applying autocratic force' to have them together? Doesn't everyone love to be a free body? Well the only two reasons to be together are 1) We build greater Value for The Customer together and/or 2) We operate in a manner that our operations gain from each other. Under these conditions, particles (business units) contribute the very essential Bonding Energy and 'Whole is greater than the Sum of Parts', as that is the only reason that makes sense for these particles to stay in 'dance' together!! In the absence of these conditions the system will become less efficient as there would obviously be an energy loss rather than a gain, by forcing togetherness.

That brings me to another version of this 1+1 mystery. Over the last few years, just before the recession hit, 'valuation' was in vogue!! Every new start up or even existing organizations started talking 'valuation'. Rather than Creating Value for The Customer, Valuation became the buzzword. It was indeed confusing to every one on the street! How do valuations shoot up like this? This was, when someone mentioned 'Sum of parts is greater than the Whole'. Now what does this mean? While till then it was considered that the 'Whole is greater than the Sum of Parts' logic. Concepts like 'Replacement Value', potential realization that could accrue of the footfalls/site traffic were to be monetized were very much in vogue.

'The Bonding Energy' should be contributed willingly by constituent particles only, towards efficiently aggregating together in the collective selfishness of "1)

We build greater Value for The Customer together and/or 2) We operate in a manner that our operations gain from each other 1) To create Value for The Customers & 2) To create Return on Investment for the Owners . . . . In that order". That is the key towards 'Whole is greater than the Sum of Parts'!! In cases where 'Sum of Parts is greater than the Whole', it is not that 'Whole' is less. It is just that the full impact of 'Whole' was never realized and nurtured to 'flower and blossom'. Eureka!!

No wonder when businesses get reduced to being seen as distinct particles, with no 'Bonding Energy', when they have no reason for being together in the first place, 'Sum of parts will be higher than the Whole'. It is this irony, driven by 'Valuation' rather than 'Value Creation', compounded by greed and short term results that lead to businesses being managed as MF portfolios rather than with an approach of 'organization building' and 'Value Creation for The Customer'. Value for the Owner is a natural outcome.

That is one flaw that the famous BCG matrix can lead to. Businesses are seen as delinked, independent entities in this approach, without looking at the 'synergistic' or 'complimentary' roles they may actually be playing in the 'dance'. This race for 'Valuation' rather than 'Value Creation for Customer' in some cases gets particularly pronounced in the 'portfolio' treatment and approach followed by some PEs. However, it is an area of caution only. Airtel and Max are cases where PE support, without losing track of Customer Value Creation led to extremely positive results. Quick valuations and selling off of parts of organizations like cattle or treating multiple organizations as merely elements of a portfolio, can be obstacles in organization building or in creating value for the customer or even for the owners. Examples of this also are many. This can be dangerous at any stage in an organization's development, but sometimes-quick valuations expected in early growth stage can ring a premature death knell for your business. Delivering a 'still born'.

I realized that:

1+1=2 is math's; can also be used by business accountants 'Whole is greater than the Sum of Parts' is sound business approach, philosophy, mindset

'Sum of Parts is greater than the Whole' is a Value Mirage in the search for Valuation.

## VALUE CREATION APPROACH—THAT BUILDS EVERLASTING COMPANIES . . .

**BUSINESSES ARE SUSTAINABLE AS LONG AS THEY CREATE A NET POSITIVE VALUE.**

If the purpose of a business is to create a net positive value for the stakeholders, the Value Creation approach differentiates, true Business Persons from Busy Fools.

A 'Busy fool' is one who toils away hard at work for hours but either fails to generate any value from his work or creates a net negative value.

Every action or a decision taken in an organization could be value accretive or value destructive. When the net value of the actions taken is value accretive in the long run, businesses prosper and continue to grow.

Successful organizations know that the purpose of any business is to create value for their investors, employees, customers, suppliers and the society.

Sustainable value can be created only when all the elements of the corporate eco-system get a perceptible share of the value created.

The Total Value created by an organization is generally equal to the sum total of:

a) Value to consumers (perceived benefit less the price paid)
b) Value to Suppliers (Cost paid to suppliers less the costs incurred by the suppliers) and
c) Value to the firm (Price realized from customer less Money paid to all suppliers and Vendors less sum total of all expenses incurred in the creation of the products and services

The term generally used globally to understand the value created by a firm to itself is quantified by EVA, defined as follows: EVA (economic value added) is the measure of output (taken as operating profit after tax and some other adjustments) less input (taken as the annual rental charge on the total capital employed, both debt and equity). As long as the EVA is positive and increasing, the firm is said to be creating value and if EVA is decreasing or negative, the firm is on the down-trend and continuing in this trend may one day lead to the non existence of the company.

Successful Organizations assess the effect on the EVA of the organization when they undertake any major investments. It must be however noted that focusing purely on the projected EVA in the short term may be detrimental to the long-term value creation process of the organization.

For example when the firm prices the products too high, their sales volumes could be adversely affected as the price may be more than the perceived benefit of the product by the consumer or the price the competitor is charging.

This will result in significant variance from the sales projections leading to piling up of inventory and blocking up of working capital. Hence the EVA projections can go haywire and the company could end up destroying the value in the process.

For example in 2004, Nokia launched value for money branded mobile phones by crashing the price-lines by over 40%. This has led to a huge surge in volumes by 3-4 times in a span of 12 months leading to tremendous value accretion. Thus while precise estimation of the effect of the company's financially linked decision are not possible always, a calculated risk with a time frame in mind is often taken by the companies to assess the net value-added.

Similarly, BPL slashed the price of its double cassette audio model SW138 by 50% in 1995 to clear excess inventories. The resultant surge in the sales of the model and its impact on the market share of BPL in the market resulted in a drastic improvement of overall sales and financial performance of BPL-Audios w.r.t competition like Philips thus adding a positive value. Economies of scale often have a suppressing effect on the costs and the customers will perceive the resultant competitive pricing positively when the selling price is lower than the benefit they perceive.

It can be understood that the factors like demand supply scenario for the product/service in the market place, strength of the competition, efforts required to communicate the proposition to the customers have a direct bearing on the value created by a company.

In a sellers market for example, the petrol market in India, where the demand is forever exceeding the supply, the organizations stand to create a huge value for their stakeholders due to their control on pricing without affecting the demand.

However when the supply far exceeds the demand, the companies with strong brands and significant competitive edge are able to enjoy positive value addition while the me-too companies struggle to survive. Innovation and strong marketing thus add a significant value and aid in the value creation process.

Organizations focused on value creation often explore ways to enhance the size of the market addressed by the products and services as the resultant increase in sales will lead to a better demand-supply scenario thus increasing the price realized from the customers leading to higher value. Value focused companies do not believe in squeezing the suppliers too much or compromise on the quality of the raw-materials used as this may have a negative effect on the quality of produce as well as the perceived benefit to consumers, resulting in lower pricing and value destruction. Net additional value creation is an important parameter that not only influences critical corporate decisions like Mergers and Acquisitions. Any corporate acquisition or takeover that results in a negative net value added due to parameters like high cost of transaction, inability to economize on common areas of expense, increased expenses due to problems associated with a more complex operation etc. will lead to destruction of organizations. Kingfisher Airlines' acquisition of Deccan Airways has resulted in a value destruction of over 75% due to negative value added.

Successful organizations have a long term and strategic perspective to value accretion in each of their activities and thus in the long run create huge values for the stakeholders and society as well.

# CAPTURE VALUE & MONETISE INNOVATION

**Creating Value but not capturing it is like investing in a river of water that flows into the sea**
— *Master Mentors*

One of the biggest challenges of the businesses and entrepreneurs today is, not only to create value from the investments they make, but also capture its value that can be monetized immediately or as a steady and growing stream of revenues.

When we invest in building a house and the house appreciates in value, a value is created that is captured in the form of the difference between the perceived value of the building and the investment done to create it. However most of the businesses today are creating intangible value in the form of software applications, web portals, music, algorithms, business ideas etc. It is indeed a challenge for smaller organizations to convert this into monetizable value that can be defended in the market place against imitation and replication.

On a routine basis, the value created by the business for itself, is reflected in the profits generated through the sale of its products and services, while the overall value generated is captured in the cumulative value to the suppliers, customers, users and the society in general.

Apart from the operational value, which will get added to the book value of the company, businesses create clusters of value that grow like a mountain, provided organizations are following right strategies. These could be termed as 'Valuemines' or 'Valuetraps' that trap the value created by the organizations.

The Valuemines created and added by the organization could be represented in the following ways:

I.  **Brand Value**—A Brand name that conjures a lot of positive impressions in the minds of a consumer and reflects a strong identity in the market place, helps a company to charge a premium on its products or services compared to smaller brands, me-too products and generic products available. Hence investments in creating strong brands supported by genuine product propositions adds lot of value to a company and is stored as an intangible in the equity created. Many times, brands have been sold for substantial values in the corporate history. Organizations like Interbrand conduct regular surveys to estimate and rank the global brands and note the appreciation or depreciation in the brand value in relation to other global brands.

II. **Intellectual Property (IP) Rights**—Patents, Copyrights, Trademarks, Industrial design rights and Trade secret protection rights are some of the protection mechanisms available to innovators or those wanted to protect their invention from getting copied by filing for Patents in relevant geographies. Similarly brands can protect their brand names from being misrepresented by others in the market place through Trademarks.

III. **Agreements with suppliers partners, clients and owners of complementary services:**—Exclusive long term agreements that give access to delivery platforms, business creating brands franchise agreements, distribution agreements, contract manufacturing agreements, service agreements or any other monetize-able agreements capture lot of value for organizations. For example, HCL Infosystems generates over 2 Billion USD revenue consistently along with a sizeable profit for many years due its exclusive distribution arrangement for Nokia cell phones. Jubiliant Organsys generated a huge business and high market capitalization from its agreement for exclusive franchising for India for Dominos Pizza. Most of the times, these agreements are win-win for both sides as the companies leverage their core strengths in maximizing the market opportunity thus generating business and profit for both the Principal and the Agent or the delivery partner. Similarly, access to a scarce raw material for a long term through an irrevocable agreement captures value for the organization, as it is able to manufacture its products and services without interruption. For example, access to gas through a long-term contract with a gas generating company by a gas based power plant or a fertilizer plant captures value for the company.

IV. **Investment in creation of own delivery networks, consumer facing infrastructure and client/user-base acquisition:**—Organizations that own a large franchise from users and customers, have immense power in the market place. Companies like Microsoft, Google for example are able to generate huge revenues by being able to launch new products and services and reach global audience instantly. HCL infosystems, India, has been able to launch a number of brands through its sales organization that can reach to the corporate and dealer outlets across the country using its own infrastructure.

This will give these organizations, immense power in acquiring smaller companies with strong IPs and generate huge scale. Microsoft was able to take over Hotmail and Google was able to take over Double click to create huge businesses from the IPs/businesses, which would have otherwise struggled to grow.

A case in point is the power 'Luxottica Spa, Italy' wielded over the global optical markets when it acquired the global optical retail chains, 'Sunglass Hut' and 'Lenscrafters'. Having controlled over 25% of the sales of the global sunglasses brands like 'Ray Ban', Luxottica, used its retail muscle to squeeze the global brands and propagated its own brands and products. Eventually, Bausch & Lomb Inc., the owner of Ray Ban had to sell out its family gold and its flagship brand to Luxottica, Italy for a meager 650 million USD (much lower than its peak value) in 1999, Ray Ban once again flourished under Luxottica to regain its global leadership position and became a highly successful and profitable brand in its portfolio.

V.  **Large scale Manufacturing/Servicing infrastructure —**
    Large plants and servicing infrastructure could potentially offer an opportunity to become low cost producers or providers of service of highest quality. This could lead to the organizations hitting sweet spots in volumes and profitability.

Innovations are one of the primary sources of value creators for an organization and create value in the long term. They need to be protected by organizations before they change the fortunes of their organizations. The innovation has to be taken to the market through an appropriate 'Business Model' that will allow the value of the innovation to be unlocked. A Business model is a description of how your company intends to create value in the marketplace. It includes that unique combination of products, services, image, and distribution that your company carries forward. It also includes the underlying organization of people, and the operational infrastructure that they use to accomplish their work' — KM Lab. A Business Model is required to capture the value of the innovation, identify the value proposition, and create an appropriate go to market strategy for unleashing the power of the same.

While generally the innovations are incremental in nature, breakthrough innovations occur rarely that change the dynamics of the industry they operate in.

Innovations could be:

A. An application like 'Instagram' or 'Angry Birds' that spread rapidly across the globe creating a huge base of users that are attractive to Social networks and Mobile Advertisers

B. A product innovation like Apple iPhone that changed the way we perceive and use a phone by providing high level of positive experience, augmented by the availability of a number of applications, useful to the consumers

C. A delivery model innovations like that of Dell Computer which changed the dynamics of the computer industry by offering direct delivery and also the power to configure their computers

D. An incremental innovation like that of 'Intel' that continuously comes out with faster and faster chips

E. An operating system innovation like Android that allowed a number of applications to be developed cheaply and ported onto the market place

F. A price based innovation like 'Walmart', 'South West Airline', 'Deccan Air'

G. A formula or a process based innovation like in Pharmaceuticals, that come out with new chemical compounds or alternate processes to manufacture off-patent products etc

In all these cases it is important to consider the market power of the innovating organization that could allow it to monetize or become a victim of imitating competitors.

When captured in the form of intellectual property (IP) or as a Copyright, innovations have the capability to create a revenue generating assets that can also be sold to others for a substantial consideration.

In case the innovator is having an extremely unique and valuable intellectual property, but is a small organization, he needs to raise money from the funds or align with a larger partner who can do the necessary investments to unlock value and also maintain entry barrier.

For example, in pharma industry, the small companies who invent new formulae tend to align with large companies to access global markets, often on very respectable terms.

If the innovation is a weak one, which is replicable, but the organization has the capability to invest in marketing and sales infrastructure, the company could quickly develop a complementary infrastructure that could help in scaling up the revenues and profits that could be used to ward off the competitors and discourage them from doing so.

A number of times, innovators welcome competition and work closely with the competition to evolve industry standards that will help the overall market for the product and the complementary products grow. It is imperative for the innovator to protect the innovation through appropriate copyrights and patents that will deter the competition in duplicating the products and services.

Inability on the part of Xerox to patent its invention of the office computer, has helped companies like IBM, Apple come out with similar products that changed the computer hardware industry landscape and also oust XEROX from the business.

Apple despite being a new entrant into the smart phone segment came out with breakthrough strategies by enabling developers to create large number of applications that enhance the user experience and break the entry barrier created by existing players.

Android, a free operating system for mobile phone has been able to make rapid inroads with its proposition that was not only free, but could compete with Apple in the ability to support applications. This was subsequently taken over by 'Google'.

It is very important for the innovator to strive and understand the full power &commercial potential of the innovation before putting in place appropriate business system to unlock the value. Then, an appropriate business model has to be selected. Also, align with complementary players in unlocking the value at the same time creating & enhancing the entry barriers for the competition.

**Any strategy is as good as its execution.**
Chanakya & Chandragupta, Krishna and Arjuna, Timmarasu and Sri Krishna Devaraya are firmly engrained in our minds as a great combination for effective strategy and exceptional execution ability.

How beautiful and long lasting is the thought of 'TajMahal' in the minds of Shahjahan if it was not translated into a historic and everlasting monument through phenomenal execution!

Any idea, which has not met with execution excellence, is as good as a piece of Plain Paper.

While actions taken without a clear strategy could lead to lot of chaos, and strategy, which is backed by strong execution on the ground, is what that leads to growth, profitability and a long lasting success.

A study of over 750 global CEOs across the globe on the top 10 challenges faced by organizations identified excellence of execution as their top challenge and keeping consistent execution of strategy by top managements their third greatest concern.

Robert Kaplan and David Norton in 'The Execution Premium: Linking Strategy to Operations for Competitive Advantage' highlighted that the ability for accompany to translate its strategies into action and deliver to their customers provides a significant advantage.

We have organizations spending lot of their resources in developing fantastic strategies for short term, medium and long term. Most of the time they take the help of high profile global consultants for these activities. Despite this, most of the time, the results are anything but spectacular. This is because executives who are entrenched firmly on their desks or boardrooms that come out with a series of steps to convert the wish list of the organization into a reality without much focus on the implementability and practicality prepare the strategies. They also lack an understanding of the ground level situation matched with their organizational capabilities.

While a lot of emphasis in management education is on learning about strategic frameworks, theories and models, very little emphasis is shown on learning the nitty-gritty of execution and the importance of execution excellence in organizational success. This is because of a variety of factors like lack of time, organizational experience, and exposure to real life situations with all their dynamic interactions. Ability to dirty their hand by getting quickly into the middle of the things in any given situation and willingness to lead from the front in any given situation are the hall mark of leaders with ability to excel in execution. The following must be taken into account while coming out with executable strategies that can add real values to organization.

A firm understanding on the ground reality is a must for development of an implementable strategy. While the steps that lead to the eventual scenario that has been mapped have to be clearly laid out, a step by step clear action plan should be laid out that is simple to understand

and is also implementable given the organizational competencies and resource availability.

The challenge of execution is mostly matter of synchronization — getting the right product to the right customer at the right time. A regional manufacturing initiative in Africa may involve reconfiguring 54 different supply chains and understanding the markets of 54 different countries.

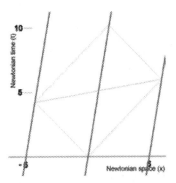

A classic case of non-synchronization leading to a grand failure is that of the takeover of Deccan Airways by Kingfisher airlines. Kingfisher Airlines, which was the most desirable airlines to travel for the airline consumers with a premium image wanted to expand its target customer base, it acquired Deccan Airways, a low cost airlines offering base and stripped down services to the consumers. The entire operation, the way it was managed not only ended up leading to lot of confusion in the minds of the consumers about the brand values of Kingfisher, but also led to enormous losses for the company leading to complete washout of the value associated with the acquisition to the company.

In the airlines business, Spicejet, Indigo airlines are classic examples of excellent execution of the strategy of low cost airlines. An effective execution will start with a good strategy and will involve the following steps:

208

- Strategy that is executable with a strong sense of on ground situation
- Strong leadership, delegation and involvement of competent persons with requisite skills.
- Continuous communication across the duration of the implementation. A number of times, the strategies fail because of lack of communication of the strategy across various levels of the organization. A infectious enthusiasm whipped up by successful communication could lead to the entire organization resonating with a single purpose to go for the success and lead to execution excellence.
- Clear measures for managing the progress of the implementation accurately. Anything that can be measured can be monitored. Hence an understanding of the metrics is a must.
- Co-ordination and synchronization across various elements of the organization till the results are achieved.

Successful organizations know the importance of 'Execution Excellence' and have this aspect ingrained well into their fabric. This also will be an important aspect of evaluation of all executives.

Any one is an effective 'Executive' or a part of the 'Executive Management' only if he has 'Execution Excellence' as his/her must possess traits.

**FOCUS ON THE USER AND ALL ELSE WILL FOLLOW**

*—GOOGLE*

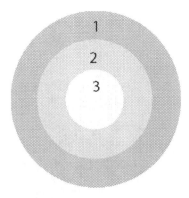

**1: Company 2: Customer 3: Consumer/User at the centre of the universe**

If there is only one thing that could create, sustain and grow businesses, then that is the focus on the Customer and the Customers of your customers (consumers). The purpose of any business is to serve its customers 'profitably' and its survival is dependent on the amount of money its customers pay or will lead to others pay to the business versus its investments. Providing the best value to the customers with respect to all the alternatives that the customer has for his money should be the single most aim of any business. The maximum size of any business is equal to the collective wallet size/ability to pay off all the customers in the target market.

**'You can grow as far as the credit limit of all your potential customers takes you . . .'**

For example:

Potential Market opportunity could be calculated for different companies could be as follows:

- Real Estate Company—Collective Credit limit of the entire potential house buyers in its target market
- Personal Computers—Collective value of the IT hardware budgets of all the targeted entities.
- Advertising Agency—Share of the Collective value of the advertising budgets of all the Advertisers
- Hotel—Collective value of the amount spent on food of all the target Customers

What is important to note is that, the Revenue potential of any organization is directly proportional to:—Market share * Purchasing power of all the potential customers * Share of wallet of the category of products to the overall purchasing power * Proportion of the share of target customers to overall size of the Potential customers base. Hence for any business to succeed, it should start from the ability of the customers to pay and what it has to do to get the maximum share of this capability. It is very important to mind the potential growth or de-growth of the target customer base and the share of the wallet as the company evaluates its areas of focus for investment. The companies, which have the ability to address global markets with relatively lower costs and ease, are the ones, which can become the biggest organizations in the fastest way. The secret behind the successes of today's rapidly growing organization is the ability to identify huge potential target customer base that is rapidly growing and provide the best possible product or service that offers the most 'Value for money' and thus address the 'WIIFM' questions best among the alternatives available and is also communicated well to the target audience.

**Its important to understand the different types & levels of customers that an organization caters to:**

While Brands and organizations are dependent on their customers for their revenue these customers are in-turn dependant on their customers who may be the ultimate consumers or users of the company's products and services.

In the picture, the company could represent the moon, while the customers could represent the earth and the ultimate resource for money in return for the product or service (consumer) could represent the sun.

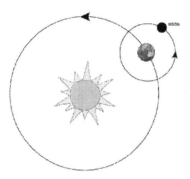

Consumer Brand (Ray Ban): Luxottica Group, Italy, manufactures While Ray Ban sunglasses; it reaches its target consumers through a network of dealers and distributors. While the dealer of Ray Ban is the customer of the organization, the user of the product is the consumer.

Hence Luxottica should ensure that both its customers are happy to deal with the brand through better policies, margins etc and the consumers are a growing clan of proud and satisfied users of the brand. Focus on building a better proposition to its ultimate consumers will lead to better business and profitability for its trade partners as well.

Google: Google believes in offering the businesses the best tools on the web to succeed on and off the web. Google derives its money from the organizations who advertise on the web and from those who use its tools for improving their productivity. These customers are further dependent on their consumers for their success and want to promote their services to their consumers in the most attractive manner, helping them in satisfying their needs and earn a share of their wallet. These consumers are the users of Google's services, which are mostly free.

Hence Google focuses on serving its users and making them swear by its products and services thus becoming a bigger and bigger clan, which in turn leads to higher and higher value for those who pay for its services, the customers.

Brand Ambassador (Sachin Tendulkar): Sachin Tendulkar also known as the God of Cricket, the most popular sport in India, derives his money from the fee paid by the cricket boards for playing and also through various endorsements and promotional activities as a Brand Ambassador. These activities are aimed at helping his clients, media channels to get much bigger wallet of their consumers that will lead to their success. As long as these consumers of his clients are a growing and happy clan, these organizations will be happy to pay higher and higher amounts to their Brand Ambassador. As long as the Brand Ambassador is delivering on his core activity that attracts the consumer through success and excellent behavior on and off the field, the clients have a higher and better chance to succeed. This will result in the Brand Ambassador obtaining more and more revenue.

Thus it is important to see that the **'Customer Centricity' has to work hand in hand with 'Consumer centricity', underlying the need to serve the consumers of the Customers better and better** apart from making it easy for the direct customers deal smoothly and easily with the organization. While most of the organizations deal with Businesses or Individuals/ groups of individuals leading to B2B or B2C type of businesses, within the organizations every department has to deal with Internal Customers.

> **An internal customer is "anyone you count on or rely upon to complete a task or a function or to provide you with information so that you can get your job done . . . and anyone who counts on you to complete a task or function or to provide them with information so that they can get their job done"**
> —*Rosenberger, 1998*

For example, HR department provides manpower, training and motivational programs for the rest of the organization and the Marketing department provides internal communication program and forecast to production department along with demand generation activities aimed at increasing the business.

Customer-centric organizations value and respect internal customers as the much as external customers. Successful Organizations are not just focused on being External Customer and Consumer Centric, but also ensure that this is internalized in all the areas at all levels of the operation within the organization as well.

## HOW GOOGLE IS CHANGING THE WORLD OF INFORMATION SEARCH AND CONSUMPTION . . .

Google, one of the finest organizations the world has ever seen, is transforming the lives of the human beings in unforeseen ways. By offering a number of tools free to its users, Google has democratized the flow of information, spreading the power of knowledge, without any limitations to billions of Internet surfers.

Google has delivered consistently phenomenal financial results with over 35% annual rate of growth even during the current year. It is slated to reach a 50 Billion US Dollar revenue mark during 2012.

The following are the most popular applications of Google along with the number of users is given below:

## Google Search:

Google Search (or Google Web Search) is a web search engine owned by Google Inc. Google Search is the most used search engine on the World Wide Web receiving several hundred million queries each day through its various services. Google's rise to success was in large part due to a patented algorithm called Page Rank that helps rank web pages that match a given search string. By delighting the customers with the quality of SERP (Search Engine Result Pages) and the speed of display of results, Google search is currently the undisputed leader of the Search market with over 80% market share. This gives it phenomenal advertising revenue making it 10 times bigger than its nearest rival in the space namely. Yahoo!. Google has been estimated to run over one million servers in data centers around the world and process over one billion search requests and about twenty four pet bytes of user-generated data every day.

## Gmail:

Gmail is a free, advertising-supported email service provided by Google. 43 million users in 54 languages across the world.

## Google plus:

Google+ (pronounced and sometimes written as Google Plus, sometimes abbreviated as G+) is a multilingual social networking and identity service owned and operated by Google Inc. It was launched in June 28, 2011. As of June 2012, it has a total of 250 million registered users.

## Android Market place (Google play):

Google Play is the Google's answer to Appstore from Apple inc. Google Play is a digital-distribution multimedia-content service from Google, which includes an online store for music, movies, books, and Android applications and games, as well as a cloud media player.

Google Play was introduced in March 2012 when Google rebranded its whole digital distribution strategy and merged Android Market and Google Music services to Google Play. As of now over 6 lakhs Android applications are available on Google Play, making it one of the fastest growing application market space and spawning a huge mobile application development industry. As Android operating system is free compared to an apple's iphone operating system (IOS), Android has enabled a drastic reduction in the pricing of smart mobile devices like phones and tablets, fuelling the demand for these high-end devices, which acts as to create a positive feedback effect to the population of Android devices.

**You tube:**

YouTube is a video-sharing website, on which users can upload, view and share videos. It uses Adobe Flash Video and HTML5 technology to display a wide variety of user-generated video content, including movie clips, TV clips, and music videos, as well as amateur content such as video blogging and short original videos. Over 300 Million users.

**Google Drive** (formerly Google Docs):

Google Drive is a file storage and sync service by Google that was released on April 24, 2012. Google Drive is an extension of Google Docs, allowing users to store all types of files on the Google servers. Google Drive gives the user a free-of-charge cloud storage of 5 gigabytes to start with.

**Google Cloud Connect:**

Google Cloud Connect is a free cloud computing plug-in for Windows Microsoft Office 2003, 2007 and 2010 that can automatically store and synchronize any Microsoft Word document, PowerPoint presentation, or Excel spreadsheet to Google Docs in Google Docs or Microsoft Office formats. The Google Doc copy is automatically updated each time the Microsoft Office document is saved. Microsoft Office documents can be edited offline and synchronized later when online. Google Cloud Sync maintains previous Microsoft Office document versions and allows multiple users to collaborate, working on the same document at the same time.

## Google Books:

Google Books (previously known as Google Book Search and Google Print) is a service from Google Inc. that searches the full text of books and magazines that Google has scanned, converted to text using optical character recognition, and stored in its digital database. As of March 2012, the number of scanned books was over 20 million out of a possible 130 million unique books in the world.

## Google Maps:

Google Maps (formerly Google Local) is a web mapping service application and technology provided by Google, that powers many map-based services, including the Google Maps website, Google Ride Finder, Google Transit,1] and maps embedded on third-party websites via the Google Maps API.2] It offers street maps, a route planner for traveling by foot, car, bike (beta), or public transport and an urban business locator for numerous countries around the world. Google Maps satellite images are not updated in real time; they are several months or years old. Google Maps uses a close variant of the Mercator projection, so it cannot show areas around the poles. A related product is Google Earth, a stand-alone program which offers more globe viewing features, including showing polar areas.

By offering so many state of the art services that dramatically enhance the productivity and performance of its users, Google is increasing its unassailable lead as the most popular technology company in the world, which is entwined in the lives of the millions of its consumers. It attracts its customers like a magnet and no one, who has experienced its service, can escape from its net. Rather, they willingly and happily get drawn into its fold increasing their engagement with the company and its services.

As Google does not charge its users for most of its services, unless they are above certain limits offered to individuals or corporate, there is no way any company can even dream of competing with Google as the base of a close to billion users is hard to be replicated or displaced by any other technology company.

Continuous innovation and pro-active engagement with its users to provide an unparalleled user experience ensure that it not only stays streets ahead of its competition, but also continuously increases its gap with the rest. By acquiring Double Click in 2007, Google cemented its place as a leader in Digital advertising by getting valuable relationships with a number of advertising agencies, advertisers and publishers.

Google's advertising programs namely Adsense and Adwords help it to monetize the huge traffic its various programs create. While Google always embodied the principles of user centricity in its marketing and product development approach with its core principle being, 'Focus on the user and everything else will follow'.

The 10 point corporate philosophy of Google celebrates, user centricity, team based approach, ethical approach, informal yet professional approach, innovation and the importance of focus that will result in excellence, when pursued with single minded dedication.

With an informal culture that supports innovation through activities like 'innovation time off' that led to the development of a number of its products & services Google has been consistently ranked as one of the best places to work for in the world. Fortune Magazine ranked Google as the best company to work for, in the year 2012.

It's going to be a no-brainer to think that Google is going to be the organization to watch for, in the 21st century, that can reach unparalleled and unforeseen heights and sky is the limit for such organizations.

It is a true model to follow for any entrepreneur or any organization in the world today.

## STAND FOR SOMETHING—MANTRA FOR MARKETING SUCCESS

> If you don't stand for something, you'll fall for anything.

Fill, Shut it, Forget it . . . The campaign that strongly associated Hero Honda with fuel efficiency leading to an undisputed leadership for Hero Honda in the two wheeler bike market.

Neighbour's envy, Owner's pride . . . The campaign that associated Onida TV with superior quality and pride of ownership that catapulted Onida to quickly climb up to value leadership in the colour television market

Thanda Matlab. A memorable campaign that has led Coca-Cola to strong choice during the season.

It's Economy Stupid—The campaign that led Bill Clinton to become the Come from behind to become the President of USA

Vote for Change—The campaign that catapulted Barack Obama to become the first Black President of USA.

History is replete with examples about overwhelming success achieved by Brands, organizations and Personalities when they get strongly associated a category or product or a name that resonates with a need or requirement or the imagination of the target audience.

Amitabh Bachan as the Angry Young Man, Sachin Tendulkar as the quintessential model human being and a cricketer par excellence, Xerox as the world's best photocopier, IBM as the personal computer, Google as the world's preferred search engine, Microsoft as the operating system and office productivity software of choice, Linux as the open source operating system etc., are a few such examples.

The most powerful organizations, brands and personalities are identified in the minds of their subjects and target audience by a single phrase or an image that represents them.

It is indeed a matter of interest that many brands and many organizations do not give any importance to this doctrine of meaning something strongly to their target audience.

While it takes lot of investment, hard work and patience to build a brand, once the brand name is established many brands try to extend the brand name to other categories in the name of extension and not only dilute the power associated with a brand name but also destroy the core values associated with the brand.

When Ray Ban, the world's famous brand of Sunglasses a name associated with premium image, high quality and pride of ownership launched Ray Ban Suntamers, a low end sunglass brand, the equity of Ray Ban took a solid beating leading to a dramatic drop in the sales of Ray Ban core brand's sunglasses. This led to Ray Ban Suntamers being scrapped and it took a lot of time and resources to undo the damage done to the premium image of Ray Ban.

When a company owning a strong brand wishes to diversify it is best done by delinking the brand/company name with the product category and launching new brands as sub brands from the same company and support the same with all its might.

Examples like iPod, iPhone, iPad from Apple which is strongly associates with a computer with a new generation operating system, You Tube, Chrome, Android etc. from Google strongly associated with the best Search engine, Lexus from Toyota, which is associated with mid range efficient cars, Lumia a new brand smart phones from Nokia are some examples of the way world's leading brands are undertaking diversification into new businesses. Tata, Godrej, Reliance, General Electric are some examples in India where the brand names have surpassed representation of just a product and stand for a set of values that these brands represent which are then imparted to the companies under respective banners. This strategy can boomerang when any of the sub brands or the parent brand fails or acquires a negative representation.

Kodak is a classic example of a manual camera brand that could not change the perception associated with its image to become a digital camera of choice to the consumers.

Kingfisher Airlines is a classic example of a high-class airlines, diluting its focus by trying to lend its name to low class and budget airlines and today, its stands for nothing in the minds of the customers.

Within the social networking space we have LinkedIn, Twitter, and Facebook, which have created their own niches while Google+ is struggling to find its space in the mind of the target audience, die its overpowering image and association with a Search engine.

Successful organizations know the value of being strongly associated with a feature or a value that strongly resonates with their target audience.

Companies, which have failed from positions of strength, are those, which have tried to extend the brand too widely, even if it comes to supporting them with huge resources. This will lead to not only wasting huge resources and time for the company, but also the drain in working capital will lead to destruction of the core brand itself.

The classic example in the Indian case is that of BPL, once an undisputed leader in Indian colour television market. As BPL diversified into telecom and cellular market by diverting huge resources as well, the resultant loss of organisational focus resulted in complete loss of market share for BPL. Finally BPL Cellular division was also sold off to competition though for a good profit, this remains etched in the minds of the BPL lovers as a classic case of misdirected brand diversification.

When Successful brands vacate their position in the minds of the customer, they should take care to replace the position with another product or proposition from their own stable but with a distinctly identifiable brand. Otherwise they stand to yield the position to the competition in a platter, which may threaten the existence of leader brand in due course.

When Deccan airlines was taken over by Kingfisher Airlines, and the brand was unsuccessfully replaced by Kingfisher Red, as a budget airline, the failure of Kingfisher airlines was successfully leveraged by Indigo to become the largest budget airliner in India. Now the existence of Kingfisher airlines is under question.

Hence strategically oriented successful organizations think in the long term and stay focused on what they and their brands stand for in the minds of their consumers.

## WALMART—THE POWER OF STANDING FOR SOMETHING . . . FOCUSEDLY . . .

World's largest discount retailer shows the importance of 'Standing for something' . . .

Sam Walton, founder of Wal-Mart, grew up in a farm community in rural Missouri during the Great Depression. The poverty he experienced while growing up taught him the value of money early in his life. Sam Walton opened the first store in 1962 in Rogers, Arkansas. Today Wal-mart has 8,500 stores in 15 countries, under 55 different names. It is also the biggest private employer in the world with over two million employees, and is the largest retailer in the word and also one of the largest global companies with annual revenue of over US$446 Billions.

Many companies have tried to replicate the model of Wal-mart but none of them have succeeded in coming close to it. There is something about Walmart that makes it unique. Wal-mart started with a simple philosophy by Sam Walton: Offer shoppers lower prices than they get anywhere else. This basic strategy has shaped Wal-Mart's strategy and drove the company's growth, making it a phenomenal success . . . Wal-Mart's slogan "our people make the difference" depicts the importance of an individual worker. Their philosophy of maintaining the highest customer service is shown with their three critical elements of the "sundown rule," the "ten-foot rule," and the "every day low prices" rule. Offering the lowest prices everyday, will increase the volume of sales, as well as bring added value for the consumers. With huge volumes of sales across the categories. Wal-mart is in a position to bargain for tremendous concessions from the vendors, which help it to offer the lowest yet profitable prices to all its customers, thus making it win-win for everyone.

Sam Walton's followed simple values focused on providing best service to its

- Customers at lowest prices. They are:
- Treat the customer right
- Take care of your people
- Be honest in your dealings
- Pass savings along to the customer
- Keep things simple, think small, control costs and
- Continuously improve operations.

Some of the key principles that enable Wal-mart to beat its competitors and succeed are:

- Commit to your business
- Share your profits with your associates, treat them as partners
- Excellent Inventory Management
- Powerful Distribution Network

- Focus on low cost to the customers
- Operate at least margins
- Focus on Volume of trade
- Striving for excellence in all operations
- Leverage Technology to gain the edge
- Plan and control to stay ahead of competition
- Rich Customer Experience

Today Wal-mart has achieved a sense of invincibility among the organizations globally and yet continuously strives to be the best in its business.

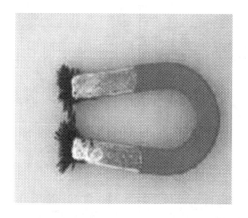

Very often, we would have heard phrases like 'Magnetic Personality', Magnetic Attraction' and Magnetic Pull. In the world of Marketing, the success stories have been written by those who have understood the power of Magnetism, applied in real life to their marketing subjects and created the aura and the story around their brand that took their target customers by awe making them yearn more and more of it till they get habituated to consuming their product or service.

In the above case, we see iron filings getting attracted and clinging onto the magnet as if they are an extension. Successful brands attract their target audience and make them their diehard fans.

Iconic Brands in the world like Apple, Google, Microsoft, Facebook, LinkedIn, Twitter, invoke a sense of dire need and/or a desire within their target audience that makes them long to be associated in the same way. What we could understand here is that, the magnets are imparted with the magnetic characteristic through a process typical to the type of magnet, either a permanent magnet or an electromagnet. They have a field of influence, intensity or strength to attract and a target set of materials they are likely to act. In some cases the magnetic power gets neutralized or lost due to external processes or over time.

The analogy of the same could be found in marketing case studies.

A case in point is that of the success of KBC on Star Plus during the year 2000.

When Star Plus was struggling for a foothold in the Indian market against the onslaught of Zee group, it pulled off a trump card by launching KBC with the Indian Super Star, Amitabh Bachan which acted like a magnet to attract the entertainment hungry star struck audience, who got glued day after day for the entire hour of the program. STAR then used the eyeballs to market its entire bouquet of Prime time programs of the K-Type, which became market leaders in their own right in due course. Here is one big magnet, spinning off more magnets (induced magnetism).

Marketers would do well to understand the key motivator that drives the purchase behavior of their target audience and strive to establish resonance between their brand and the target audience. The bond that could be established could last longer and grow stronger only if the brand lives up to its promise and continues to excite its audience through innovation and reinvention lest it should lead to brand fatigue and falling out of terms with the ever moving profile of its target audience. Or else the magnetic power will be lost like that of an electromagnet that loses its magnetism, when the current across its coil of wire is cut off.

How does one transform one's brand from being just an "attractive" one to one that is "magnetic" in its qualities—ability to draw consumers to it like iron filings are drawn to a magnet!!

The key ingredient in a magnetic brand is passion— it is the single largest differentiator for a brand to draw customers to itself. A study of some of the finest brands like Apple, Apollo Hospital Care, Apcolite from Asian Paints, Ray Ban and Swarovski etc. has shown that these brands are magnetic and not just attractive.

Successful brands and by extension, Successful Organizations, have passion as a common thread in the organization—Passion in manufacturing the products without a flaw (visible or perceived), passion in the packaging and passion in ensuring that the goods reach the user in the way the creator envisaged it to be.

Apple, with its no compromise approach to create the world's finest products, gave the world, killer products like Mac Book, iPod, iPhone, iPad, each of which created their own markets and die-hard followers, across the world. The passion of the founder, the legendary Steve Jobs, percolated down to each and every employee in the organization, influenced each and every aspect of the product and service created by the organization.

In the world's leading brand of Crystal, Swarovski, the brand was in the centre of everything. When the goods were packed and shipped from a single warehouse in Europe, they were packaged individually in gift boxes with a protective sponge in them. Then they were packed in a cardboard carton and wrapped in waterproof film. The water proof film was wiped clean before sending to the stores." It was not necessary", said many but the credo in the organization was that when you sell beautiful products you need to present it in his finery even when it is being handed over to a delivery boy. That is passion and hence brand magnetism for you. Not only was Swarovski attractive but also was magnetic because the way the product was packaged, the consumer got convinced that this brand cares for him or her and is drawn to it. No other brand has been able to do the same.

Sunglasses have made the journey from eye protection goggles to fashion statements over the years. As it is the most visible accessory on a person, it needs to communicate to the world at large as to who the wearer is! A successful brand like Ray Ban managed to do that by not only developing styles but also packaging them in apt sunglass cases! Here again the packaging was the magnet which drew the customers to it and made Ray Ban a must have personal accessory. The Signet—a dressy model and the General—named after a World War II Hero—had special sunglass cases, which reflected the design. The former was in a 'faux leather" dressy case and the latter in a black case with the 50 years of Ray Ban mentioned which communicated authority and seniority—hall marks of a General

These two examples show as to how you can magnetize your brand. Look beyond the obvious—the core product or service is often copied by others. However if you focus on the smaller details, you can find that magnetic quality. This can be in terms of packaging, a warranty card or sometimes the wrapping paper! If even the smallest detail is well executed, magnetic attraction sets in.

Walk the talk—If you are offering heath care services, it is not enough that you offer a top class medical service. The smaller detail like the warmth and understanding in the smile of the receptionist is magnetic. It should be a warm smile to cheer them up but not an expansive one like one would see in a hotel!! The wrong smile or choice of greeting can turn the magnetic power off.

Magnets also repel—We must ensure that in our quest of creating a magnetic effect, we do not overdo it. Customers get turned off when they see an "over the top" welcome or greeting.

We therefore should be careful that we consciously create magnetic qualities in our brand that of an attraction force and not a repulsion force!

# W I I F M
## What's, in it for me?

**A MUST RECIPE OF ORGANISATIONS WHO ACHIEVE
AND KEEP UP WITH SUCCESS . . .**

Successful organizations unequivocally address 'What's in it for me' question addressing various levels of stake holders like customers — internal and external, share holders and promoters, employees, business associates, the society and the government.

While every day, thousands of businesses are being born aiming to focus on a number of business opportunities, it is indeed surprising to note that most of them fall drastically short when posed with the above question with respect to their stake holders.

Any action aiming to motivate others to perform an action has to compellingly address the question,

'What is in it for me?' Otherwise, the desired action may just not take place or even if it takes place comes at an undue cost that makes it unprofitable in the first place.

Customers expect Value for money, Convenience, Psychological Gratification or an approval in the Society for being seen to be a consumer of a product or a service that they consume, Shareholders expect dividend and value appreciation, Employees expect salaries, status and job satisfaction, Government expects taxes and compliance, Vendors & partners expect fair dealing and timely account settlements in a win-win manner etc.

Successful Organizations not only aim to achieve that the above are taken care, but also are competently addressed better than the rest of the competitors offering similar services.

**'Explain what is in it For me and you have my attention'**

*—Anonymous . . .*

Let us take the example of Google Inc: It may happen that the Market shares are determined by how long and how well a company consistently scores well on the above parameters, it is important to note that the relative performance at any given point of time determines the financial performance of the company.

| Stake Holder | What is in it for me . . . ? |
|---|---|
| User | Best in class Search Experience, mail and related applications |
| Advertiser | Hi quality reach and an excellent gang for the buck . . . |
| Employee | Amazing work life experience, job satisfaction and above par perks, Status in society . . . |
| Shareholder . . . | Consistently top class returns for their investments |
| Government | Access to Information, compliance and taxes from the company and its employees, empowerment of the citizens through information access. |

There are a number of cases which we observe, when the organizations which have hit the right formula in all these aspects, lose sight of these very fundamentals and slip out of the minds of their stake holders, but not keeping up with the dynamic and ever changing environment.

For example, My Space and Orkut used to rule the Social Media space before new entrants

Face Book and Twitter swept the ground under their feet, while LinkedIn continues to hold its ground by reinventing itself continuously and improving its score on all the above parameters day by day.

This situation can be applied to any field and any situation and you can observe that the real winners are those who consistently offer something better than the rest to those who deal with them.

While Bill Clinton won the Presidential elections with his promise to further the economic strength of United Sates and delivered on the same successfully, Obama came to power by his focused agenda to restore the pride of Americans through a badly needed economic turnaround.

Successful Organizations in any walk of life are forever asking themselves. 'Are we addressing the 'WIIFM' question and put in place systems and action plans that consistently increase the gaps with respect to their competitors.

## THE 3 HOCK THEORY IN MARKETING . . .

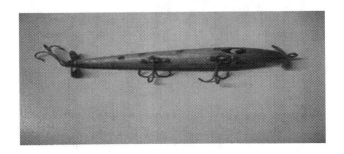

What are the 3 strong hooks you have to catch your customers?

**Successful companies understand this and have this invariably as a part of their proposition to customers . . .**

Marketing is all about attracting the customers to the company's products and service. While target marketing is about reaching out to the right customers in the right place, the brand should have strong hooks to catch the customers, engage them and draw them its net.

IN 1993, BPL launched Car Stereos in Delhi. The sales head at Delhi was the best and the brightest with a track record of being a star sales manager. Once the briefing on the product pertaining to the launch was completed, the USPs, the competition, the pricing and the positioning etc., the sales head requested for the 3 compelling things that he can tell the trade to convince them about our proposition to ensure a great launch'. Once the team could brainstorm on this, prioritize the communicable benefits regarding the product and zero in on 3 USPs of the product, the field was in a much better position to launch the product and could indeed do a great job.

In 2001, the National Marketing at Ray Ban Sunglasses was into a brainstorming session with the account director at the advertising agency. While working on the campaign creative, the account director mentioned, 'Can you please tell 3 distinctive and desirable features of Ray Ban that would attract the consumers?'

The team could figure out that, the requirement for a healthy & safest gadget for sun protection, the prestige value associated along with a favorable value for money trade off and the strong perception of being the highest quality and durable product are strong hooks for the consumers to patronize the brand. This insight invariably formed the cornerstone for all communication campaigns of Ray Ban, which continues to the best choice in its category for discerning customers globally.

It is indeed relevant even today, as it is observed that, it generally takes at least 3 parameters to stand out from the rest in our mind and perception, for any product or service to be adopted.

Why 3? Because human minds find it difficult to register more than 3 items in any attribute at the same time. Outclassing the competition on 3 items will indeed represent a good barrier to competition and seems no flash in the pan! This also has the ability to attract a wider range of audience for which the relative importance of the parameter may wary from item to item. For example for those who travel by air, the 3 must have hooks would be Convenience, Safety and Time saved and for those using Google, they would be Speed, Relevance and Simplicity of search.

While there could be more hooks (more the better), 3 strong hooks covering the most desirable features of the product or the service as differentiated from the alternatives will go a long way in attracting the target customers. What are the various aspects of these hooks and how do we communicate them to the prospective customers?

For maximum effectiveness,

- The hooks have to be universally appealing and make strong sense for majority of the consumers as a major factor affecting the purchase. Ideally these hooks have to encompass the most sought after needs meant to be addressed by their consumption
- The target consumer should be able to immediately able to understand how the hook is indeed relevant to his needs personally and how the brand, the product or the service stands out on these features w.r.t competition and his/her needs
- The hook should be visually communicated to the target consumers for establishing the relevance
- The communication of the hook to lead to a curiosity build-up in the minds of the consumers for maximum effectiveness. Remember, Onida ad 'Don't envy it, Buy it!
- The hook can work if the product is in immediate reach of the target consumer and hence take care to make the product accessible in an easy manner. The hook should not be in a place that is out of reach for the targets or in a location that is not frequented by the targets
- There should be a call for action and an associated trigger for the target to come and try out the product

With the above strategy we can come out with compelling marketing programs to attract the target consumer, engage them and get hooked on forever . . .

# GREAT EXPERIENCE—THAT RESULTS IN ACCELERATING GROWTH

**GIVE A GOOD EXPERIENCE—GET LOYALTY**
**GIVE A GREAT EXPERIENCE—GET AN ADVOCATE**

Successful Companies have realized that while the attention spans have gone down for people with their employers and suppliers due to the multiplicity of options competing for their attention, it is the quality of the engagement you do with these important stake holders in the business that differentiates great performance from the poor.

Engagement and Positive Experience are the new mantras of success in the 21st century . . .

HAPPY EMPLOYEES + DELIGHTED CUSTOMERS
= EXPLOSIVE BUSINESS GROWTH

A Positive Experience will provide not only a reason to repeat the experience but also leads to a viral effect of recommending to the friends, relatives and social circles thus leading to an increased equity and more business.

Citibank, one of the finest global banks that has survived many ups and downs through its life of over 200 years, is a great example of what a positive customer experience can do to an organization. Customers who have used the credit cards of Citibank for over 20 years have found the experience to be consistently excellent and recommendation worthy.

Apple Computer achieved great strides as a global Technology company with the innovative features of its operating system and cutting edge products that consistently provided superior customer experience which were copied by their competitors.

Google surged far ahead of its older rivals and astonished their competition with their motto of providing best possible user experience. By providing a 'Search' facility that was faster, reliable and more relevant to the needs of its users, Google consistently increased its lead over some of its finest competitors like Yahoo and Microsoft to unassailable levels.

Happy customers who have their problems resolved will tell 4-6 people about their positive experience. Source: the White House Office of Consumer Affairs, Washington, DC.

In his book 'How to win customers and keep them for life', Michael Leboeuf has stated some interesting facts as a finding from his research:

- 1% die
- 3% move away
- 68% quit because of an attitude of indifference towards the customer by the staff
- 14 % is dissatisfied with the product
- 9% leave because of competitive reasons.

It is important to see the importance of 'ENGAGEMENT' with the customers that will help in retaining over 60% of the business effectively giving a potential to double the business with minimum effort.

Customer loyalty is, in most cases worth 10 times the price of a single purchase. Source: "Understanding Customers" by Ruby Newell-Legner

With the advent of Social Media on the internet and the empowerment of the individual consumers to influence large circles of potential consumers with viral effect through blogs, reviews, Facebook, Twitter and corporate sites apart from the traditional channels which are generally non viral and limited, in reach, organizations that have effectively provided enhanced experience and get a net positive word of mouth (reflected by a Net Promoter Score) creates a platform for success in today's competitive market scenario. This catapults great organizations to leadership and helps them thrive in today's networked economy.

How do we define Customer Experience?

Customer experience (CX) is the sum of all experiences a customer has with a supplier of goods or services, over the duration of their relationship with that supplier. From awareness, discovery, attraction, interaction, purchase, use, cultivation and advocacy. It can also be used to mean an individual experience over one transaction; the distinction is usually clear in context.

—Wikipedia

A customer or an user interacts with a company, its products and services at various 'Touch-points' through personal visits to stores—online and offline, chatting on the web, interacting through queries and complaints on the phone, apart from other one to one interactions with various employees/parties partnering the companies in their delivery.

It has now become imperative for the organizations to take a holistic view of the Customer Experience through the life cycle of the interactions across the various touch-points with the company from awareness to interaction to purchase and post purchase.

By delighting the customers through the life-cycle of the relationship and by providing excellent service making periodic contacts through courtesy calls, wishes, incentives, schemes etc., companies aim to convert the customers from being loyal to advocates thus increase the life time value of the customers to the company.

Today's customer focused organizations have a clear-cut strategy and a number of tools to pro-actively manage their customer relationships and enhance the user experience.

The tools encompass some of the following activities:

Define the parameters that reflect the customer experience. For example, the ratings of the customers on the services provided by the company across the touch points. One such parameter is the Net Promoter Score that is defined by the net of the positive opinions to the negative opinions expressed on the web

Consciously strive to provide excellent quality of interactions with low tolerance to failure across the spectrum of interactions. High Quality Retail Ambience and Accessible locations for offline companies and user friendly interfaces provide the hard elements of the experience for customers while the competence, behavior, responsiveness and the sensitivity of the employees handling the customers providers provides the softer elements

Measure the various parameters continuously to keep track of the improvement or deterioration of the company across all these parameters. This involves listening to the customers intensively and extensively and asking for feedback on regular basis "80% of complaints received by an organization are likely to have poor communication as their root cause, either with the customer or within the organization itself. Source: Unknown"

Take action consistently to reinforce positive experience through rewards and rout out negative experience through remedial measures

Once the feedback is received, positive feedback could be used as reference to promote to new customers and reinforced to build better bridge with such customers providing positive feedback while negative feedback should be immediately acted upon and the remedial measures undertaken. "56%-70% of the customers who complain to you will do business with you again if you resolve their problem. If they feel you acted quickly and to their satisfaction, up to 96% will do business with you again, and they will probably refer other people to you. Source: the White House Office of Consumer Affairs, Washington, DC".

While Loyalty cards and special offers are repeatedly used by companies to get the customers to do repeat business, companies who work on delighting their customers by working on the Quality of products and services, Value for Money and in providing excellent support to their customers get not only repeated customers but also a positive viral buzz that widens their gap with the competition.

## APPLE COMPUTER—COMPANY THAT CHANGED THE WORLD

Apple computer Inc, founded by Steve Jobs on the April fool's day of 1976, demonstrated to the world, the power of innovation, when harnessed in conjunction with execution excellence. Passion, Uncompromising attitude to pursuit of excellence in every sphere of work and attention to the smallest detail, combined to deliver amazing results at Apple Computer, under the legendary Steve Jobs. The world of technology will never be the same after the demise of Steve Jobs, a person who created one of the finest and the most innovative technology companies in the world. Apple created the Mac operating systems, a series of graphical user interface-based operating systems in 1984, that consistently endeared the Apple Macintosh computers, integrated with them, to their users and put Apple computers streets ahead of the rest of the brands using any other operating system.

Apple's Macintosh computers had a fierce fan following and those who saw the demonstration of an Apple computer, regretted for their life, when they were unable to buy one. After being unceremoniously ousted from Apple in 1985, 9 years after he founded the company along with Steve Wozniak, Steve Jobs created another iconoclastic computer company called the NeXT. He also got into animation by buying out Pixair Animation studio and produced some of the finest animation movies like A Bug's Life and Toy Story. As Apple's fortunes hit rock bottom, post his exit from the company, he was requested by the board of Apple Computer to return back to resurrect his baby. What followed was history. After launching iMac, with the iconic operating system, ilife, Steve Jobs, launched the ugly but sensational iPod that revolutionized the world's music industry in conjunction with the on-line e-commerce music platform, namely, iTunes, which empowered the music lovers to legally down load their favorite numbers as per their wish instead of buying as albums. IPod was followed by iPhone, which revolutionized the smart phone category of mobile phones by offering unforeseen features to its users. The experience its delivered to it's users amazed the world and it became an instant hit despite any shortcomings in the early versions. iPad, one of the greatest tablets ever to adorn the hands of the tech-freaks, followed iPhone and the rest is history. Apple not just created products, but also enabled the proliferation and entire eco-system that thrived on creating applications and accessory products that enhanced the user experience of the Apple's products. Today, there are over 5 lakh applications in the App Store, created by a number of third party developers who continue to churn out more and more. These applications vie with each other to get downloaded onto the iPhone or the iPad with a promise to create newer and better experiences to its users. Thus Apple is now aided by vast brigades of brilliant mobile application developers that increase the entry barriers for competition like Samsung, Nokia and Blackberry. Another interesting aspect of Apple's marketing strategy is that, for many years, as it concentrated on building one blockbuster product after the other, Apple never really had to advertise and waste valuable marketing dollars. The power of the performance of its products and the viral buzz they created with an immensely positive user experience, ensured that its products were always in huge demand, way ahead of its ability to supply and flew off the shelves from the very first day they are launched. Apple kept its ears firmly on the ground to ensure that any loopholes in its products are plugged at an early stage and improvised versions are launched quickly to delight their users.

Today Apple Inc sells over 35 million iPhone per quarter and over 11 million iPods per quarter and the sales keep hitting new records every new quarter. (http://aaplinvestors.net/stats/iphonevsipod/)

No wonder, even after the death of Steve Jobs on the 5th of October 2011, at an age of just 56, Apple has become the most valued companies in the world with a market capitalization of over 500 Billion US Dollar, a neat 30% above its nearest rival, Exxon Mobil, the largest corporation in the world.

The following table gives the Market capitalization of the top 20 companies in the world as on 25th July 2012.

## SERVICE EXCELLENCE—A KEY CONTRIBUTOR TO CUSTOMER DELIGHT . . .

**THERE IS PLACE IN THE WORLD FOR ANY BUSINESS THAT TAKES CARE OF ITS CUSTOMERS—AFTER THE SALE.**

*—Harvey MacKay*

Successful Companies understand the importance of delivering unparalleled service to their customers, without any compromise, as this will lead to an excellent experience. A delighted customer spreads a positive word of mouth to other potential customers leading to more business for the company.

**A customer is the most important visitor on our premises; he is not dependent on us. We are dependent on him. He is not an interruption in our work. He is the purpose of it. He is not an outsider in our business. He is part of it. We are not doing him a favor by serving him. He is doing us a favor by giving us an opportunity to do so. . . .**

*—Mahatma Gandhi*

Customers can afford to do without their vendor, but a company cannot survive without a satisfied customer. The linchpin of any business is the customer. Customers lay the foundation of businesses today. In this consumer driven age, what sets apart great companies is the service they provide to their customers. Great companies invest in customers because, that is where the business lies. The business decisions of the leading brands across the globe today, are driven to satisfy and exceed the expectations of their customers that will create impregnable entry barriers for any competitor to overcome.

**The goal as a company is to have customer service that is not just the best but legendary . . .**
— *Sam Walton, Founder of Wal-Mart*

Customer is the King Maker. Several studies have shown that it costs nearly six times more to win a new customer than to keep an existing one. Customers are powerful marketing agents; a satisfied customer can help win more deals than the best marketing personnel. They become more important in the digital age, where people can give feedback and influence the buyers at the click of a mouse.

**IF WE DON'T TAKE CARE OF OUR CUSTOMERS, SOMEONE ELSE WILL**
— *Unknown*

The customers today are bombarded with options, sometimes more than what they can handle. So, what differentiates a business is the service it provides to its customers. The best agents for marketing the products and services are the customers. A reputation is built on what people talk about their experience. How a company is perceived in the market determines its brand image. Their customers build the best brands. Fascinatingly a great number of companies like Facebook, Twitter and pinterest are prime examples of companies that have sky rocketed due to their customers and the empowerment they have provided to their customers to express their opinions. This has led to the customer's voice becoming very potent enough to make or break any businesses.

**"If you do build a great experience, customers tell each other about that. Word of mouth is very powerful."**

*Jeff Bezos, CEO Amazon.com*

Excellent service is the best marketing strategy for a business. The world is a place where the speed of communication keeps increasing. Things propagate and travel faster than ever before. Whether it is good or bad reviews, it can affect the performance of a brand in the competitive market place.

Amazon, founded in 1994 is the world's largest online retailer today. The story of Amazon is a story of excellence in service that propelled it to great heights. The business model makes them one of the most successful modern companies and a technological giant. Amazon has transformed the industry in its own ways. It has done it through remarkable customer service. They made shopping possible at a click. They empowered users to give ratings, review and provide feedback on all products and services. It enables the users to pick and choose the best products.

Google, Apple, GE, and Toyota motors, etc are other companies to have emerged as global leaders due to their excellent Services. The core essence of these top companies is in providing great services to their customers. These companies have focused on customer delight and enhanced customer experience making them truly world class. When the customer feels good it promotes your brand and organization. This is how great companies are built. Customer service is imperative for the success of a company. Most successful companies, who focus on customer delight, advocate the following that leads them to achieving service excellence:

- ✓ Know your customers. Build a customer profile. Each and every customer is special and they must feel it

✓ Look at your business from the customer's perspective and then communicate

✓ Make a great first impression. Whether it is the logo, salesman or the business cards of company, all this speaks about your company

✓ Build trust by giving the best quality. Be reliable and do what you say

✓ Each genuine complaint is a great chance to improve upon the products/services that you are offering. Develop a system where customer complaints can be gathered easily

✓ Have an excellent complaint handling system that is transparent to the customers. Intimate the customers about the action plan for the complaints and communicate regularly

✓ Be proactive and responsible in solving the pain points of the customer

✓ Do something pleasantly surprising that leaves a wow effect on your customer

✓ The key to customer satisfaction is to exceed expectations of your customers

✓ Be honest with your customers; never lie, over promise or under deliver

✓ Make it easy for the customers to give their feedback and register complaints. Be accessible via internet, phone calls and customer service centers

✓ Differentiate yourself from the market, offer something unique

✓ Develop means to get the customer satisfaction and feedback. Measure customer service level & ask your customers about their expectations

✓ Create a compelling customer experience, one that urges them to recommend your products or services to others

✓ Leverage the power of online monitoring tools to know more about your brand. See what people are saying about your products and services. Do something exceptionally good to get their attention. Create your presence, help your customers and be noticed

✓ Bring in experts and a trained staff that deals with customers. Share relevant information about your products and services with your customers. Help them use it better

✓ Create a customer interaction plan. The idea is to communicate effectively with your customers. Too much or too little communication can hinder your business, it is important to get the balance right.

   o *When creating a customer plan, address the following questions:*
   o *How do you communicate with your customers?*
   o *How often do you communicate with them?*
   o *What do you need to tell your customers?*
   o *When you need to talk to them?*

✓ Thank your customers for the business. A hand written or prewritten note can do wonders & make the customer feel great. When you care, it shows in your attitude

✓ When you cannot fix the customer's problem, apologize sincerely. If possible, offer them some discounts, refunds or credit accounts for future

✓ Innovate, experiment and execute with customer at the heart of your organization

Nothing promotes a business more than a satisfied customer. The best advertisement media in the digital age is the word of mouth. Great service invariably builds and boosts your brand. Be exceptional and be talked about.

The most successful companies are not only known by their results, but also the confidence and satisfaction they produce for their customers. There is a strong correlation between the customer satisfaction level and the brand equity of a company. Studies from American

Customer Satisfaction Index and other agencies seem to corroborate the same.

The American Customer Satisfaction Index has shown that the stock prices of companies ranking higher for customer service tend to do better than those with lower value. According to Forbes magazine, between 1994 and 2007, companies ranking in the top 25% of the index created $420 billion in wealth for shareholders versus $111 billion for those in the bottom 25% — in other words, companies that please their customers are shown to create four times the wealth.

**ONE CUSTOMER WELL TAKEN CARE OF COULD BE MORE VALUABLE THAN $10,000 WORTH OF ADVERTISING**
*—Jim Rohn*

Customer service is the best advertisement for any business. It is imperative to make sure that it is as impressive as it can be. Great services produce the best returns on investment. Service excellence builds the foundation on which great organizations are operated. Successful Organizations know that that their entire stakes are dependent on their services excellence and hence the need to be never compromising in investing to achieve the best service levels they can offer to their customers, which in turn will not only let their business survive, but also multiply.

**AMAZING CUSTOMER SERVICE @ AMAZON.**
AMAZING CUSTOMER EXPERIENCE

**"The most important single thing is to focus obsessively on the customer. Our goal is to be earth's most customer-centric company"**
*—Jeff Bezos, CEO & President of Amazon.com*

The dot com bubble that bust in the early 2000, took away a number of companies into the oblivion. But a few companies in the world like Apple, Google, Amazon, EBay and Zappos have survived the bouts of recession and tough times and grew from strength to strength.

This is because, despite growing so big and leaders in their respective spheres of operation, they never forgot the basics about what got them to existence in the first pace.

While Apple believed in delivering amazing experience to its customers through its products, Google empathies with its users to provide them the best possible user experience, redefining the way information is searched, consumed and put to use productively, Amazon under Jeff Bezos, has come up as an amazing customer focused organization. In the words of Jeff Bezos, 'If you build a great experience, customers tell each other about that. **"Word of mouth is very powerful"**

One of the lessons which Jeff Bezos, learnt and implemented at Amazon is that, satisfied and delighted customers are the best advertisement & publicity, a company can invest in, as they not only give more businesses in their life-time association with the company, but also bring their friends to become the customers. Hence Amazon focuses heavily in providing an excellent service to all its customers and keeps them delighted.

A similar culture and attitude is seen at Zappos, a wholly owned subsidiary of Amazon. At Zappos, the business model is developed around the goal of maximizing the customer and employee happiness. While every call centre, measures its success by the number of successful calls handled in a given time, Zappos measures its success by the number of calls leading to excited customers. It celebrates the fact that customers love to spend more time talking to their call centers on an average call as, this in turn leads to more business per call and higher repeat order percentage as they satisfy their customers with best-fit solutions.

When we learn that the CEO of Amazon believes that each and every one of his global customers have be treated like a welcome guest to his party, by all his employees, we know the secret behind a vibrant & growing US$ 50 Billion, most admired global corporation!

Business is all about making commitments and delivering on the same in return for a consideration. In any transaction that includes a delivery of a promise and a payment for the same in cash, kind or a returning action, a win-win approach will make the partners want to continue their dealings and value exchanges forever. Most important transactions for any business are:

- Commitment of return on investment by the business to its shareholders
- Commitment of brand/product or service proposition by the business to its customers & consumers from the quality of the product to redresses of their complaints if any
- Commitment of working environment, salaries, incentives and rewards to the employees and associates
- Commitment of profitable association to the trade partners promoting the products, services and the plans of the business to consumers and users
- Commitment of the business to Government, Society and the environment &
- Commitment to the vendors of inputs, necessary services and support required by the company, for healthy and prompt transactions including proper accounting practices and prompt payments . . .

In each of the above it is imperative for the organization to stick to its commitments as basic requirement, not only for survival, but also as an ethical and healthy practice.

Successful organizations make it a practice to strive for exceeding the expectations of their associates that results in the delight of their associates making them want not only to repeat the transaction again and again, but also to be an ambassador for the organization.

Exceeding the expectations thus becomes an important aspect of the customer experience that an organization should master. How does an organization ensure that they consistently meet and exceed expectations of their partners, associates, stakeholders, employees etc . . . ?

Great organizations invariably, do the following:

- Believe in offering honest, credible and deliverable commitments
- Have a thorough understanding of the situation in which the commitments are given
- Are always transparent with the associates and the transacting party about the issues, limitations and risk factors affecting the delivery of the commitments
- Arrive at an agreement with the transacting party for a sign-off of the commitment
- Always ensure that the commitments are recorded in writing to ensure no ambiguity. Though, it a common practice to boast of being a person of words who never goes back on his/her word, successful organizations never encourage oral commitments ass this will lead to adhocism and heart burns at times
- Possess and reflect courage to lose business than fall short on commitments
- Have a long-term approach in favor of a short-term approach. While short sightedness and short term approach are thoroughly reflected in an urge on the part of the organization to undertake a transaction somehow, the long term approach takes into account the need to be associated

profitably for a long time and should never end up in loss of face for falling short on commitments.

- A bias for a win-in approach as against, winner takes all or I win—You lose approach and finally
- Give whatever it takes to deliver on the commitments and give more value than promised even if has to entail sacrifices on the part of the organization for the same.

Successful Organizations, who consistently exceed expectations, endear themselves to the investors and always get a high rating from them, making themselves financially more viable than their counterparts who lack on this vital aspect. This is indeed a value enhancer.

Managing Expectations is thus a vital strategy for the 21st century's successful organizations

## CISCO—A GREAT EMPLOYER . . .
COMMITMENT TO CUSTOMERS & EMPLOYEES . . .

Founded in 1984 by Leonard Bosack & Sandy Lerner, Cisco takes its name from the American city of SanFrancisco. A global leader in the networking equipment, with a turnover in excess of 43 Billion US Dollars, CISCO is one of the most valuable technology companies in the world today. John Chambers groomed as a successor to take over as CEO from John Morgridge in 1995, took the company from a turnover of $1.2 billion in annual revenue into $43 billion in 17 years, with the employee count rising from 2200 to 65000 in the same period. Today, Cisco has a market share in excess of 60% in the networking infrastructure space with the nearest competitors like Juniper Networks, HP, and IBM etc. having less than just 10%. An incredible leadership led the organization to become an extremely customer centric organization with a penchant for execution excellence in its areas of focus.

The reason for Cisco's success could be summarized as follows;

- It is a well known fact that Cisco as an organization is extremely customer focused. Every customer of Cisco has a number of positive experiences to recount regarding the response from the customer service department of Cisco in times of breakdown or any other contingency
- Cisco is credited with the most exhaustive product range that anticipates every possible need of the potential customer, at the same time offering unbeatable quality, rated ahead of its competitors. It is said that Cisco is the no 1 company in the consideration set of every customer wanting to buy networking equipment and infrastructure
- Strategic Acquisitions: Cisco is credited with an incredibly shrewd and successful acquisition strategy. Cisco acquired a variety of companies to spin products and talent into the company. In 1995-1996 the company completed 11 acquisitions. Several acquisitions, such as Stratacom, were the biggest deals in the industry when they occurred. Though a number of the acquisitions did not pay off, the calculated risk taken by Cisco continues to pay rich dividends as it grows from strength to strength. With a cash reserve in excess of US $ 40 Billion, Cisco is forever scouting for opportunities that would help it maintain its edge and give the best in networks to its customer
- Focus on quality of employees and performance focus: Cisco believes in being ahead of its competition in recruiting the best of the talent, offering the best product, supporting the customers with service levels that exceeds expectation and also by coming out with new products & technologies through continuous innovation

- Focus on training and creation of an eco-system for adoption of Cisco's products by its clients. Cisco has become a truly global transnational organization and has spread its tentacles into every nook and corner of the world. By establishing a widespread training network to train workforce on Cisco products and technologies, across the world through Cisco Certification Courses, it ensured that its clients and partners are well supported and staffed with trained engineers. This has resulted in an excellent & unparalleled eco-system in which Cisco brand can thrive and be streets ahead of any of its competitors

- Focus on Employee satisfaction: While being very much performance focused and is very demanding on its employees, has always been ranked as one of the best companies to work for globally. John Chambers believes in empowering the employees and in participatory leadership that helps in employees being more responsible, at the same time focused on delivering the best results in the area of their operation. Cisco's employee friendly policies ensure a tremendous fit between the talent of its employees and the job they are given, focus on taking care of the employees' personal requirements as and when required within a reasonable flexibility. This results in delighted employees acting as the ambassadors of the company and giving their best at all times

- Focus on innovation and planning for the future: Cisco has always stayed ahead of the curve in its core area of operations and is now very focused on the next wave of technological revolution, namely the Cloud Computing based technologies & services with the launch of Cloud Verse, a framework to link public, private and hybrid clouds. Cisco has always been on the cutting edge in its domain and led the changing technology landscape by appropriate investments and timely & strategic acquisitions for a quick take off. These strategies have helped Cisco to be a leading, globally successful organization of the 21st century.

In the survey launched by Silicon India, known to be the largest community of Indian professionals, Cisco Systems has been raked highly in the list of Top 10 Best Multinational companies in the world
(http://www.siliconindia.com/news/business/10-Best-Multinational-Companies-nid-112182-cid-3.html)
& And Top 10 most ethical companies in the world ((http://www.siliconindia.com/news/business/Worlds-10-Most-Ethical-Companies-nid-124169-cid-3.html).
Cisco is a living example of a company that believes in exceeding expectations of its customers, employees and the society it operates in.

**The web attacks traditional ways of doing things and elites, and this is very uncomfortable for traditional businesses to deal with**

*—Sir Martin Sorrell, CEO, WPP Group*

There was a time, when we used to send 100% of our communication through courier/fax/telex/ letters and phone calls. We used to spend our free time watching television or visiting a shopping complex to shop for our wares or for entertainment.

There has been an irreversible trend across all aspects of our life leading us to do most of the above activities in the four confines of our rooms whether at house or at a work place or in any other 3rd party location.

People now communicate mostly through emails, relax by playing games on their computers, shop and bank over the net and watch movies and TV programs over the net as well. With the rapid growth of the Social media, now even we tend to make friends and maintain our relationships over the net as well!

More than 50% of the free time of a typical consumer today is spend browsing over the net for information, shopping, entertainment, socializing or any other form of communication and networking. This has been a rapid one way trend up and expected to grow further

As Mr. Rupert Murdoch suggested in 2006, "To find something comparable, you have to go back 500 years to the printing press, the birth of mass media. Technology is shifting power away from the editors, the publishers, the establishment, and the media elite. Now it's the people who are taking control"

The explosion of the internet over the years has brought within the reach of every consumer, unforeseen power to access & process information, network effectively across the world and leave their footprints in a variety of forums, groups and their own platforms like websites, emails, blogs etc. There has been a dramatic change in proportion of time spent by the people on the web w.r.t. that on the television.

Some statistics courtesy Entwined Digital:

- More uploads to YouTube in 60 days than all 3 major US networks created in 60 years
- 110 million tweets are sent per day on Twitter or 4+million per hour (Twitter)
- Facebook generates 770 Billion page views, 700+ Billion minutes, every month
- Stumble Upon (43%) has overtaken Facebook (38%) as #1 source for US social media traffic
- In 2010, Asia Pacific had more than 825 million internet users, 42% of the global total.

In 2011 Google suggested that digital media has transformed our buying decisions. Marketing has a Changing Rulebook based on Zero Moment of Truth or ZMOT, "the moment when you grab your laptop, mobile phone or some other wired device and start learning about a product or service." Google provides core digital training in ZMOT for all members of their sales team internationally.

These statistics tell the story of how our buying behaviors have changed:

- 65% of Asian Pacific consumers use online services to locate nearby products and brands
- 70% of Americans say they look at online product reviews before making a purchase

- 79% of consumers say they use a Smartphone to help with shopping
- 83% of moms say they do online research after seeing TV commercials for products that interest them
- When people surf the web, they are in complete control of their actions and experience. They have an option to interact with the advertisements and promotions that are targeted at them.

This power in the hands of today's consumers has brought in a sea change in the way the marketers need to look at their approach and is a result of the digital revolution brought by the explosion of internet through a devices ranging from standard computers to highly personalized and extremely capable mobile devices.

Old-school marketers are used to one-way marketing communication and a sales approach that talks at the customer rather than with the customer. That just doesn't work anymore. Newt Barrett, contentmarketingtoday.com

Marketing always starts with the consumer in mind. Top Marketers are successful in influencing the need perception of the consumers, understanding their needs and wants, creating products and services to meet their needs, communicating effectively with their targeted consumers and in putting in place a mechanism to fulfill their needs and manage their lifetime relationship with the brand. Most of these principals are universal and evergreen. While these do not change constantly, what is changing today is the ability on behalf of the consumers to explore constantly, compare efficiently, comment and convince other co-customers for a given product or a service. The people who are surfing on the web are mostly doing to so at their own volition and are out there to spend their time purely at their wish. The intrusive advertisements that they are subjected to in their real life can be avoided on the net and they can be drawn to see interact and participate in only those advertisements, promotions and activities that they choose. The near total belief in the minds of consumers today that any information they is need is available and easily accessible on the new has led to the growth of the internet based advertisement industry on a rapid basis.

**The tipping point is that magic moment when an idea, trend, or social behavior crosses a threshold, tips, and spreads like wildfire**
    —*Malcolm Gladwell—from The Tipping Point*

This brings us to the issue that the traditional approach of mass advertising can be ineffective and needs to take into account the changes in the consumer lifestyle and need for self-expression.

The rapid advancement of technology in the recent past has brought to the quiver of the marketers, a tremendous computing, storage and processing power. This coupled with innovative products and solutions developed by thought leaders like Sergey Brin, Larry Page, Jerry Yang, David Filo, Mark Zuckerberg, Eduardo Saverin, Dustin Moskovitz, Chris Hughes, Jack Dorsey, Steve Jobs in the recent past have put in the hands of people, unforeseen capabilities to create applications, choose the ways they want to participate, limited only by their own mind and extended competencies.

**We have technology, finally, that for the first time in human history allows people to really maintain rich connections with much larger numbers of people**
    —*Pierre Omidyar, founder, eBay.*

On the other hand, marketers are able to precisely target individual consumers as they get on to the net for their needs and their entertainment.

This has led to the marketers to abandon their one-sided communication approach and start involving with their target consumers, existing consumers and society in general for the prosperity of their businesses.

**We will no longer view you as "consumers". Instead, you are co-creators, participants, and advocates**

*—David Armano—Logic + Emotion*
*and Edelman Digital*

There has been rapid growth of online organizations and businesses and most of the new businesses are increasingly diverting their marketing spends on-line.

Google, one of the greatest companies ever, has taken full advantages of this changing face of marketing.

Google strongly feels that the Marketing strategies of companies has to keep in pace with this change in dynamics in the nature of shopping behavior of the 21st century consumers.

Google, Facebook, YouTube, Twitter, MySpace, Yahoo, LinkedIn, Amazon are a few of the new generation of businesses that get 100% of their revenue from the net based activities and their share in the global revenue generation is surging north rapidly year after year.

With increased spend happening on the net, there is now a requirement of analyzing the spends and calculating the ROI of the investments that are happening in this area. With precise targeting of potential customers and personalized communication to each individual possible in an extremely cost effective manner, the marketing arms of organizations are increasingly getting confident in spreading their wings on the net and are diverting their spends in large proportions.

While the entire marketing approach is undergoing a sea change with individual consumers now driving the character of marketing activities, there has been a corresponding and significant change in the competencies and profile expectation from the employees of the advertising and marketing industry.

**The new types of employees that are going to fill the marketing, communications and sales departments of the most successful**

**companies are going to have job titles like community manager, editor in chief, blogger, podcaster, videographer and social media director**

*—Mitch Joel—Twist Image*

## FACEBOOK: THE ANTHEM OF THE 21st CENTURY YOUTH . . .

Facebook has revolutionized the way people connect, communicate and socialize around the globe. With over 900 million users as of May 2012, Facebook has more people than most countries in the world. It is the mostly actively used social networking site in the world today.

Facebook founded in 2004, it has grown exponentially surpassing all other competitors. FB was not meant to be a company but provide the user with the best user experience. In his own words Zuckerberg, CEO, Facebook said, "Simply put: we don't build services to make money, We make money to build better services." Today, Facebook is already generating highly profitable annual revenue of over one billion US Dollars and is valued over 50 Billion US Dollars, a proud achievement for a company less than 10 years old . . .

Here is a look at things that make Facebook so successful:

### Socializing

Facebook has become the new means for socializing. People can connect, communicate and share events about their lives on Facebook. It has become a way people express themselves.

### Focus on Users

Facebook is a tool that gives the user a freedom to share his thoughts, events, opinions with the rest. It is built around the user. All the services and usability aspects are user centric and that makes FB so popular.

## Smart ways to connect people

One of the smartest algorithms devised by FB is to connect people who know each other. The intuitive and smart features make FB popular. The recommendations are based on similar preferences, likes and interests. Like-minded people can communicate with each other easily and develop their social networks effectively. This enables millions of people with diverse interests, backgrounds and cultures to interact with each other.

## Simplicity

Facebook has a simple and elegant user interface. It is very intuitive and requires very little effort on the part of the user to use it. It has a consistent layout and good graphic design which makes it appealing to the users.

## Dynamic

While Facebook was started in a dorm room, it has certainly lived up to the growing needs of the users. The initial idea was to allow campus students to communicate freely with each other. However, with strategic insights and promotions they built an exponential user base. The Facebook team has been dynamic and adaptive to the growing user base and its needs. The FB timeline, tickers and several other features are prime examples of the dynamic nature of FB.

## Entertainment

Facebook has become the ultimate source of entertainment for the youth. There are many games that have become increasingly popular due to FB. Farmville, Backyard Monsters are just some of them. The games coupled with social networking provide a fun filled platform for the youngsters.

## Facebook Ads

Digital marketing campaigns are revolved around FB users. A lucrative user base of more than 900 million attracts advertisers and companies. The Facebook ads are shown based on the likes, comments and profile of the user, making advertising more relevant.

## Facebook Pages

Most of the fortune 500 companies have a Facebook corporate page. It allows them to talk about their products/services, interact with the users, get a real world feedback and enable communication. Most of these companies regularly update their pages, post relevant contents and offer something for the end users too. Facebook pages have become an effective way of engaging potential customers. It has become a social business tool too.

## Facebook Aps

Facebook has created an amazing eco-system with lakhs of applications being built by third part developers, which help in engaging the members. Facebook has devised a unique win-win system that enables the third party developers to not only further the user experience and engagement levels on this fantastic social media portal, but also enables them to successfully monetize them depending on their popularity.

Today, with over 800 million users worldwide and average user engagement levels spanning the highest number of hours per user for any online platform, Facebook nation could be the third largest and the richest nation in the world.

## DIGITAL MEDIA MARKETING—MAKES THE MOST OF YOUR ADVERTISING INVESTMENT.

**Digital Marketing Strategy**

The world is changing at the speed of thoughts. The digital landscape has created a virtual world where physical boundaries have disappeared. The leading companies around the globe are prominently investing more and more resources to ensure a strong presence in the virtual world. "Every consumer-facing business absolutely had to be experimenting in virtual worlds if it wanted to get the attention of the under 30s" [Richards, 2008]. All the top organizations around the globe are now coming up with their digital marketing strategy to leverage the power of social media. The digital marketing outlines all brand communications through various social channels, setting up content for attracting qualified leads, talent, selling and executing a vision, from delivering stand alone projects to integrated campaigns, developing brand presence, tracking online and delivering brand email.

**Why is it important?**

The key areas of responsibility for Digital Marketing include:

- Creating an online brand and visibility
- Means to attract the highest quality talent
- Managing communications and maintain an online marketing campaign
- Knowledge Sharing by creating content that has the ability to create a viral effect

- Use the digital landscape to more effectively carrying out the business objectives
- Attracting Qualified leads
- Create a social media presence.
- Driving results by bring more traffic to the company website using SEO. To increase the number of page views, unique visitors, average time per visit and stickiness factor for website.
- Review and analyze the performance using web-analytic tools. Understanding the visitor patterns and customer behavior. Setting business goals and tracking conversions.
- Creating a social media presence and growing online reputation.

**Understanding the customer**

The hardest thing to buy in the twenty first century is the attention of the consumer. You cannot buy user attention, you have to earn it. As long as you offer something incredibly exciting people are going to promote it. If it made sense to them, they will share it. You cannot beg user attention; you need to command it by sheer quality. Any digital marketing campaign is driven by content. The first step of the marketing campaign is to create compelling content.

Who is your customer? What are his needs? Address them and create contents that help the customer in engaging the customer, if possible solve some of his problems. Build a rapport with him by providing him something he needs and make him come back to you with more expectations.

Top companies invest their resources in creating core content built around the customers. These organizations are creating blogs, articles, presentation and templates to help customers.

The proverbial saying goes like content is the king. What you promote must promote itself. People influence the digital media presence. The famous analogy that works with digital media is that it should not be 100% of one person's job but 1% of 100 persons' job. Everyone is important to the campaign for bringing in the desired results.

## Steps to ensure a successful Digital Marketing Campaign

Once the target audience is identified, the following steps can be taken to create a high impact digital marketing campaign. The idea is to create a campaign that promotes itself. Here is a look at the different digital channels and avenues that are used by the top organizations in the world for a successful digital marketing campaign.

### 1. Authority Core Content

The content should pull the visitors. It should be sticky, relevant and have the ability to go viral. It should make an impression and retain the visitors.

People should find value in sharing the stuff.
What is the content that you are offering?
Essays, How-to articles, Tip sheets, Checklists, Guidebooks, Interviews Audio/video podcast: downloadable audios/videos
Blogs, Articles, Info graphics: Information with graphs/charts. e-Books: Something that people can share.
Presentations: Strategy presentations and how to guides
Press releases and newsletters
Widgets: Links that can be embedded.
Blog Posts: There is a detailed description of blog section below.

The companies maintain information pool and volunteer to share information with their customers. This creates an information pool that attracts users and qualified traffic.

## 2. Social Media Marketing

Creating a social presence for the organization on different social media networks. This helps an organization maintain online reputation and build brand awareness. When creating a profile for the company, the following needs to be considered:

### Viral Market: How viral is the content?

Regularly updating the content is a must.

Leverage two-way conversations and interact with your audience.

Building Followers on LinkedIn, Face Book, twitter etc.

Contests and special offers for enticing the users.

Identifying influencers and getting them to promote your campaign.

## 3. Leverage Online Communities for your organization

The successful organizations leverage online communities for discussions, expert opinions, customer feedback and various presentations. Working with Online Communities enables posting information on discussion forums and get live feedback. Some companies participate and involve in online/offline seminars and conferences also. This helps in attracting talent as well as business leads. These are communities, which can bring quality traffic.

## 4. Referral Marketing what is in it for those who refer your organization?

A lot of companies use free gifts to those who follow and refer the organization using social media networks like FB, twitter, pinterest etc. This helps in building the momentum and traffic initially. What does your customer get when he makes a recommendation for you? Organizations give free bees to generate good recommendations.

## 5. Use article directory submissions & content distribution networks

There are plenty of content sharing websites where content can be distributed. The idea is to accumulate back links, bring brand awareness and get qualified traffic on the company's website. Some of the websites wherein members can post stuff are as follows.

Leverage the power of free content distribution and article submission directories to get quality traffic. Some of the most popular websites for sharing content are as follows:

http://www.scribd.com/
http://www.docstoc.com/
http://issuu.com/http://ezinearticles.com/
http://calameo.com/

## 6. Blog

Business blogs that convey a purpose generates quality traffic and leads. The key question is what are you trying to convey to the potential customer? Building a niche is tough. Most effective bloggers do not talk about their products/services but about the common industry issues and the problems.

They convey to the users how their product/service can solve those problems. Another great way is to invite industry leaders for featured posts and interviews on the website.

Make a list of 10 most common questions that the prospective customers will ask. Address those questions by creating articles and giving detailed answers to those questions. When this is repeated for a period of 3 months, it will generate a good information base to attract potential clients. Making the content interesting and appealing is paramount.

## 7. Search Engine Optimization

Search Engine Optimization is the art of influencing search engines in order to improve rankings and secure top positions for keywords. SEO can improve website rankings, boost brand awareness, drive high quality website traffic and increase conversions. Here is a brief introduction on what you can do with it:

- Technical SEO and data analysis: Any SEO project requires data analysis in the form of keyword research, traffic measurement and goal evaluation
- Content creation: In many cases, SEO activities require large amounts of new content in the form of articles, info graphics and other images. So a creative mind is a must on your SEO team
- Link building: Because back links can play a tremendous role in your website's rankings, SEO teams should have at least one person who will pursue link-building opportunities and generate back links
- Web development: In addition to back links, a number of other variables figure into SEO, including site speed, internal linking and navigation, and content indexing. All design and development aspects that have a high impact high on search results will be implemented during website development

Broadly speaking the SEO can be divided into two categories

- On Page SEO: This will be implemented during design/development of the web pages
- Off Page SEO: This involves all promotional activities outside the design of the website. This area involves link building, registering with directories relevant to the industry and getting more content for search engine listing.

Identifying Keywords for which contents need to be created. Share content, blogs, articles links to drive traffic. Google Analytics: Define goals using analytics. This is an excellent tool for gauging your website traffic, their conversion ratio and goal conversion etc.

## 8. Inorganic Promotion

Outsourcing the contents to agencies, which can take care of the PR related activities for your organization. These agencies typically promote content on social media like twitter, FB, YouTube and other content sharing sites. These agencies can help us reach a minimum level of user impressions.

## 9. Email Marketing:

Identify the Core content that needs to be circulated. Sharing useful content, taking the user feedback and surveys. Encourage discussion and two-way communications using emails. Can use Auto responder setup. The free offers on the website can be posted via emails or RSS auto responders to ensure that you are in touch with the prospects. Email can be circulated for creating brand awareness. Readers can post their feedback, inputs and suggestions, which can be posted on the website. The updates and latest developments can also be posted to the users who sign up with the company.

## 10. Mobile Marketing

Mobile Marketing involves communicating with the consumer via mobile device, either to send a simple marketing message, to introduce them to a new audience participation-based campaign or to allow them to visit a mobile website. Many successful organizations successfully employ mobile sms marketing strategy to promote their schemes. Some companies also use mobile apps for disseminating information and contents for quality leads. Creating the website which can be navigated using mobile phones. Create an SMS marketing campaigns that offers something to the users and calls for some action. It could be a discount coupon, free gift or a voucher that the customer can redeem.

## 11. Tools to measure Success of Digital Media Campaign

The following tools are useful in gauging the performance of digital media campaign. A successful Digital Media campaign requires regular upkeep and requires monitoring the user trends and traffic analysis. It should keep track of PPC and other strategies for achieving the conversions. What people are saying about you? What all things are happening around you in social media?

Some of the Tracking Tools that can be used for measuring success of the campaign are as follows:

Social Media: http://www.icerocket.com/

Web Analytics:https://www.google.com/webmasters/ tools and http://www.google.com/analytics/

SEO Analytics: Google analytics, Google webmaster guidelines and many analytics tools are available for managing SEO.

Online Reputation and Management:http:// socialmention.com/ Know the top influencers in your field:http://tweetlevel.edelman.com/

How far your message has travelled and impressions:http://tweetreach.com/

These tools are excellent to monitor the digital media presence and progress of a company. It is important to have social mentions for creating a brand. No brand campaign today is complete without the inclusion of a digital media-marketing plan. Whether it is the presidential campaign of Barack Obama, the corporate blogs of the fortune 500 companies or start-ups, everyone is looking to create an online brand presence.

You cannot buy user attention for long, you have to earn it. When you offer something incredibly exciting, people will promote it. If it adds value and makes sense to them, they will share it. You cannot beg user attention; you need to command it by sheer quality. This is how great brands flourish in the 21stcentury.

## LINKEDIN—THE POWER OF BUSINESS NETWORKING ...

LinkedIn is the world's largest community of professionals across the world. Its website says "LinkedIn is a networking tool that helps you discover inside connections to recommended job candidates, industry experts and business partners. It strengthens and extends your existing network of trusted contacts."

Founded by Reid Hoffman in December 2002, LinkedIn remains the strongest marketing channel for professionals around the globe. There are over 50 million LinkedIn members in over 200 countries. In short, LinkedIn is an ultimate business networking platform to drive businesses and connect professionals.

An estimate study says that over 10% of the world's professionals are already on LinkedIn. And with the speed the professionals are signing up, it wouldn't be long before LinkedIn will have a major share of the remaining 90% too.

A look at what makes LinkedIn the most successful social networking site for the professionals:

### Freemium Model

LinkedIn allows the user to create professional networks free of cost. It is a place meant which provides professionals with networking opportunities and career opportunities.

### Network with professionals

Whether it is a company looking for a good candidate or a candidate looking for a good opportunity. LinkedIn combines them both and provides a great platform for job seekers, job providers for networking.

### References

It is a place where you get companies/professionals with qualified references from professionals. The referrals and recommendations provide a powerful means of increasing credibility.

## Knowledge about Employers or Clients

A great deal of information about potential employers and clients can be obtained from the profile. It enables one to make informed decisions whether is recruiting a candidate or making a business decision. An employee can get the latest company updates and industry news.

## Search

The LinkedIn Search facility makes it easy for someone to find specific services from a company or for a company to find employees with relevant skill sets.

## Publicity

It provides a network and groups to promote articles, blog post, or research papers. There are user created groups on LinkedIn, which provide a segmented audience.

## LinkedIn Answers

As a professional you can showcase your expertise and receive exposure and credibility in your field.

## Find Events

Use LinkedIn Events to find conferences, workshops and other types of events that would be useful to you, based on your professional profile. You can also see who else within your network is attending!

## Promote Your Event

LinkedIn Events can promote your event to potential attendees based on their profile information. It will also add the events to your professional profile so that others can see that you have presented at conferences or events.

## Company Page

It provides a tool to create a corporate page, which can act as a vehicle for driving quality business leads for its products/services, attracts professionals and company news. It helps one create a brand presence and awareness about the company.

# THRIVING IN THE FACE OF COMPETITION . . .

**Competition is the keen cutting edge of business, always shaving away at costs**

*—Henry Ford*

Emergence of new competition for any product or service could be seen as an endorsement of the attractiveness of the market and an opportunity togrow the demand by investing together to educate the customers and offer better and better features. By staying competitive and through constructive approach, smart organizations try to garner higher and higher share of the market.

In India, Hero Honda started offering a range of 100cc Bikes in 1985, the two wheeler market was largely dominated by Bajaj Auto with its traditional scooters. As the market for the 100cc bikes, which happened to be a disruptive innovation at that time, with a far superior mileage to the existing competition, Bajaj took little time in responding to the challenge.

In 1986, Bajaj Auto launched a range of motorcycles and fought fiercely with the fast emerging blue chip company, Hero Honda Ltd. While a number of other companies who got into the two wheeler market perished along the way, Bajaj Auto managed to survive the competition and grew to an annual revenue of over US$3.5 Billion as seen today.

Over the last decade, the company has successfully changed its image from a scooter manufacturer to a two-wheeler manufacturer. Its product range encompasses scooterettes, scooters and motorcycles. Its real growth in numbers has come in the last four years after successful introduction of a few models in the motorcycle segment

Together, Bajaj, TVS Motor and Hero Motors (formerly Hero Honda) have grown the Indian market for 100cc Bikes to over US$10 Billion in the past 28 years from almost nil levels.

Fierce competitive spirit in the market place leads to continuous improvement of the features and improved value for money for the consumer due to the efforts of the organizations to be the preferred vendor. Rise of Bharti Airtel, as a global organization despite being faced with disruptive price competition from Reliance communication during the past 10 years is another classic example of a great organization. While a number of organizations have perished being unable to cope up with the competition, the successful companies display the following traits:

A) **Monitoring competition**—Continuously study the competition and strive to keep ahead of them with distinctive and unique selling propositions. Look for opportunities to learn and replicate/surpass in the good features and avoid mistakes done by the competition. Monitoring the competition will allow the company to study the response of others to similar environment and hence will help in evolving the right response. Various online and offline sources like websites, news reports, annual reports, report by funds, advertisements for products and people, patent applications, market surveys are used to monitor the competition. Schemes, New product launches, Pricing movements Production reports, Demand and Inventory reports are continuously monitored by the market intelligence wings in successful organizations.

B) **Watch out & Respond to New developments—**
Look for disruptive innovations or competition from alternate product/service—markets that could evolve as an opportunity to compete it in or as potential competitors. A number of times most dangerous competition stems from new companies that have worked in stealth mode. Successful companies use brute force to dominate such market, stifle growth of such companies or sometimes buy out the competition. For example, Nirma was a classic example in the Indian scenario, which as a new entrant into the detergent market gave tough time to the market leader with disruptive innovation in product/pricing/packaging w.r.t Hindustan lever's Surf. Very often innovation in the form institutional disruption and country disruptions seep the companies off their feet if the threats are not proactively handled.

C) **Co-existing with competitor as Partners—**
Constructive approach to competition has helped companies evolve new markets together with joint investments in setting uniform standards necessary for productive use of resources, share capital resources required for product development, distribution etc while making operations more profitable and viable leading to a higher net addition of economic value. Apple

Computer's decision to use Intel's processors and also 'Windows Operating System' in a dual mode in its personal computers in 20042005 leads to a dramatic growth in the sale of its PCs and gave a new growth curve to its business.

Mark Cataldo, Chairman of the Board of the Open Mobile Alliance, a network of leading telecom companies in the world announced, "The Open Mobile Alliance is very pleased that our organizations have come together to address this key technology area. By cooperating, our organizations, OMA's service enablers and APIs will enrich the support of multimedia services across the rapidly diversifying range of devices."

*http://news.yahoo.com/major-standards-organisationscooperate-drive-development-home-environment-125007624.html*

This is a great example of the cooperation among competitors to evolve industry standards. Similarly, the cooperation between the Indian cellular companies to share cell tower infrastructure by forming joint venture companies is another classic example of co-competition (cooperation between competitors).

Formation of CIBIL by financial services companies in India is another classic case of competitors coming together to share information to help in credit rating verification of their applicants to reduce delinquencies and Non Performing Assets, thus improving their performance.

Today's successful companies have a clear constructive approach that enables them to leverage competition for business growth than be intimidated by them and be insecure. This is the hallmark of thriving organizations.

# LESSONS FROM THE FAILURES THAT SHOOK THE WORLD . . .

*Titanic, name and thing, will stand as a monument and warning to human presumption. The Bishop of Winchester, preaching in Southampton, 1912.*

TITANIC, which was supposed to be an unsinkable ship, sank without a trace after hitting an iceberg in the early hours of April 15th, 1912 in the North Atlantic seas.

In the recent history, we have seen a number of large companies, which were successful in their own way for a long time, suddenly loose way and disappear from the corporate landscape. While a number of factors have to fall in place together to create a successful organization, a few factors are sufficient to cause the companies to fail, just like how a few unplugged leaks caused by a rock hit could sink a huge ship if not plugged in time.

Let us review some recent corporate failures and the reasons that caused them.

## Lehman Brothers

Lehman Brothers was one of the biggest investment banks in the world, when it declared bankruptcy on 15th September 2008. A fall from a market capitalization of USD 60 Billion in February 2007 to almost zero in around 19 months, this is one of the most spectacular failures of a blue chip corporate with over 25000 employees. Reckless exposure to low quality assets and unbridled aggression in acquiring subprime mortgage business after a rapid rise in prices led to its fall. Holding over 639 Billion USD of assets at notional value and over 620 Billion USD of liabilities at the time of filing for bankruptcy, Lehman's fall was one of the biggest collapses of all time. Lehman's high degree of leverage with debt over 30 times the shareholder's equity, and a rapidly falling value of its mortgage portfolio in a weak market, led to huge losses and inability to cope with the situation leading to its ultimate filing of bankruptcy. Lehman Brothers brushed many loopholes in its accounting practices under the carpet by regular window dressing of accounts and ignored many early warning signals. Lack of fiscal discipline and ethical accounting practices led to this giant crash and vanish into oblivion. This shows that, lack of transparency, undue aggression in the market place, lack of fiscal discipline can mean an end to any large organization and hence no one is infallible.

## Enron

Rated, "America's Most Innovative Company" by Fortune for six consecutive years, from 1996 to 2001, listed on the Fortune's "100 Best Companies to Work for in America" in 2000, and having offices that were stunning in their opulence, Enron, once one of the largest American corporations with a market capitalization of over 70 Billion USD. When it filed for bankruptcy in December 2001, its supposed financial strength was managed through a set of fraudulent and innovative accounting practices termed later as "Enron scandal" and its claimed turnover of 101Billion USD was found to be mostly fudged and non-existent.

The fraud committed by Enron led to the fall of a Global Accounting Consultancy firm, Arthur Anderson and also led to the creation of Sarbanes-Oxley act 2002 to guard against such fraudulent corporate accounting practices in the US. This shows how greed, lack of ethics, manipulation of accounts and fraudulent managements can destroy the wealth of the society.

## Swiss Air

The formal National Airline of Switzerland, was once known as the 'Flying Bank' due its financial strength till it followed an aggressive loan backed acquisition strategy also known as the 'Hunter Strategy' in the late 1990s. The economic downturn that followed the September 2011, attack on the World Trade Centre, led to a severe drop in its turnover and profits, making it difficult to pay back the loans it had taken leading to operations becoming unsustainable and subsequent closure of the airlines on 31st March 2002.

## BPL Limited

BPL Limited, the promoter of BPL TV was the most admired company and a leader in the consumer electronics space in India with a market capitalization of over Rs 1300 crores. BPL had a rapidly growing portfolio of Consumer Electronics/Appliances products till the group diversified into Telecom and Power Generation business in the mid 1990s. Diversion of resources to other businesses from the core business and inability to feed its core businesses with requisite funds and also inability to raise funds due to stock market related issues, led to the downfall of BPL Limited. It not only lost market share rapidly, but also had to close down all its manufacturing facilities, sales & marketing operations and lost all its net worth.

## Subhiksha

Subhiksha was once the fastest growing retail chain in India with over 1600 retail outlets selling groceries, fruits & vegetables, medicines and mobile phones. Having grown rapidly in just 12 years of existence, Subhiksha had to shut its shop in 2009 owing to severe cash crunch stemming from financial mismanagement. Starting as a discount retailer and a price warrior, Subhiksha aimed to become a chain of Super Markets offering a shopping experience coupled with discount pricing to the consumers. This led to a dramatic increase in its working capital requirements as it rapidly expanded its outlet base across the country backing them with high decibel advertisement campaigns. Frequently changing business models, too fast an expansion without the backing of sufficient funds, lack of appropriate systems to handle growth and poor supplier and principal relations led to the downfall of the retailer, once hailed as a star on the Indian organized retail landscape.

## Global Trust Bank

Run by the eminently successful Ramesh Gelli, known as the super banker who was behind the success of Vysya Bank, GTB was once the darling of investors and account holders. One of the earliest new generations Private Sector Banks in India, GTB expanded its operations and grew rapidly till the early 2000s. It's over exposure to risky assets against the prevalent norms that crashed in value due to the economic downturn in early 2000s led to a rapid worsening of its financial health. It was forced to stop operations before being taken over by Oriental Bank of Commerce by the intervention of the RBI to protect the account holders. Its efforts to be taken over by Axis Bank failed when Axis Bank got a scent of the asset quality of GTB leaving it high and dry.

Chasing growth by throwing caution to winds, compromising on ethics and involving in malpractices, manipulation and dressing up of accounts, share price manipulation, excessive focus on providing return to promoters at the cost of depositors, minority shareholders and borrowers were considered to be the main contributors for the fall of the Global Trust Bank.

## Satyam Computers Ltd

Satyam Computer Services Ltd (Satyam) was once looked upon as the poster boy of Indian IT Outsourcing Industry and was ranked among the top 4 IT Companies of India. With more than one third of Fortune 500 companies as its clients, Satyam was one of the most admired companies from India. A command and control style of functioning by the promoters who showcased a galaxy of eminent persons as board members and a globally admired auditor in Price Waterhouse, led to the external world being completely oblivious to the happenings in the organization.

Underneath an image of respectability the company undertook massive window dressing of accounts, inflating the accounts consistently over a number of years, showing much higher sales and profits than actual figures thus defrauding the shareholders, investors and the media by lying about its actual performance. When the problems and real issues were coming to light, the promoter of Satyam Mr Ramalinga Raju admitted to fudging the accounts for several years and also about overstating the cash balances of the company by thousands of crores that were supported internally by duplicate demand drafts.

The problems came to the surface when Satyam wanted to merge with the real estate and infrastructure companies owned by the sons of Mr. Ramalinga Raju, Maytas Infrastructure and Maytas Properties, which led to suspicion & uproar in the investor fraternity and subsequent exposure of the fraud. Excessive promoter greed, diversion of promoter's interests into other areas like infrastructure, falling short on integrity and ethical approach, lack of internal controls and poor corporate governance led to the fall from grace of an enterprise and destruction of the shareholder value.

While these are the companies that have failed their investors, employees and the society, there are many companies that have failed to read the signals from the market place and were swept aside by the changing dynamics. The rapid loss of market shares of brands like Nokia and Blackberry, the flight to oblivion of brands like Ambassador, LML, Lambretta on the Indian roads, the bankruptcy in 2005 of Polaroid, the makers of Polaroid camera are a few examples of the companies unable to take corrective action in the right time to reinvent themselves and keep up their growth and profitability.

Most often, organizational failures happen when the managements are unable to forecast the changing situations that affect the fortunes of the company and take appropriate actions when it is very much in their realms to do so.

Failures can be arrested if the organizations:

- Stick to the core values and maintain their focus on adding value through their business
- Act on problems that may arise during the operations immediately with foresight
- Maintain ethical and transparent approach
- Be pro-active in guarding themselves against factors that destroy value like complacency and putting self-interests in front of their stakeholders and the society and
- Adhere to the very principles that have led them to success in the first place. If not, they are either wanting to fail or preparing for their failure

The early part of this century has gone into exploring the frontiers of a 'Solution Based Approach' to solving the customers' problems for gaining their business. While solution based selling is an evergreen concept, the greatest organizations of the 21st century are being rapidly built around their ability to unearth new & yet undiscovered needs of their target customers, creating a surge of requirement for newer experiences that take the world by storm and satisfying the same with breathtaking agility.

**The greatest good you can do for another is not to share your riches, but to reveal to him his own.**

*—Benjamin Disraeli*

Many companies discovered products and solutions that could potentially capture the imagination of users, a number of such companies could not capitalize on them, as they neither had the vision of what their invention/discovery could achieve in the long term, nor had the staying power including patience for sticking to the same till it caught on. For example, Xerox corporation was one of the first organizations to work on commercially developing the personal computer, but gave up the idea of scaling up the product in the early stages, which was capitalized by IBM & Apple. Hence the true credit and the fruits of these inventions have repeatedly gone to those, who have discovered the need of their target customers, for these potential blockbusters and fuelled

283

the demand so generated, by producing breathtaking products & solutions and propagating them with amazing speed and efficiency. Some of the finest examples of long-lasting organizations that have been created in front of our eyes are:

**MICROSOFT**—Discovered and fuelled the needs for a standard & smart operating system to power the growing number of personal computer in the world

**WALMART**—Discovered and fueled the need for a no frills—lowest priced economical solution of a huge majority of the customers

**INTEL**—Discovered and fuelled the need for faster and faster computing

**INFOSYS**—Discovered and fuelled the need for increasing productivity through outsourcing by high Cost-of-Living economies and the need for clients to focus on their core strengths to win their battles in the market

**GOOGLE**—Discovered and fuelled the needs of Information Hungry Internet Surfers

**NOKIA**—Discovered and fuelled the needs for a smarter, economical, signal and battery efficient mobile phones for users on the move

**APPLE**—Discovered and fuelled the need for a great user experience in technology product usage

**FACEBOOK**—Discovered and fuelled the need for a great Social Networking Platform for friends

**TWITTER**—Discovered and fuelled the need to express oneself to the world while on the move

**LINKEDIN**—Discovered and fuelled the need to have an online career profile to network with like minded professionals

**AMAZON**—Discovered and fuelled the need for quick, instantaneous and online purchases through e-commerce and then the emerging unlimited and flexible storage requirements by today's rapidly escalating memory needs of organizations

**CISCO**—Discovered and fuelled the needs of today's networked economies to create the networking infrastructure backbone

**DELL**-Discovered and fuelled the need for cutting the cost and configuring their own systems

**SAMSUNG**-Innovation in display technologies powering the TVs, Mobile Screens and Computer screens coupled with an urge to create faster, better and cheaper products in consumer technology domain

Apart from these, even companies like **Subway, McDonald and Starbucks** who have come about by creating an experience/unique need based approach are reinventing themselves to be able to read the trends and create their own markets. The list can include a number of more winning companies which have rapidly grown to grace the Fortune 500 list in a double quick time.

While there have been a few and far companies in the last century, which challenged the status quo and created new markets, this century is seeing a explosion of such companies which are not only creating fantastic unforeseen products and technologies but are also creating world scale capacities and capabilities to satisfy and service the demand so created.

When winning companies discover a potential blockbuster product/service that caters to an unearthed need, they just do not create a product or a service, but create a widespread eco-system that goes to create a medium in which their core proposition swims and multiplies.

When Apple created an iPhone, it rapidly grew iStore to satisfy the growing demand for legalized music by iPhone users. Similarly, when it created iPhone, it enabled an entire Application Development industry to create lakhs of applications that would engage its customers and enhance their experience.

A Brief Comparison on the 3 main approaches of marketing for organizations:

| FACTOR | PRODUCT/ SERVICE BASED APPROACH | SOLUTION BASED APPROACH | INSIGHT BASED APPROACH |
|---|---|---|---|
| Approach | A proactive approach without a clear customer focus. Create a product or service around core competence and try to fuel demand for the same. Based on own strengths and capabilities | A reactive approach Identify the customer problems and needs, ask questions to unearth possible solutions with end in mind. Arrive at a solution and keep fine-tuning till the client is satisfied. Network, integrate with partners as required to create an integrated solution to solve customer's problem. | A well-directed, strategized proactive approach. Study pain points not yet addressed, identify potential trends and demand fuelling situations (for example, rapid growth in technology usage leads to increased storage demand while the investments are limited and need to be optimized. Solution to solve customer's problem. |

| Customer Focus | Low. More focus on own interests than the requirements. Self-driven than market driven. More focus on Push than pull. | High. Focused on selected base of targeted customers. Customer Driven. Combinations of push & pull strategies with a fine balance between the two. | Very High, aimed at large segments of potential customers. Market driven & Customer Centric. Focus on creating massive customer pull |
|---|---|---|---|
| Attitude | Prescriptive | Analytical, Prescriptive & Incremental | Disruptive |
| Customer Engagement | Mostly after creating the product/service | During the period of engagement. | Before engagement with the customer and for the rest of the life time to come out with continuous upgrades |
| Customer Engagement | Mostly after creating the product/service | During the period of engagement. | Before engagement with the customer and for the rest of the life time to come out with continuous upgrades |
| Risk Involved | Medium. Build capacities as you grow or scrap project if not taking off. | Low. Higher chance of success than other strategies we are trading on a relative known path to solve discovered problems. | High. As apart from the need to hit the right button, the company also has to ward off potential competitors who can upstage in execution and incremental up-gradations. |

| Critical success factor | Economies of scale, Value for Money and an element of luck. | Customer relationships and close coordination with the markets, Analytical approach, Flexibility to adapt and consider wide alternatives and continuously fine-tune to hit the nail on the head and arrive at desirable end points. | Innovation, executive excellence & staying power. Proactive approach with eyes and ears not just focused on the market but also working along with the mind, other parts, brain and the other sense to create earthshaking solutions. |
|---|---|---|---|
| Relevance today | Limited | High. This is a minimum requirement for survival in today's customer driven markets. | Very high. A must strategy for the organizations aiming for success in the 21st century. |

How do the 21st century companies adopt the insight selling approach to stay ahead and create long lasting enterprises?

- Focus on the segments of the market generally populated by progressive customers who are looking for newer experiences and are willing to adapt to new paradigms quickly
- Challenge status quo and look for disruptive ways to solve existing products and dramatically improve the user experiences
- Focus on creating a good first impression with early adopters that snowballs into a much larger demand with positive feedback loops that makes it multiply through viral effects
- Make it easy for early adopters through low barriers for adoption like, free trials, introductory offers, reach out programs etc.

- Offer incentive programs to create a viral effect by rewarding those taking part in the buzz creation
- Focus on PR activities extensively instead of bombarding with advertisement campaigns till the volume scales up to support much larger promotional engagements. This will improve staying power without compromising the awareness creation programs. Focus on emotional and rational elements in communication rather than just being analytically and objectively persuasive
- Be obsessive about listening to customers and evolve the value proposition as the novelty will result in unforeseen glitches in the early stages of market creation
- Focus on customer education and concept selling through various channels as the more the customers know about the usage, the better it is for them to experience and spread the good word
- Communicate with an intention to create a pull rather than be seen as an obsessively aggressive sales promoter. Sometimes, companies create artificial scarcity as a strategy to create an excessively high-pressured demand funnel to develop, which will rocket the sales with a much higher surge.

A calculated and a balanced strategy with course correcting elements and an understanding that, great strategies fail to resurrect faulty product/service offerings, will enable organizations to create successful brands in the 21st century.

## INSPIRATIONAL BUSINESS QUOTES

1. I have not failed. I've just found 10,000 ways that won't work. — Thomas Edison
2. Logic will get you from A to B. Imagination will take you everywhere. — Albert Einstein
3. Coming together is a beginning. Keeping together is progress. Working together is success. — Henry Ford
4. Without continual growth and progress, such words as improvement, achievement, and success have no meaning. — Benjamin Franklin
5. No culture can live if it attempts to be exclusive. — Mahatma Gandhi
6. Live as if you were to die tomorrow. Learn as if you were to live forever. — Mahatma Gandhi
7. Strength does not come from physical capacity. It comes from an indomitable will. — Mahatma Gandhi
8. You can't ask customers what they want and then try to give that to them. By the time you get it built, they'll want something new. — Steve Jobs
9. Be a yardstick of quality. Some people aren't used to an environment where excellence is expected." — Steve Jobs
10. "I'm convinced that about half of what separates the successful entrepreneurs from the non — successful ones is pure perseverance. — Steve Jobs
11. High expectations are the key to everything." — Sam Walton
12. Your most unhappy customers are your greatest source of learning. — Bill Gates
13. Success is a lousy teacher. It seduces smart people into thinking they can't lose." — Bill Gates

14. My interest in life comes from setting myself huge, apparently unachievable challenges and trying to rise above them. — Richard Branson

15. If you do build a great experience, customers tell each other about that. Word of mouth is very powerful. — Jeff Bezos

16. "Your brand is what people say about you when you are not in the room." — Jeff Bezos

17. "When you innovate, you've got to be prepared for everyone telling you you're nuts." — Larry Ellison

18. Face reality as it is, not as it was or as you wish it to be. — Jack Welch

19. If you don't have a competitive advantage, don't compete. — Jack Welch

20. As long as you're going to be thinking anyway, think big. — Donald Trump

21. I don't know the key to success, but the key to failure is trying to please everybody. — Bill Cosby

22. The best way to predict the future is to create it. — Peter Drucker

23. The function of leadership is to produce more leaders, not more followers. — Ralph Nader

24. Don't just read the easy stuff. You may be entertained by it, but you will never grow from it. — Jim Rohn

25. Make your product easier to buy than your competition, or you will find your customers buying from them, not you. — Mark Cuban

26. In the modern world of business, it is useless to be a creative, original thinker unless you can also sell what you create. — David Ogilvy

27. It is always the start that requires the greatest effort. — James Cash Penney

28. I can accept failure, everyone fails at something. But I can't accept not trying. — Michael Jordan

29. If you are not willing to risk the unusual, you will have to settle for the ordinary. — Jim Rohn

30. The way to get started is to quit talking and begin doing. — Walt Disney

31. "The very first company I started failed with a great bang. The second one failed a little bit less, but still failed. The third one, you know, proper failed, but it was kind of okay. I recovered quickly. Number four almost didn't fail. It still didn't really feel great, but it did okay. Number five was PayPal."—Max Levchin, former CTO of PayPal

32. "So often people are working hard at the wrong thing. Working on the right thing is probably more important than working hard."—Caterina Fake, co—founder of Flickr

33. "Not having a clear goal leads to death by a thousand compromises"—Mark Pincus, founder of Zynga

34. "There is no luck, you work hard and study things intently. If you do that for long and hard enough you're successful."—Jason Calacanis, founder CEO of Mahalo.com

35. "Markets come and go. Good businesses don't.—Fred Wilson, co—founder of Union Square Venture

36. "We are really competing against ourselves. We have no control over how other people perform."—Pete Cashmore, founder of Mashable

Quotes of well known entrepreneurs/biz leaders like Steve Jobs, Edison, Jeff Bezos, Kack Welch etc . . .

| Sl. No | DOMAIN | ORGANIZATION | FOUNDED YEAR | COUNTRY | LOCATION | T/O LATEST KNOWN | NO OF EMPLOYEES |
|---|---|---|---|---|---|---|---|
| 1 | ENERGY | EXXON MOBIL | 1870 | USA | TEXAS | 486.50 | 83600 |
| 2 | ENERGY | ROYAL DUTCH SHELL PLC | 1907 | UK | LONDON | 470.00 | 90000 |
| 3 | RETAIL | WAL-MART STORES INC | 1962 | USA | ARKANSAS | 447.00 | 2200000 |
| 4 | ENERGY | BP PLC | 1909 | UK | LONDON | 386.50 | 79700 |
| 5 | ENERGY | CHEVRON | 1879 | USA | CALIFORNIA | 253.70 | 63000 |
| 6 | AUTOMOBILES | MITSUBISHI | 1870 | JAPAN | TOKYO | 250.00 | 350000 |
| 7 | AUTOMOBILES | TOYOTA MOTOR CORPORATION | 1937 | JAPAN | TOKYO | 230.00 | 325000 |
| 8 | AUTOMOBILES | VOLKSWAGEN AG | 1937 | GERMANY | WOLFSBURG | 200.00 | 369000 |
| 9 | AUTOMOBILES | GENERAL MOTOR COMPANY | 1908 | USA | DETROIT | 150.00 | 207000 |
| 10 | TECH-CONGLOMERATE | SAMSUNG ELECTRONICS | 1969 | SOUTH KOREA | SEOUL | 149.00 | 160000 |
| 11 | CONGLOMERATE | GENERAL ELECTRIC CO | 1892 | USA | CONNECTICUT | 147.00 | 301000 |
| 12 | FINANCE | BERKSHIRE HATHWAY INC | 1839 | USA | NEBRASKA | 144.00 | 260000 |
| 13 | RETAIL | CARREFOUR S.A. | 1957 | FRANCE | LEVALLOIS PERRET | 138.07 | 471755 |
| 14 | AUTOMOBILES | FORD MOTOR COMPANY | 1903 | USA | MICHIGAN | 136.00 | 164000 |

| Sl. No | DOMAIN | ORGANIZATION | FOUNDED YEAR | COUNTRY | LOCATION | T/O LATEST KNOWN | NO OF EMPLOYEES |
|---|---|---|---|---|---|---|---|
| 15 | AUTOMOBILES | DALMIER AG | 1883 | GERMANY | STUTTGART | 135.00 | 265000 |
| 16 | TECHNOLOGY | HEWLETT-PACKARD COMPANY | 1939 | USA | CALIFORNIA | 127.00 | 349600 |
| 17 | FINANCE | UBS AG | 1854 | SWITZERLAN | D BASEL & ZURICH | 47.00 | 64000 |
| 18 | PHARMA | BAYER AG | 1863 | GERMANY | LEVERKUSEN | 44.93 | 111800 |
| 19 | TELECOM | NOKIA CORP | 1865 | FINLAND | EXPOO | 47.54 | 122148 |
| 20 | FOOD INDUSTRY | NESTLE | 1867 | SWITZERLAN | D VEVEY | 84.73 | 328000 |
| 21 | FINANCE | GOLDMAN SACHS GROUP IN | C 1869 | USA | NEWYORK | 28.81 | 33300 |
| 22 | ENERGY | EXXON MOBIL | 1870 | USA | TEXAS | 486.50 | 83600 |
| 23 | AUTOMOBILES | MITSUBISHI | 1870 | JAPAN | TOKYO | 250.00 | 350000 |
| 24 | CONSULTING | KPMG | 1870 | NETHERLAND | S AMSTELVEEN | 22.70 | 145000 |
| 25 | FINANCE | JP MORGAN CHASE | 1871 | USA | NEWYORK | 90.00 | 260000 |
| 26 | TELECOM | ERICSSON | 1876 | SWEDEN | STOCKHOLM | 32.69 | 104525 |
| 27 | FMCG | HENKEL AG & CO | 1876 | GERMANY | DUSSELDORF | 19.20 | 47753 |
| 28 | ENERGY | CHEVRON | 1879 | USA | CALIFORNIA | 253.70 | 63000 |
| 29 | GARMENTS | PHILIPS VAN HEUSEN | 1881 | USA | MANHATTAN | 5.89 | 12000 |
| 30 | AUTOMOBILES | DALMIER AG | 1883 | GERMANY | STUTTGART | 135.00 | 265000 |
| 31 | METALS & MINING | BHO BILLITON | 1885 | AUSTRALIA | MELBOURNE | 71.70 | 40757 |
| 32 | PHARMA | JOHNSON & JOHNSON | 1886 | USA | NEWBURNSWICK | 65.00 | 117900 |
| 33 | FMCG | PROCTER & GAMBLE CO | 1837 | USA | CONNECTICUT | 82.55 | 129000 |
| 34 | TECH-CONGLOMERATE | TOSHIBA | 1939 | JAPAN | TOKYO | 81.51 | 212000 |

| Sl. No | DOMAIN | ORGANIZATION | FOUNDED YEAR | COUNTRY | LOCATION | T/O LATEST KNOWN | NO OF EMPLOYEES |
|---|---|---|---|---|---|---|---|
| 35 | TECH-CONGLOMERATE | SONY CORPORATION | 1946 | JAPAN | TOKYO | 80.58 | 162700 |
| 36 | FINANCE | AVIVA PLC | 2000 | UK | LONDON | 79.09 | 36600 |
| 37 | FINANCE | AIG INC | 1967 | USA | NEWYORK | 77.00 | 77000 |
| 38 | AUTOMOBILES | BMW | 1917 | GERMANY | MUNICH | 75.00 | 100306 |
| 39 | TELECOM | VODAFONE | 1991 | UK | LONDON | 71.76 | 83862 |
| 40 | METALS & MINING | BHO BILLITON | 1885 | AUSTRALIA | MELBOURNE | 71.70 | 40757 |
| 41 | TECHNOLOGY | MICROSOFT CORP | 1975 | USA | WASHINGTON | 69.94 | 90000 |
| 42 | RETAIL | TARGET CORP | 1902 | USA | MINNESOTA | 69.87 | 365000 |
| 43 | AVIATION | BOEING CO | 1916 | USA | CHICAGO | 69.00 | 165000 |
| 44 | RETAIL | HOME DEPOT | 1978 | USA | GEORGIA | 68.00 | 321000 |
| 45 | PHARMA | PFIZER INCORPORATED | 1849 | USA | NEWYORK | 67.00 | 103700 |
| 46 | FOOD INDUSTRY | PEPSICO | 1902 | USA | NEWYORK | 66.50 | 297000 |
| 47 | PETRO CHEM | RELIANCE INDUSTRIES LTD | 1966 | INDIA | MUMBAI | 66.18 | 23166 |
| 48 | FINANCE | CITIGROUP INC | 1812 | USA | NEWYORK | 66.00 | 266000 |
| 49 | PHARMA | JOHNSON & JOHNSON | 1886 | USA | NEWBURNSWICK | 65.00 | 117900 |
| 50 | TECHNOLOGY | DELL INC | 1984 | USA | TEXAS | 63.00 | 110000 |
| 51 | METALS & MINING | POSCO | 1968 | SOUTH KOREA | POHANG | 61.00 | 29648 |
| 52 | PHARMA | NOVARTIS INTERNATIONAL AG | 1996 | SWITZERLAND | BASEL | 58.57 | 119418 |
| 53 | TELECOM | ORANGE | 1994 | FRANCE | PARIS | 57.44 | 168694 |
| 54 | FMCG | UNILEVER | 1930 | UK | LONDON | 57.16 | 171000 |

| SI. No | DOMAIN | ORGANIZATION | FOUNDED YEAR | COUNTRY | LOCATION | T/O LATEST KNOWN | NO OF EMPLOYEES |
|---|---|---|---|---|---|---|---|
| 55 | TECHNOLOGY | FUJITSU | 1935 | JAPAN | TOKYO | 57.09 | 172336 |
| 56 | TELECOM | COMCAST | 1963 | USA | MISSISSIPPI | 56.00 | 126000 |
| 57 | AUTOMOBILES | CHRYSLER | 1925 | USA | MICHIGAN | 55.00 | 52000 |
| 58 | FOOD INDUSTRY | KRAFT FOODS INC | 1903 | USA | ILLINOIS | 54.37 | 126000 |
| 59 | TECHNOLOGY | INTEL CORP | 1968 | USA | CALIFORNIA | 54.00 | 100100 |
| 60 | TELECOM | NTT DOCOMO | 1991 | JAPAN | TOKYO | 53.85 | 22954 |
| 61 | AUTOMOBILES | RENAULT SA | 1899 | FRANCE | BoulogneBillancourt | 53.00 | 129000 |
| 62 | COURIER | UNITED PARCEL SERVICE INC | 1907 | USA | GEORGIA | 53.00 | 398300 |
| 63 | FINANCE | BARCLAYS PLC | 1690 | UK | LONDON | 50.37 | 146100 |
| 64 | AUTOMOBILES | FIAT SPA | 1899 | ITALY | TURIN | 50.00 | 138000 |
| 65 | TECH-CONGLOMERATE | LG ELECTRONICS | 1958 | SOUTH KOREA | SEOUL | 49.00 | 91000 |
| 66 | PHARMA | MERCK & CO | 1891 | USA | NEWJERSEY | 48.00 | 86000 |
| 67 | INTERNET | AMAZON.COM INC | 1994 | USA | WASHINGTON | 48.00 | 65000 |
| 68 | TELECOM | NOKIA CORP | 1865 | FINLAND | EXPOO | 47.54 | 122148 |
| 69 | FINANCE | UBS AG | 1854 | SWITZERLAND | BASEL & ZURICH | 47.00 | 64000 |
| 70 | FOOD INDUSTRY | THE COCA-COLA CO. | 1892 | USA | GEORGIA | 46.54 | 146200 |
| 71 | PHARMA | BAYER AG | 1863 | GERMANY | LEVERKUSEN | 44.93 | 111800 |
| 72 | CONSUMER ELECTRONICS | CANON INC | 1937 | JAPAN | TOKYO | 44.82 | 198307 |
| 73 | TECHNOLOGY | CISCO SYSTEMS INC | 1984 | USA | CALIFORNIA | 43.00 | 71025 |
| 74 | PHARMA | ROCHE LTD | 1896 | SWITZERLAND | BASEL | 42.96 | 80129 |

| Sl. No | DOMAIN | ORGANIZATION | FOUNDED YEAR | COUNTRY | LOCATION | T/O LATEST KNOWN | NO OF EMPLOYEES |
|---|---|---|---|---|---|---|---|
| 75 | PHARMA | GLAXO SMITHKLINE PLC | 1904 | UK | LONDON | 42.73 | 96500 |
| 76 | MEDIA | WALT DISNEY & COMPANY | 1923 | USA | CALIFORNIA | 41.00 | 156000 |
| 77 | AVIATION | AIRBUS | 1970 | FRANCE | Blagnac | 40.71 | 63000 |
| 78 | COURIER | FEDEX CORP | 1971 | USA | MEMPHIS | 39.30 | 290000 |
| 79 | Technology | QUANTA COMPUTER | 1988 | TAIWAN | TAIPEI | 38.00 | 60000 |
| 80 | INTERNET | GOOGLE INC | 1998 | USA | CALIFORNIA | 38.00 | 55000 |
| 81 | TECHNOLOGY | ORACLE CORP | 1977 | USA | CALIFORNIA | 37.00 | 115166 |
| 82 | MEDIA | VIVENDI | 1853 | FRANCE | PARIS | 35.42 | 58000 |
| 83 | AVIATION | LUFTHANSA AG | 1926 | GERMANY | COLOGNE | 35.00 | 117000 |
| 84 | AUTOMOBILES | TATA MOTORS | 1945 | INDIA | PUNE | 35.00 | 60000 |
| 85 | FINANCE | NEW YORK LIFE INSURANCE CO. | 1845 | USA | NEW YORK | 34.95 | 12650 |
| 86 | MEDIA | NEWS CORP | 1979 | USA | NEWYORK | 33.00 | 51000 |
| 87 | TELECOM | ERICSSON | 1876 | SWEDEN | STOCKHOLM | 32.69 | 104525 |
| 88 | AUTOMOBILES | SUZUKI MOTOR CORP | 1909 | JAPAN | SHIZUOKA | 32.00 | 52000 |
| 89 | CONSUMER ELECTRONICS | PHILIPS | 1891 | NETHERLANDS | AMSTERDAM | 31.27 | 114500 |
| 90 | FINANCE | AMERICAN EXPRESS CO | 1850 | USA | NEWYORK | 30.00 | 62500 |
| 91 | RETAIL | IKEA | 1943 | SWEDEN | SMALAND | 29.15 | 127000 |
| 92 | CONSULTING | PRICE WATER HOUSE COOPERS | 1849 | UK | LONDON | 29.00 | 169000 |
| 93 | MEDIA | TIME WARNER | 1990 | USA | MANHATTAN | 29.00 | 34000 |

| Sl. No | DOMAIN | ORGANIZATION | FOUNDED YEAR | COUNTRY | LOCATION | T/O LATEST KNOWN | NO OF EMPLOYEES |
|---|---|---|---|---|---|---|---|
| 94 | FINANCE | GOLDMAN SACHS GROUP INC | 1869 | USA | NEWYORK | 28.81 | 33300 |
| 95 | CONSULTING | DELOITTE & TOUCHE | 1845 | UK | LONDON | 28.80 | 182000 |
| 96 | METALS | TATA STEEL | 1907 | INDIA | MUMBAI | 27.70 | 81622 |
| 97 | CONSULTING | ACCENTURE PLC | 1953 | IRELAND | DUBLIN | 27.35 | 251000 |
| 98 | TELECOM | TELSTRA | 1975 | AUSTRALIA | MELBOURNE | 26.03 | 35790 |
| 99 | FOOD INDUSTRY | MC DONALD'S | 1940 | USA | CALIFORNIA | 24.00 | 400000 |
| 100 | CONSULTING | ERNST & YOUNG | 1849 | UK | LONDON | 22.90 | 152000 |
| 101 | CONSULTING | KPMG | 1870 | NETHERLANDS | AMSTELVEEN | 22.70 | 145000 |
| 102 | TECHNOLOGY | XEROX | 1906 | USA | NEWYORK | 22.62 | 139650 |
| 103 | TECHNOLOGY | LENOVO | 1984 | CHINA | BEIJING | 21.60 | 26341 |
| 104 | CONGLOMERATE | VIRGIN GROUP LIMITED | 1970 | UK | LONDON | 21.30 | 50000 |
| 105 | GARMENTS | NIKE INC | 1964 | USA | WASHINGTON | 20.86 | 38000 |
| 106 | FMCG | LOREAL GROUP | 1909 | FRANCE | HAUTS-DE-SEIN | E 19.95 | 66620 |
| 107 | MEDICAL EQUIPMENT | FRESENIUS | 1912 | GERMANY | BAD HOMBURG | 19.64 | 137552 |
| 108 | FMCG | HENKEL AG & CO | 1876 | GERMANY | DUSSELDORF | 19.20 | 47753 |
| 109 | CONSUMER ELECTRONICS | WHIRLPOOL | 1911 | USA | MICHIGAN | 18.34 | 71000 |
| 110 | FOOD INDUSTRY | SUBWAY | 1965 | USA | CONNECTICUT | 18.00 | 234000 |
| 111 | TECHNOLOGY | SAP | 1972 | GERMANY | Weinheim | 17.26 | 59420 |
| 112 | FMCG | COLGATE PALMOLIVE CO | 1806 | USA | NEWYORK | 16.72 | 39200 |
| 113 | CONGLOMERATE | YAMAHA | 1887 | JAPAN | SHIZUOKA | 16.00 | 51474 |

| Sl. No | DOMAIN | ORGANIZATION | FOUNDED YEAR | COUNTRY | LOCATION | T/O LATEST KNOWN | NO OF EMPLOYEES |
|---|---|---|---|---|---|---|---|
| 114 | AVIATION | QANTAS AIRWAYS LTD | 1920 | AUSTRALIA | SYDNEY | 16.00 | 33000 |
| 115 | AVIATION | BRITISH AIRWAYS PLC | 1974 | ENGLAND | LONDON | 15.44 | 57000 |
| 116 | TELECOM | ALCATEL–LUCENT | 1898 | FRANCE | PARIS | 15.42 | 76000 |
| 117 | MEDIA | VIACOM | 1971 | USA | NEWJERSEY | 15.00 | 10580 |
| 118 | TELECOM | QUALCOMM | 1985 | USA | CALIFORNIA | 15.00 | 17500 |
| 119 | GARMENTS | ADIDAS AG | 1924 | GERMANY | HERZOGENAURACH | 14.75 | 42540 |
| 120 | AVIATION | EMIRATES | 1985 | UAE | DUBAI | 14.69 | 39000 |
| 121 | CONSUMER ELECTRONICS | ELECTROLUX GROUP | 1919 | SWEDEN | STOCKHOLM | 14.63 | 52916 |
| 122 | METALS | HINDALCO | 1958 | INDIA | MUMBAI | 14.38 | 19341 |
| 123 | FINANCE | ICICI BANK | 1955 | INDIA | MUMBAI | 13.81 | 80000 |
| 124 | FOOD INDUSTRY | STARBUCKS | 1971 | USA | SEATTLE | 11.70 | 37000 |
| 125 | INTERNET | EBAY INC | 1995 | USA | CALIFORNIA | 11.65 | 27770 |
| 126 | AVIATION | CATHAY PACIFIC | 1946 | CHINA | HONGKONG | 11.57 | 29000 |
| 127 | METALS | VEDANTA RESOURCES PLC | 1976 | UK | LONDON | 11.42 | 31171 |
| 128 | AVIATION | SINGAPORE AIRLINES | 1947 | SINGAPORE | SINGAPORE | 11.20 | 13500 |
| 129 | FMCG-NETWORK | AMWAY CORP | 1959 | USA | MICHIGAN | 10.90 | 20000 |
| 130 | FMCG | SARA LEE CORP | 1939 | USA | ILLINOIS | 10.80 | 33000 |
| 131 | INFRASTRUCTURE | LARSEN & TOUBRO | 1938 | INDIA | MUMBAI | 10.00 | 45117 |
| 132 | TELECOM | BHARTI AIRTEL | 1995 | INDIA | DELHI | 10.00 | 20500 |
| 133 | FOOD INDUSTRY | KFC CORP | 1930 | USA | KENTUCKY | 9.20 | 455000 |
| 134 | TECHNOLOGY | TCS | 1968 | INDIA | MUMBAI | 8.89 | 243545 |

| Sl. No | DOMAIN | ORGANIZATION | FOUNDED YEAR | COUNTRY | LOCATION | T/O LATEST KNOWN | NO OF EMPLOYEES |
|---|---|---|---|---|---|---|---|
| 135 | FOOD INDUSTRY | CADBURY PLC | 1824 | UK | LONDON | 8.40 | 71657 |
| 136 | TELECOM | MOTOROLA CORP | 1928 | USA | ILLINOIS | 8.20 | 23000 |
| 137 | FINANCE | VISA INC | 1970 | USA | CALIFORNIA | 8.00 | 6900 |
| 138 | EYEWEAR | LUXOTTICA | 1961 | ITALY | MILAN | 7.65 | 65611 |
| 139 | AUTOMOBILES | MAHINDRA & MAHINDRA | 1945 | INDIA | MUMBAI | 7.40 | 15500 |
| 140 | TECHNOLOGY | WIPRO | 1945 | INDIA | BANGALORE | 7.30 | 135920 |
| 141 | CONSULTING | MCKINSEY | 1926 | USA | CHICAGO | 7.00 | 17000 |
| 142 | TECHNOLOGY | INFOSYS | 1981 | INDIA | BANGALORE | 7.00 | 151151 |
| 143 | FMCG | ITC LTD | 1910 | INDIA | KOLKATTA | 6.43 | 24027 |
| 144 | TECHNOLOGY | COGNIZANT TECHNOLOGY | 1994 | USA | NEWJERSEY | 6.12 | 140500 |
| 145 | GARMENTS | PHILIPS VAN HEUSEN | 1881 | USA | MANHATTAN | 5.89 | 12000 |
| 146 | FINANCE | HDFC BANK | 1994 | INDIA | MUMBAI | 5.60 | 55752 |
| 147 | FINANCE | MASTERCARD WORLDWIDE | 1966 | USA | NEWYORK | 5.50 | 5600 |
| 148 | AUTOMOBILES | HARLEY DAVIDSON | 1903 | USA | MILWAUKEE | 5.30 | 6000 |
| 149 | ENERGY | SUZLON ENERGY | 1995 | INDIA | PUNE | 5.25 | 15000 |
| 150 | INTERNET | YAHOO! INC | 1995 | USA | CALIFORNIA | 5.00 | 14100 |

# APPENDIX 2

# OVER 100 YEARS OLD & THRIVING

| Sl. No | DOMAIN | ORGANIZATION | FOUNDED YEAR | COUNTRY | LOCATION | T/O LATEST KNOWN | NO OF EMPLOYEES |
|---|---|---|---|---|---|---|---|
| 1 | FINANCE | BARCLAYS PLC | 1690 | UK | LONDON | 50.37 | 146100 |
| 2 | FMCG | COLGATE PALMOLIVE CO | 1806 | USA | NEWYORK | 16.72 | 39200 |
| 3 | FINANCE | CITIGROUP INC | 1812 | USA | NEWYORK | 66.00 | 266000 |
| 4 | FOOD INDUSTRY | CADBURY PLC | 1824 | UK | LONDON | 8.40 | 71657 |
| 5 | FMCG | PROCTER & GAMBLE CO | 1837 | USA | CONNECTICUT | 82.55 | 129000 |
| 6 | FINANCE | BERKSHIRE HATHWAY INC | 1839 | USA | NEBRASKA | 144.00 | 260000 |
| 7 | FINANCE | NEW YORK LIFE INSURANCE CO. | 1845 | USA | NEW YORK | 34.95 | 12650 |
| 8 | CONSULTING | DELOITTE & TOUCHE | 1845 | UK | LONDON | 28.80 | 182000 |
| 9 | TECH-CONGLOMERATE | SIEMENS | 1847 | GERMANY | BERLIN/ MUNICH | 90.41 | 360000 |
| 10 | PHARMA | PFIZER INCORPORATED | 1849 | USA | NEWYORK | 67.00 | 103700 |
| 11 | CONSULTING | PRICE WATER HOUSE COOPERS | 1849 | UK | LONDON | 29.00 | 169000 |
| 12 | CONSULTING | ERNST & YOUNG | 1849 | UK | LONDON | 22.90 | 152000 |
| 13 | FINANCE | AMERICAN EXPRESS CO | 1850 | USA | NEWYORK | 30.00 | 62500 |
| 14 | MEDIA | VIVENDI | 1853 | FRANCE | PARIS | 35.42 | 58000 |
| 15 | GARMENTS | LEVI STRAUSS & CO | 1853 | USA | SANFRANCISCO | 4.40 | 16200 |
| 16 | EYECARE | BAUSCH & LOMB | 1853 | USA | NEWYORK | 2.51 | 13000 |
| 17 | FINANCE | UBS AG | 1854 | SWITZERLAN | D BASEL & ZURICH | 47.00 | 64000 |

| Sl. No | DOMAIN | ORGANIZATION | FOUNDED YEAR | COUNTRY | LOCATION | T/O LATEST KNOWN | NO OF EMPLOYEES |
|---|---|---|---|---|---|---|---|
| 18 | PHARMA | BAYER AG | 1863 | GERMANY | LEVERKUSEN | 44.93 | 111800 |
| 19 | TELECOM | NOKIA CORP | 1865 | FINLAND | EXPOO | 47.54 | 122148 |
| 20 | FOOD INDUSTRY | NESTLE | 1867 | SWITZERLAN | D VEVEY | 84.73 | 328000 |
| 21 | FINANCE | GOLDMAN SACHS GROUP IN | C 1869 | USA | NEWYORK | 28.81 | 33300 |
| 22 | ENERGY | EXXON MOBIL | 1870 | USA | TEXAS | 486.50 | 83600 |
| 23 | AUTOMOBILES | MITSUBISHI | 1870 | JAPAN | TOKYO | 250.00 | 350000 |
| 24 | CONSULTING | KPMG | 1870 | NETHERLAND | S AMSTELVEEN | 22.70 | 145000 |
| 25 | FINANCE | JP MORGAN CHASE | 1871 | USA | NEWYORK | 90.00 | 260000 |
| 26 | TELECOM | ERICSSON | 1876 | SWEDEN | STOCKHOLM | 32.69 | 104525 |
| 27 | FMCG | HENKEL AG & CO | 1876 | GERMANY | DUSSELDORF | 19.20 | 47753 |
| 28 | ENERGY | CHEVRON | 1879 | USA | CALIFORNIA | 253.70 | 63000 |
| 29 | GARMENTS | PHILIPS VAN HEUSEN | 1881 | USA | MANHATTAN | 5.89 | 12000 |
| 30 | AUTOMOBILES | DALMIER AG | 1883 | GERMANY | STUTTGART | 135.00 | 265000 |
| 31 | METALS & MINING | BHO BILLITON | 1885 | AUSTRALIA | MELBOURNE | 71.70 | 40757 |
| 32 | PHARMA | JOHNSON & JOHNSON | 1886 | USA | NEWBURNSWICK | 65.00 | 117900 |
| 33 | CONGLOMERATE | YAMAHA | 1887 | JAPAN | SHIZUOKA | 16.00 | 51474 |
| 34 | INFRASTRUCTURE | THYSSEN KRUPP | 1891 | GERMANY | ESSEN | 53.33 | 180050 |
| 35 | PHARMA | MERCK & CO | 1891 | USA | NEWJERSEY | 48.00 | 86000 |
| 36 | CONSUMER ELECTRONICS | PHILIPS | 1891 | NETHERLAND | S AMSTERDAM | 31.27 | 114500 |
| 37 | CONGLOMERATE | GENERAL ELECTRIC CO | 1892 | USA | CONNECTICUT | 147.00 | 301000 |
| 38 | FOOD INDUSTRY | THE COCA-COLA CO. | 1892 | USA | GEORGIA | 46.54 | 146200 |

| Sl. No | DOMAIN | ORGANIZATION | FOUNDED YEAR | COUNTRY | LOCATION | T/O LATEST KNOWN | NO OF EMPLOYEES |
|---|---|---|---|---|---|---|---|
| 39 | FINANCE-GOVT OWNED | PUNJAB NATIONAL BANK | 1895 | INDIA | MUMBAI | 6.59 | 57000 |
| 40 | PHARMA | ROCHE LTD | 1896 | SWITZERLAN | D BASEL | 42.96 | 80129 |
| 41 | TELECOM | ALCATEL-LUCENT | 1898 | FRANCE | PARIS | 15.42 | 76000 |
| 42 | AUTOMOBILES | RENAULT SA | 1899 | FRANCE | BoulogneBillancourt | 53.00 | 129000 |
| 43 | AUTOMOBILES | FIAT SPA | 1899 | ITALY | TURIN | 50.00 | 138000 |
| 44 | RETAIL | TARGET CORP | 1902 | USA | MINNESOTA | 69.87 | 365000 |
| 45 | FOOD INDUSTRY | PEPSICO | 1902 | USA | NEWYORK | 66.50 | 297000 |
| 46 | AUTOMOBILES | FORD MOTOR COMPANY | 1903 | USA | MICHIGAN | 136.00 | 164000 |
| 47 | FOOD INDUSTRY | KRAFT FOODS INC | 1903 | USA | ILLINOIS | 54.37 | 126000 |
| 48 | AUTOMOBILES | HARLEY DAVIDSON | 1903 | USA | MILWAUKEE | 5.30 | 6000 |
| 49 | PHARMA | GLAXO SMITHKLINE PLC | 1904 | UK | LONDON | 42.73 | 96500 |
| 50 | TECHNOLOGY | XEROX | 1906 | USA | NEWYORK | 22.62 | 139650 |
| 51 | FINANCE-GOVT OWNED | CANARA BANK | 1906 | INDIA | BANGALORE | 4.67 | 44450 |
| 52 | ENERGY | ROYAL DUTCH SHELL PLC | 1907 | UK | LONDON | 470.00 | 90000 |
| 53 | COURIER | UNITED PARCEL SERVICE INC | 1907 | USA | GEORGIA | 53.00 | 398300 |
| 54 | METALS | TATA STEEL | 1907 | INDIA | MUMBAI | 27.70 | 81622 |
| 55 | AUTOMOBILES | GENERAL MOTOR COMPANY | 1908 | USA | DETROIT | 150.00 | 207000 |
| 56 | ENERGY | BP PLC | 1909 | UK | LONDON | 386.50 | 79700 |
| 57 | AUTOMOBILES | SUZUKI MOTOR CORP | 1909 | JAPAN | SHIZUOKA | 32.00 | 52000 |
| 58 | FMCG | LOREAL GROUP | 1909 | FRANCE | HAUTS-DE-SEINE | 19.95 | 66620 |
| 59 | TECH-CONGLOMERATE | HITACHI | 1910 | JAPAN | TOKYO | 123.52 | 372360 |

| Sl. No | DOMAIN | ORGANIZATION | FOUNDED YEAR | COUNTRY | LOCATION | T/O LATEST KNOWN | NO OF EMPLOYEES |
|--------|--------|--------------|--------------|---------|----------|------------------|-----------------|
| 60 | FMCG | ITC LTD | 1910 | INDIA | KOLKATTA | 6.43 | 24027 |
| 61 | TECHNOLOGY | IBM | 1911 | USA | NEWYORK | 107.00 | 433362 |
| 62 | CONSUMER ELECTRONICS | WHIRLPOOL | 1911 | USA | MICHIGAN | 18.34 | 71000 |
| 63 | CONSUMER ELECTRONICS | SHARP CORPORATION | 1912 | JAPAN | TOKYO | 31.37 | 57200 |
| 64 | MEDICAL EQUIPMENT | FRESENIUS | 1912 | GERMANY | BAD HOMBURG | 19.64 | 137552 |

# WORLD'S FINEST BILLION DOLLAR ORGANIZATIONS

# APPENDIX 3

| Sl. No | DOMAIN | ORGANIZATION | FOUNDED YEAR | COUNTRY | LOCATION | T/O LATEST KNOWN | NO OF EMPLOYEES |
|---|---|---|---|---|---|---|---|
| 1 | TECH-CONGLOMERATE | SAMSUNG ELECTRONICS | 1969 | SOUTH KOREA | SEOUL | 149.00 | 160000 |
| 2 | TECHNOLOGY | HEWLETT-PACKARD COMPANY | 1939 | USA | CALIFORNIA | 127.00 | 349600 |
| 3 | TELECOM | AT&T INC | 1983 | USA | TEXAS | 127.00 | 256420 |
| 4 | TECH-CONGLOMERATE | HITACHI | 1910 | JAPAN | TOKYO | 123.52 | 372360 |
| 5 | TELECOM | VERIZON | 1983 | USA | NEWYORK | 110.00 | 188200 |
| 6 | TECHNOLOGY | APPLE INC | 1976 | USA | CALIFORNIA | 108.25 | 60400 |
| 7 | TECHNOLOGY | IBM | 1911 | USA | NEWYORK | 107.00 | 433362 |
| 8 | CONSUMER ELECTRONICS | PANASONIC | 1918 | JAPAN | OSAKA | 99.96 | 330767 |
| 9 | TECH-CONGLOMERATE | SIEMENS | 1847 | GERMANY | BERLIN/MUNICH | 90.41 | 360000 |
| 10 | TECH-CONGLOMERATE | TOSHIBA | 1939 | JAPAN | TOKYO | 81.51 | 212000 |
| 11 | TECH-CONGLOMERATE | SONY CORPORATION | 1946 | JAPAN | TOKYO | 80.58 | 162700 |
| 12 | TELECOM | VODAFONE | 1991 | UK | LONDON | 71.76 | 83862 |
| 13 | TECHNOLOGY | MICROSOFT CORP | 1975 | USA | WASHINGTON | 69.94 | 90000 |
| 14 | TECHNOLOGY | DELL INC | 1984 | USA | TEXAS | 63.00 | 110000 |
| 15 | TELECOM | ORANGE | 1994 | FRANCE | PARIS | 57.44 | 168694 |
| 16 | TECHNOLOGY | FUJITSU | 1935 | JAPAN | TOKYO | 57.09 | 172336 |

| Sl. No | DOMAIN | ORGANIZATION | FOUNDED YEAR | COUNTRY | LOCATION | T/O LATEST KNOWN | NO OF EMPLOYEES |
|---|---|---|---|---|---|---|---|
| 17 | TECHNOLOGY | INTEL CORP | 1968 | USA | CALIFORNIA | 54.00 | 100100 |
| 18 | TELECOM | NTT DOCOMO | 1991 | JAPAN | TOKYO | 53.85 | 22954 |
| 19 | TECH-CONGLOMERATE | LG ELECTRONICS | 1958 | SOUTH KOREA | SEOUL | 49.00 | 91000 |
| 20 | INTERNET | AMAZON.COM INC | 1994 | USA | WASHINGTON | 48.00 | 65000 |
| 21 | TELECOM | NOKIA CORP | 1865 | FINLAND | EXPOO | 47.54 | 122148 |
| 22 | CONSUMER ELECTRONICS | CANON INC | 1937 | JAPAN | TOKYO | 44.82 | 198307 |
| 23 | TECHNOLOGY | CISCO SYSTEMS INC | 1984 | USA | CALIFORNIA | 43.00 | 71025 |
| 24 | INTERNET | GOOGLE INC | 1998 | USA | CALIFORNIA | 38.00 | 55000 |
| 25 | TECHNOLOGY | ORACLE CORP | 1977 | USA | CALIFORNIA | 37.00 | 115166 |
| 26 | TELECOM | ERICSSON | 1876 | SWEDEN | STOCKHOLM | 32.69 | 104525 |
| 27 | CONSUMER ELECTRONICS | SHARP CORPORATION | 1912 | JAPAN | TOKYO | 31.37 | 57200 |
| 28 | CONSUMER ELECTRONICS | PHILIPS | 1891 | NETHERLANDS | AMSTERDAM | 31.27 | 114500 |
| 29 | TELECOM | TELSTRA | 1975 | AUSTRALIA | MELBOURNE | 26.03 | 35790 |
| 30 | TECHNOLOGY | XEROX | 1906 | USA | NEWYORK | 22.62 | 139650 |
| 31 | TECHNOLOGY | LENOVO | 1984 | INDIA | BEIJING | 21.60 | 26341 |
| 32 | CONSUMER ELECTRONICS | WHIRLPOOL | 1911 | USA | MICHIGAN | 18.34 | 71000 |
| 33 | TECHNOLOGY | SAP | 1972 | GERMANY | Weinheim | 17.26 | 59420 |
| 34 | TELECOM | ALCATEL-LUCENT | 1898 | FRANCE | PARIS | 15.42 | 76000 |
| 35 | TELECOM | QUALCOMM | 1985 | USA | CALIFORNIA | 15.00 | 17500 |

| SI. No | DOMAIN | ORGANIZATION | FOUNDED YEAR | COUNTRY | LOCATION | T/O LATEST KNOWN | NO OF EMPLOYEES |
|---|---|---|---|---|---|---|---|
| 36 | CONSUMER ELECTRONICS | ELECTROLUX GROUP | 1919 | SWEDEN | STOCKHOLM | 14.63 | 52916 |
| 37 | INTERNET | EBAY INC | 1995 | USA | CALIFORNIA | 11.65 | 27770 |
| 38 | TELECOM | BHARTI AIRTEL | 1995 | INDIA | DELHI | 10.00 | 20500 |
| 39 | TECHNOLOGY | TCS | 1968 | INDIA | MUMBAI | 8.89 | 243545 |
| 40 | TELECOM | MOTOROLA CORP | 1928 | USA | ILLINOIS | 8.20 | 23000 |
| 41 | TECHNOLOGY | WIPRO | 1945 | INDIA | BANGALORE | 7.30 | 135920 |
| 42 | TECHNOLOGY | INFOSYS | 1981 | INDIA | BANGALORE | 7.00 | 151151 |
| 43 | TECHNOLOGY | COGNIZANT TECHNOLOGY | 1994 | USA | NEWJERSEY | 6.12 | 140500 |
| 44 | TECHNOLOGY | HCL TECHNOLOGIES | 1991 | INDIA | NOIDA | 3.83 | 82464 |
| 45 | INTERNET | YAHOO! INC | 1995 | USA | CALIFORNIA | 4.98 | 14100 |
| 46 | TELECOM | RELIANCE COMMUNICATIONS | 2004 | INDIA | MUMBAI | 4.54 | 20000 |
| 47 | TECHNOLOGY | ADOBE SYSTEMS | 1982 | USA | SANJOSE | 4.21 | 9925 |
| 48 | CONSUMER ELECTRONICS | VIDEOCON | 1979 | INDIA | AURANGABAD | 4.00 | 50000 |
| 49 | INTERNET | FACEBOOK | 2004 | USA | CALIFORNIA | 3.71 | 3200 |
| 50 | TELECOM | IDEA CELLULAR | 1995 | INDIA | MUMBAI | 3.07 | 6500 |
| 51 | TECHNOLOGY | TECH MAHINDRA | 1986 | INDIA | PUNE | 1.06 | 42746 |
| 52 | INTERNET | LINKEDIN | 2006 | USA | CALIFORNIA | 0.52 | 2447 |
| | | | | | | 2273.97 | 6080011 |

# WORLD'S FINEST BILLION DOLLAR ORGANIZATIONS

# APPENDIX 4

| Sl. No | DOMAIN | ORGANIZATION | FOUNDED YEAR | COUNTRY | LOCATION | T/O LATEST KNOWN | NO OF EMPLOYEES |
|--------|--------|--------------|--------------|---------|----------|------------------|-----------------|
| 1 | TELECOM | AT&T INC | 1983 | USA | TEXAS | 127.00 | 256420 |
| 2 | FINANCE | BANK OF AMERICA CORP | 1998 | USA | NORTH CAROLINA | 115.00 | 282000 |
| 3 | TELECOM | VERIZON | 1983 | USA | NEWYORK | 110.00 | 188200 |
| 4 | FINANCE | HSBC HOLDINGS PLC | 1991 | UK | LONDON | 105.80 | 285000 |
| 5 | RETAIL | COSTCO | 1983 | USA | WASHINGTON | 89.00 | 147000 |
| 6 | FINANCE | AVIVA PLC | 2000 | UK | LONDON | 79.09 | 36600 |
| 7 | TELECOM | VODAFONE | 1991 | UK | LONDON | 71.76 | 83362 |
| 8 | TECHNOLOGY | DELL INC | 1984 | USA | TEXAS | 63.00 | 110000 |
| 9 | PHARMA | NOVARTIS INTERNATIONAL AG | 1996 | SWITZERLAND | BASEL | 58.57 | 119418 |
| 10 | TELECOM | ORANGE | 1994 | FRANCE | PARIS | 57.44 | 168694 |
| 11 | TELECOM | NTT DOCOMO | 1991 | JAPAN | TOKYO | 53.85 | 22954 |
| 12 | INTERNET | AMAZON.COM INC | 1994 | USA | WASHINGTON | 48.00 | 65000 |
| 13 | TECHNOLOGY | CISCO SYSTEMS INC | 1984 | USA | CALIFORNIA | 43.00 | 71025 |
| 14 | INTERNET | GOOGLE INC | 1998 | USA | CALIFORNIA | 38.00 | 55000 |
| 15 | Technology | QUANTA COMPUTER | 1988 | TAIWAN | TAIPEI | 38.00 | 60000 |
| 16 | MEDIA | TIME WARNER | 1990 | USA | MANHATTAN | 29.00 | 34000 |
| 17 | TECHNOLOGY | LENOVO | 1984 | CHINA | BEIJING | 21.60 | 26341 |

| Sl. No | DOMAIN | ORGANIZATION | FOUNDED YEAR | COUNTRY | LOCATION | T/O LATEST KNOWN | NO OF EMPLOYEES |
|---|---|---|---|---|---|---|---|
| 18 | TELECOM | QUALCOMM | 1985 | USA | CALIFORNIA | 15.00 | 17500 |
| 19 | AVIATION | EMIRATES | 1985 | UAE | DUBAI | 14.69 | 39000 |
| 20 | INTERNET | EBAY INC | 1995 | USA | CALIFORNIA | 11.65 | 27770 |
| 21 | TELECOM | BHARTI AIRTEL | 1995 | INDIA | DELHI | 10.00 | 20500 |
| 22 | AUTOMOBILES | MARUTHI SUZUKI | 1982 | INDIA | DELHI | 7.50 | 7000 |
| 23 | TECHNOLOGY | INFOSYS | 1981 | INDIA | BANGALORE | 7.00 | 151151 |
| 24 | TECHNOLOGY | HCL TECHNOLOGIES | 1991 | INDIA | NOIDA | 3.83 | 82464 |
| 25 | TECHNOLOGY | COGNIZANT TECHNOLOGY | 1994 | USA | NEWJERSEY | 6.12 | 140500 |
| 26 | FINANCE | HDFC BANK | 1994 | INDIA | MUMBAI | 5.60 | 55752 |
| 27 | ENERGY | SUZLON ENERGY | 1995 | INDIA | PUNE | 5.25 | 15000 |
| 28 | INTERNET | YAHOO! INC | 1995 | USA | CALIFORNIA | 4.98 | 14100 |
| 29 | TELECOM | RELIANCE COMMUNICATIONS | 2004 | INDIA | MUMBAI | 4.54 | 20000 |
| 30 | TECHNOLOGY | ADOBE SYSTEMS | 1982 | USA | SANJOSE | 4.21 | 9925 |
| 31 | INTERNET | FACEBOOK | 2004 | USA | CALIFORNIA | 3.71 | 3200 |
| 32 | FINANCE | AXIS BANK | 1995 | INDIA | MUMBAI | 3.60 | 21640 |
| 33 | TELECOM | IDEA CELLULAR | 1995 | INDIA | MUMBAI | 3.07 | 6500 |
| 34 | AVIATION | JET AIRWAYS | 1992 | INDIA | MUMBAI | 2.90 | 15000 |
| 35 | INFRASTRUCTURE | RELIANCE INFRASTRUCTURE | 2002 | INDIA | MUMBAI | 2.80 | 8988 |
| 36 | PHARMA | DR REDDY'S LABS | 1984 | INDIA | HYDERABAD | 2.10 | 14923 |
| 37 | RETAIL DIVERSIFIED | TITAN | 1987 | INDIA | CHENNAI | 1.30 | 3000 |

| SI. No | DOMAIN | ORGANIZATION | FOUNDED YEAR | COUNTRY | LOCATION | T/O LATEST KNOWN | NO OF EMPLOYEES |
|--------|--------|--------------|--------------|---------|----------|------------------|-----------------|
| 38 | RETAIL | SHOPPERS STOP | 1991 | INDIA | MUMBAI | 1.10 | 14000 |
| 39 | TECHNOLOGY | TECH MAHINDRA | 1986 | INDIA | PUNE | 1.06 | 42746 |

# WORLD'S FINEST BILLION DOLLAR ORGANIZATIONS

## APPENDIX 5

| Sl. No | DOMAIN | ORGANIZATION | FOUNDED YEAR | COUNTRY | LOCATION | T/O LATEST KNOWN | NO OF EMPLOYEES |
|---|---|---|---|---|---|---|---|
| 1 | AUTOMOBILES | TATA MOTORS | 1945 | INDIA | PUNE | 35.00 | 60000 |
| 2 | AUTOMOBILES | MARUTHI SUZUKI | 1982 | INDIA | DELHI | 7.50 | 7000 |
| 3 | AUTOMOBILES | MAHINDRA & MAHINDRA | 1945 | INDIA | MUMBAI | 7.40 | 15500 |
| 4 | AUTOMOBILES | HERO MOTO CORP | 1956 | INDIA | LUDHIANA | 3.92 | 20000 |
| 5 | AUTOMOBILES | BAJAJ AUTO | 1945 | INDIA | PUNE | 3.40 | 10250 |
| 6 | AUTOMOBILES | ASHOK LEYLAND | 1948 | INDIA | CHENNAI | 2.40 | 15800 |
| 7 | AUTOMOBILES | TVS MOTORS | 1978 | INDIA | CHENNAI | 1.26 | 5000 |
| 8 | AVIATION | JET AIRWAYS | 1992 | INDIA | MUMBAI | 2.90 | 15000 |
| 9 | DIVERSIFIED | VIDEOCON | 1979 | INDIA | AURANGABAD | 4.00 | 50000 |
| 10 | ENERGY | SUZLON ENERGY | 1995 | INDIA | PUNE | 5.25 | 15000 |
| 11 | ENERGY-GOVT OWNED | INDIAN OIL | 1964 | INDIA | NEWDELHI | 80.00 | 36198 |
| 12 | ENERGY-GOVT OWNED | BPCL | 1976 | INDIA | MUMBAI | 41.00 | 14154 |
| 13 | ENERGY-GOVT OWNED | HPCL | 1974 | INDIA | MUMBAI | 37.00 | 11226 |
| 14 | ENERGY-GOVT OWNED | ONGC | 1956 | INDIA | DEHRADUN | 30.75 | 32862 |
| 15 | ENERGY-GOVT OWNED | COAL INDIA | 1975 | INDIA | DELHI | 11.30 | 383347 |
| 16 | ENERGY-GOVT OWNED | NTPC | 1975 | INDIA | DELHI | 11.23 | 26000 |
| 17 | ENERGY-GOVT OWNED | GAIL | 1984 | INDIA | NEW DELHI | 7.27 | 3703 |

| Sl. No | DOMAIN | ORGANIZATION | FOUNDED YEAR | COUNTRY | LOCATION | T/O LATEST KNOWN | NO OF EMPLOYEES |
|---|---|---|---|---|---|---|---|
| 18 | ENGINEERING-GOVT OWN | BHELED | 1953 | INDIA | DELHI | 8.68 | 46500 |
| 19 | FINANCE | ICICI BANK | 1955 | INDIA | MUMBAI | 13.81 | 80000 |
| 20 | FINANCE | HDFC BANK | 1994 | INDIA | MUMBAI | 5.60 | 55752 |
| 21 | FINANCE | AXIS BANK | 1995 | INDIA | MUMBAI | 3.60 | 21640 |
| 22 | FINANCE | HDFC LTD | 1977 | INDIA | MUMBAI | 2.70 | 1607 |
| 23 | FINANCE-GOVT OWNED | STATE BANK OF INDIA | 1955 | INDIA | MUMBAI | 37.00 | 292215 |
| 24 | FINANCE-GOVT OWNED | PUNJAB NATIONAL BANK | 1895 | INDIA | MUMBAI | 6.59 | 57000 |
| 25 | FINANCE-GOVT OWNED | CANARA BANK | 1906 | INDIA | BANGALORE | 4.67 | 44450 |
| 26 | FMCG | ITC LTD | 1910 | INDIA | KOLKATTA | 6.43 | 24027 |
| 27 | FMCG | HINDUSTAN UNILEVER LTD | 1933 | INDIA | MUMBAI | 3.50 | 16500 |
| 28 | FMCG | ASIAN PAINTS | 1942 | INDIA | MUMBAI | 1.55 | 5000 |
| 29 | FMCG | NIRMA | 1969 | INDIA | AHMEDABAD | 1.12 | 5000 |
| 30 | INFRASTRUCTURE | LARSEN & TOUBRO | 1938 | INDIA | MUMBAI | 10.00 | 45117 |
| 31 | INFRASTRUCTURE | RELIANCE INFRASTRUCTURE | 2002 | INDIA | MUMBAI | 2.80 | 8988 |
| 32 | MEDIA | ESSEL GROUP | 1976 | INDIA | MUMBAI | 2.50 | 8000 |
| 33 | METALS | TATA STEEL | 1907 | INDIA | MUMBAI | 27.70 | 81622 |
| 34 | METALS | HINDALCO | 1958 | INDIA | MUMBAI | 14.38 | 19341 |
| 35 | PETRO CHEM | RELIANCE INDUSTRIES LTD | 1966 | INDIA | MUMBAI | 66.18 | 23166 |
| 36 | PHARMA | DR REDDY'S LABS | 1984 | INDIA | HYDERABAD | 2.10 | 14923 |

| Sl. No | DOMAIN | ORGANIZATION | FOUNDED YEAR | COUNTRY | LOCATION | T/O LATEST KNOWN | NO OF EMPLOYEES |
|---|---|---|---|---|---|---|---|
| 37 | PHARMA | RANBAXY LABS | 1961 | INDIA | GURGAON | 1.99 | 10435 |
| 38 | PHARMA | CIPLA | 1935 | INDIA | MUMBAI | 1.26 | 16000 |
| 39 | PHARMA | LUPIN LABS | 1968 | INDIA | MUMBAI | 1.04 | 6000 |
| 40 | REAL ESTATE | DLF LTD | 1946 | INDIA | NEWDELHI | 1.60 | 5542 |
| 41 | RETAIL | SHOPPERS STOP | 1991 | INDIA | MUMBAI | 1.10 | 14000 |
| 42 | RETAIL DIVERSIFIED | TITAN | 1987 | INDIA | CHENNAI | 1.30 | 3000 |
| 43 | TECHNOLOGY | TCS | 1968 | INDIA | MUMBAI | 8.89 | 243545 |
| 44 | TECHNOLOGY | WIPRO | 1945 | INDIA | BANGALORE | 7.30 | 135920 |
| 45 | TECHNOLOGY | INFOSYS | 1981 | INDIA | BANGALORE | 7.00 | 151151 |
| 46 | TECHNOLOGY | HCL TECHNOLOGIES | 1991 | INDIA | NOIDA | 3.83 | 82464 |
| 47 | TECHNOLOGY | HCL INFOSYSTEMS | 1976 | INDIA | NOIDA | 2.18 | 6500 |
| 48 | TECHNOLOGY | TECH MAHINDRA | 1986 | INDIA | PUNE | 1.06 | 42746 |
| 49 | TELECOM | BHARTI AIRTEL | 1995 | INDIA | DELHI | 10.00 | 20500 |
| 50 | TELECOM | RELIANCE COMMUNICATIONS | 2004 | INDIA | MUMBAI | 4.54 | 20000 |
| 51 | TELECOM | IDEA CELLULAR | 1995 | INDIA | MUMBAI | 3.07 | 6500 |
| | | | | | | 568.65 | 2336191 |

315

# WORLD'S FINEST BILLION DOLLAR ORGANIZATIONS

# APPENDIX 6

| Sl. No | DOMAIN | ORGANIZATION | FOUNDED YEAR | COUNTRY | LOCATION | T/O LATEST KNOWN | NO OF EMPLOYEES |
|---|---|---|---|---|---|---|---|
| 1 | PETRO CHEM | RELIANCE INDUSTRIES LTD | 1966 | INDIA | MUMBAI | 66.18 | 23166 |
| 2 | AUTOMOBILES | TATA MOTORS | 1945 | INDIA | PUNE | 35.00 | 60000 |
| 3 | METALS | TATA STEEL | 1907 | INDIA | MUMBAI | 27.70 | 81622 |
| 4 | METALS | HINDALCO | 1958 | INDIA | MUMBAI | 14.38 | 19341 |
| 5 | FINANCE | ICICI BANK | 1955 | INDIA | MUMBAI | 13.81 | 80000 |
| 6 | TELECOM | BHARTI AIRTEL | 1995 | INDIA | DELHI | 10.00 | 20500 |
| 7 | INFRASTRUCTURE | LARSEN & TOUBRO | 1938 | INDIA | MUMBAI | 10.00 | 45117 |
| 8 | TECHNOLOGY | TCS | 1968 | INDIA | MUMBAI | 8.89 | 243545 |
| 9 | AUTOMOBILES | MAHINDRA & MAHINDRA | 1945 | INDIA | MUMBAI | 7.40 | 15500 |
| 10 | TECHNOLOGY | WIPRO | 1945 | INDIA | BANGALORE | 7.30 | 135920 |
| 11 | TECHNOLOGY | INFOSYS | 1981 | INDIA | BANGALORE | 7.00 | 151151 |
| 12 | FMCG | ITC LTD | 1910 | INDIA | KOLKATTA | 6.43 | 24027 |
| 13 | FINANCE | HDFC BANK | 1994 | INDIA | MUMBAI | 5.60 | 55752 |
| 14 | ENERGY | SUZLON ENERGY | 1995 | INDIA | PUNE | 5.25 | 15000 |
| 15 | CONSUMER ELECTRONIC | S VIDEOCON | 1979 | INDIA | AURANGABAD | 4.00 | 50000 |
| 16 | AUTOMOBILES | HERO MOTO CORP | 1956 | INDIA | LUDHIANA | 3.92 | 20000 |
| 17 | TECHNOLOGY | HCL TECHNOLOGIES | 1976 | INDIA | NOIDA | 3.83 | 82464 |

| Sl. No | DOMAIN | ORGANIZATION | FOUNDED YEAR | COUNTRY | LOCATION | T/O LATEST KNOWN | NO OF EMPLOYEES |
|---|---|---|---|---|---|---|---|
| 18 | AUTOMOBILES | BAJAJ AUTO | 1945 | INDIA | PUNE | 3.40 | 10250 |
| 19 | TECHNOLOGY | HCL INFOSYSTEMS | 1976 | INDIA | NOIDA | 2.18 | 6500 |
| 20 | AVIATION | JET AIRWAYS | 1992 | INDIA | MUMBAI | 2.90 | 15000 |
| 21 | AUTOMOBILES | ASHOK LEYLAND | 1948 | INDIA | CHENNAI | 2.40 | 15800 |
| 22 | PHARMA | DR REDDY'S LABS | 1984 | INDIA | HYDERABAD | 2.10 | 14923 |
| 23 | PHARMA | RANBAXY LABS | 1961 | INDIA | GURGAON | 1.99 | 10435 |
| 24 | FMCG | ASIAN PAINTS | 1942 | INDIA | MUMBAI | 1.55 | 5000 |
| 25 | RETAIL DIVERSIFIED | TITAN | 1987 | INDIA | CHENNAI | 1.30 | 3000 |
| 26 | PHARMA | CIPLA | 1935 | INDIA | MUMBAI | 1.26 | 16000 |
| 27 | TECHNOLOGY | TECH MAHINDRA | 1986 | INDIA | PUNE | 1.06 | 42746 |
| 28 | PHARMA | LUPIN LABS | 1968 | INDIA | MUMBAI | 1.04 | 6000 |
| | | | | | | 257.87 | 1268759 |

# WORLD'S FINEST BILLION DOLLAR ORGANIZATIONS

## APPENDIX 7

| Sl. No | DOMAIN | ORGANIZATION | FOUNDED YEAR | COUNTRY | LOCATION | T/O LATEST KNOWN | NO OF EMPLOYEES |
|---|---|---|---|---|---|---|---|
| 1 | INDIAN-CONGLOMERATES | RELIANCE GROUP | 1966 | INDIA | MUMBAI | 90.00 | 14000 |
| 2 | INDIAN-CONGLOMERATES | TATA GROUP | 1868 | INDIA | MUMBAI | 83.00 | 424365 |
| 3 | INDIAN-CONGLOMERATES | ADITYA BIRLA GROUP | 1857 | INDIA | MUMBAI | 40.00 | 133000 |
| 4 | INDIAN-CONGLOMERATES | ESSAR GROUP | 1969 | INDIA | MUMBAI | 17.00 | 75000 |
| 5 | INDIAN-CONGLOMERATES | JINDAL GROUP | 1952 | INDIA | NEWDELHI | 12.00 | |
| 6 | INDIAN-CONGLOMERATES | BHARTI ENTERPRISES | 1976 | INDIA | MUMBAI | 10.00 | 30000 |
| 7 | INDIAN-CONGLOMERATES | ADANI GROUP | 1988 | INDIA | AHMEDABAD | 7.12 | 9000 |
| 8 | INDIAN-CONGLOMERATES | HCL GROUP | 1976 | INDIA | NOIDA | 6.01 | 88964 |
| 9 | INDIAN-CONGLOMERATES | GODREJ GROUP | 1897 | INDIA | MUMBAI | 3.30 | 9700 |
| 10 | INDIAN-CONGLOMERATES | FUTURE GROUP | 1981 | INDIA | MUMBAI | 3.00 | 30000 |

| Sl. No | DOMAIN | ORGANIZATION | FOUNDED YEAR | COUNTRY | LOCATION | T/O LATEST KNOWN | NO OF EMPLOYEES |
|---|---|---|---|---|---|---|---|
| 11 | INDIAN-CONGLOMERATES | MODI GROUP | 1933 | INDIA | DELHI | 2.80 | 28000 |
| 12 | INDIAN-CONGLOMERATES | JAYPEE GROUP | 1957 | INDIA | NOIDA | 2.11 | 20000 |
| | | | | | | 276.34 | 862029 |